This Could Be the Start
of Something Big

This Could Be the Start of Something Big

HOW SOCIAL MOVEMENTS FOR REGIONAL EQUITY ARE RESHAPING METROPOLITAN AMERICA

Manuel Pastor Jr., Chris Benner,
and Martha Matsuoka

Cornell University Press
Ithaca and London

First published 2009 by Cornell University Press
First printing, Cornell Paperbacks, 2009

Printed in the United States of America

Library of Congress Cataloging-in-Publication Data

Pastor, Manuel.
    This could be the start of something big : how social move-
ments for regional equity are reshaping metropolitan America /
Manuel Pastor, Jr., Chris Benner, and Martha Matsuoka.
        p. cm.
    Includes bibliographical references and index.
    ISBN 978-0-8014-4721-1 (cloth : alk. paper)—
    ISBN 978-0-8014-7462-0 (pbk. : alk. paper)
  1. Regional planning—Social aspects—United States.
2. Regionalism—Social aspects—United States.   3. Regional
disparities—United States.   4. Community development,
Urban—United States.   5. Community organization—
United States.   6. Metropolitan areas—United States.   7. Social
movements—United States.   I. Benner, Chris.   II. Matsuoka,
Martha, 1961–   III. Title.
    HT392.P37   2008
    307.1'20973—dc22   2008038071

Cornell University Press strives to use environmentally responsible suppliers and materials to the fullest extent possible in the
publishing of its books. Such materials include vegetable-based,
low-VOC inks and acid-free papers that are recycled, totally
chlorine-free, or partly composed of nonwood fibers. For further
information, visit our website at www.cornellpress.cornell.edu.

Cloth printing   10 9 8 7 6 5 4 3 2 1
Paperback printing   10 9 8 7 6 5 4 3 2 1

To Betsy, Gwynn, and Anthony,
for their love, leadership, and patience.

Contents

Acknowledgments

When we first sat down to write our thanks, we realized that making a full list of our debts would result in an acknowledgments section as long as the book itself. More than most academic endeavors, this has been a well-supported enterprise: several funders, many colleagues, and an army of research assistants have contributed to the data and analysis that we offer here. But the real source of support has been not the usual academic and philanthropic suspects but rather all those in the social movements for regional equity that we describe in this volume. They are the subjects of our study, but they are also the actors who have provided us with guidance, challenged us with criticism, and inspired us with leadership—and so we start with our thanks to them.

For teaching us about how regional equity might scale to power via faith-based networks, we thank the Reverend Cheryl Rivera, Pat Jackson, Ponsella Hardaway, Vicki Kovari, Ana Garcia Ashley, Greg Galuzzo, Mike Kruglik, and Paul Sculley, as well as the Reverends Patrick Gahegan, Bart Beebe, Joseph Barlow, Kevin Turman, Patrick Johnson, and Cindy Reese; in the same vein, we offer profound appreciation to Bethel New Life's Mary Nelson and Steven McCullough, partly for explaining the role of religious institutions and partly for questioning the very premises of our work.

For educating us about the role of labor in regional struggles, we thank Madeline Janis of the Los Angeles Alliance for a New Economy; Donald Cohen of the Center for Policy Initiatives; Kent Wong of the UCLA Labor Center; Leslie Moody of Partnerships for Working Families; Phaedra Ellis-Lampkins and Bob Brownstein of Working

Partnerships USA; and Eric Parker, John Goldstein, Phil Neuenfelt, Sheila Cochran, and Bruce Colburn, all from various labor groupings in Milwaukee.

For getting us to think more carefully about the power of organizing and the issues of scale, we thank Anthony Thigpenn, Jennifer Ito, Sabrina Smith, and Elsa Barboza of SCOPE in Los Angeles; Gilda Haas of Strategic Actions for a Just Economy, also in Los Angeles; Juliet Ellis of Urban Habitat in Oakland; and Gihan Perera of the Miami Workers Center. For reminding us that building organizational capacity matters in regional equity, we thank Dwayne Marsh at PolicyLink for his reflections on ACTION! in Boston and Massachusetts, and Deborah Scott for sharing her time and vision for the new labor-community effort STAND UP! in Atlanta, Georgia.

For sharing key lessons with regard to the intersection of community development and regional equity, we thank James Head of the San Francisco Foundation; Alvertha Penny of the California Community Foundation; Anika Goss-Foster and Kari Sederburg (formerly of Detroit LISC); Jeremy Nowak and Pat Smith of the Reinvestment Fund; Miguel Garcia of the Ford Foundation; Denise Fairchild of the Community Development Technology Center; Rick Cole, city manager of Ventura, California; Katherine Perez of The Urban Land Institute–Los Angeles; Von Nkosi and Hattie Dorsey, both formerly with the Atlanta Neighborhood Development Corporation; and consultants (and so much more!) Rebecca Riley and Jim Gibson—additional thanks to Jim for his thorough and thoughtful review of an earlier draft of this work.

For specific guidance with regard to implementing community-based regionalism "on the ground," we thank Jaime Alvarado of Somos Mayfair, Allen Edson, James "Tim" Thomas, Margaret Gordon, and Rosalinda Palacios, formerly of the 7th Street/McClymonds Initiative of West Oakland; Will Mollard, Stewart Hyland, and Julio Garcia, formerly of One East Palo Alto; Ritchie Harrison, Maria Zardis, Gaylotta Murry, Pat Bosch, Anthony Williams, Denise Dorz, and Dora Mattuci from the Van Dyke–8 Mile Collaborative in Detroit; and Sony Grant-Pierson, Jason Dietrick, Maggie DeSantis, and Charlie Mahony, all involved in the Detroit–Grosse Point Park Collaborative. For helping us see the intersections of regionalism and environmental justice, we thank the Southeast Los Angeles Regional Environmental Justice Collaborative (Communities for a Better Environment, East Yard Communities for Environmental Justice, Coalition for a Safe Environment, Comité Pro Uno, and the

Liberty Hill Foundation), and all the member organizations of the Bay Area Environmental Health Collaborative.

For helping us understand the role of business in regional equity partnerships, we thank Doug Henton and John Melville of Collaborative Economics; Kim Walesh of the City of San Jose; Sunne McPeak (formerly of the Bay Area Council); Brian Bosworth of FutureWorks; the late Nick Bollman of the California Center for Regional Leadership; Mark Pisano of the Southern California Association of Governments; Ben Starrett of the Funders' Network for Smart Growth and Livable Communities; and Julia Taylor in Milwaukee.

For helping us see how all the strands of regional equity can come together, we thank the participants in the Ford-sponsored Conversation on Regional Equity: Angela Glover Blackwell of PolicyLink, Amy Dean of Building Partnerships USA, Cynthia Duncan of the Carsey Institute, Mary Gonzalez of the Gamaliel Foundation, Bart Harvey (formerly of the Enterprise Foundation), Heeten Kalan of the New World Foundation, Bruce Katz and Alice Rivlin of the Brookings Institution, john powell of the Kirwan Institute at Ohio State, and the very independent (and independent-minded) David Rusk.

For their academic advice and (sometimes gentle, sometimes not) critiques along the way, we thank Peter Dreier and Bob Gottlieb of Occidental's Urban and Environmental Policy Institute; Myron Orfield of the Institute for Race and Poverty; Margaret Weir of UC Berkeley; Rolf Pendall and Susan Christopherson of Cornell; Phil Thompson and Xavier Briggs of MIT; and Jackie Leavitt, Paul Ong, and Abel Valenzuela of UCLA. Our most profound thanks in this regard go to Robert Kleidman of Cleveland State University and Todd Swanstrom of St. Louis University; their careful reviews of an earlier draft greatly influenced our thinking. Although we suspect that we could have achieved an even better reworking of the book had we simply turned the task over to them, we hope this final version meets the high standards they both sought and expected.

For research assistance in this project, we thank Rachel Rosner, Julie Jacobs, Miranda Schirmer, Javier Huizar, and Justin Scoggins of the Center for Justice, Tolerance and Community (CJTC) at UC Santa Cruz; Jennifer Tran, Jennifer Renteria, and Vanessa Carter of the Program for Environmental and Regional Equity at USC; and consultant Serena Lin. For managing our budgets and staff with a combination of good cheer and ruthless efficiency, we thank Susan Welch of CJTC; Susan also helped with editing and organizing various versions of the manuscript, never (well, almost never) complaining about the odd mix of writing styles, citation formats, and even theoretical frameworks.

Sources of funding for this endeavor included the Hewlett Foundation, which supported our work with three neighborhood initiatives in the Bay Area (from which we learned about the challenges of making region-community links), and the MacArthur Foundation's "Building Resilient Regions" project (from which we learned to think about regional equity as embedded in a broader set of issues that regions must confront to succeed). The primary and most important source of funding, however, was the Ford Foundation, an institution that has shown a strong commitment to developing this field as a new way to think about community development. Among supportive people there, we specifically thank Pablo Arias, Melvin Oliver (now at UC Santa Barbara), and Susanne Siskell.

Our most profound debt at Ford and beyond is to our program officer, Carl Anthony. As those in this field know, Carl made a significant difference by helping to steer both funds and philanthropic attention in the direction of regional equity and community organizing. The field would not be where it is today without his constant prompting about its possibilities, a conviction that grew out of his long history as an organizer and leader in the area of environmental justice and urban design. He was an able mentor to all of us, pioneering the concepts of regional equity and providing key support (as well as intellectual provocation and committed friendship) along the way. If regional equity ever fully catches fire, it will be partly due to his tireless efforts.

Finally, we have enjoyed the love and support of a patient set of friends and family members—too many to be named—who have often wondered why we crisscrossed the country for site visits to Gary or Camden, why we worked late at night when sleep (and partners) beckoned, and why we then named the resulting book after a song written by Steve Allen and made popular by Ella Fitzgerald. The answer is simple: just as Ella broke racial and other barriers to bring the country together around the sheer artistry of America's finest contribution to music, jazz, the regional equity movement is crossing once-hard lines of race and space in pursuit of America's finest values of community, inclusion, and participation.

It's music to our ears—and, as in jazz, there's more than a bit of improvisation occurring as these new metropolitan organizers scramble to help all of us live up to America's democratic promise. We dedicate this book to them and hope that it will make a useful contribution not just to the realm of research but to the world of action and change.

MANUEL PASTOR, CHRIS BENNER,
AND MARTHA MATSUOKA

—Los Angeles

This Could Be the Start
of Something Big

CHAPTER ONE

Something's Happening Here

For nearly two decades, progressives have been dismayed by the steady rise of the right in U.S. politics and political discourse. Seeking to respond, some analysts have focused on the need to re-frame progressive ideas, arguing that staying on message, but with new words and new ideas, could return the country to a fabled liberal past. Others have focused on the need to infuse progressive politics with values, including those more rooted in the faith-based traditions so often rejected by an agnostic left. Still others have stressed the importance of designing policy remedies that can reconcile the demands of a global market with the growing concerns of an anxious middle class.[1]

Often lost in the debate—and the occasional gloom and doom about American politics—is a striking and sometimes underanalyzed phenomenon: the resurgence of progressive politics and movements at a local level.[2] Clearly, there has been a rightward drift in some states and localities—or else, we could not have a book like *What's the Matter with Kansas?* (Frank 2004)—but against that backdrop has emerged a quiet groundswell of new coalitions, policies, and models that seem to stress equity, inclusion, and opportunity.

---

[1] For more on reframing and values, see Lakoff (2004); on the need to stress faith, see Wallis 2005 and Lerner 2006; for more on policy approaches, see Krugman 2003.

[2] For a succinct analysis of this surge of local progressive politics, see Nichols 2005. See also a recent superb collection on community organizing and cities edited by Marion Orr (2007); some of the ideas there are similar to ours although we put much more focus on the regional equity strand of this organizing and the issue of geographic scales.

Across the country, urban coalitions—including labor, faith groups, and community-based organizations—have come together to support living-wage laws and to fight for transit policies that can move the needle on issues of working poverty. Neighborhood groups have allied with labor leaders to fight for community benefits agreements that link economic growth with affordable housing and job training. Environmental activists and minority leaders, often gazing warily across the chasms of race at a national level, have forged multiracial regional alliances to reduce pollution and transform contaminated or vacant urban lands by useful development.

Just as striking as the rise of this progressive resurgence has been its reception among unlikely allies. In places as diverse as Chicago, Atlanta, and San Jose the usual business resistance to pro-equity policies has changed, particularly when issues essential to restoring regional competitiveness, such as increased affordable housing and more efficient transportation systems, are raised. City-suburb differences, while still profound, are more frequently giving way to a process of finding political and policy common ground, especially now that older suburbs find themselves facing the same demographic and economic challenges that have long plagued central cities. Public officials, traditionally satisfied with the local fragmentation that enhances their influence, have begun considering how to change the rules of the game in a way that will forge better interjurisdictional cooperation.

There's something happening here—although the rather clouded picture it presents may seem to echo the next words from that famous tune from the 1960s—"What it is ain't exactly clear." Is the rise of these progressive experiments simply a local phenomenon, worthy of academic contemplation but just an anomaly in the national body politic? Or is there something going on at the local and regional levels that can offer guidance for building national social movements and governing coalitions to revitalize the promise of America?

Looking Down but Building Up

In our view, there is something happening—and it could be, in the words of another popular song from a slightly earlier era, "the start of something big." But to see it and its possibilities requires that we recognize a new thread running through many local efforts: a perspective and politics that emphasizes "regional equity."

This regional equity view operates at three levels. *Analytically,* it takes as a bedrock principle that many of our country's most challenging urban problems are created by our patterns of metropolitan development, particularly the spatial configuration of cities and suburbs. *Practically,* it suggests that new metropolitan strategies—on housing, economic development, and workforce—are crucial to tackling these problems and may be more effective at generating equitable outcomes than either traditional community development efforts or broad national policy. *Politically,* it suggests that the region is a productive place for new progressive organizing, partly because it is on the regional scale that many problems are experienced and partly because a confluence of interests make it possible to create new sustainable coalitions among unlikely partners.

The regional equity perspective also pays attention to issues of economic competitiveness and sustainability in ways that appeal beyond the usual low-income constituencies. Indeed, it argues that inclusion of low-income groups is central to recovering regional economies and, hence, is in everyone's interest. As a result, regional equity proponents have been experimenting with policies that would not have been traditionally associated with antipoverty efforts or community development—fields historically concerned with building low-income housing, launching local job-training programs, and reconstructing distressed neighborhoods. Likewise, these same proponents have sought to move beyond a traditional left politics sometimes characterized by oppositional protest against business, casting aspersions on suburbs, and arguing for localist and often inward-looking neighborhood development.[3]

In Los Angeles, for example, an organizing and advocacy group from South Central L.A., the historic heart of black L.A., challenged a $70 million city subsidy given to the DreamWorks studio—famously headed by Steven Spielberg, Jeffrey Katzenberg, and David Geffen—as an incentive to locate in the city. But rather than derailing the tax break or insisting that the jobs be located in distressed neighborhoods, advocates fought for a training program for inner-city community college students attached

---

[3] Bruegmann (2005) lumps the regional equity proponents with the new urbanist design aficionados who he thinks are contemptuous of suburbs and suburban life. We would argue that Bruegmann has an overly broad characterization of most of the new urbanist and Smart Growth movements—and it is very inaccurate with regard to regional equity advocates. The latter deeply understand the suburban impulse to flee the problems of the central city but argue that our fates are linked, particularly in the inner-ring suburbs now facing urban-style problems.

to entertainment industry jobs, wherever they might be in the regional economy. As it turned out, DreamWorks decided not to build a new studio, and the subsidy was withdrawn—but the process of negotiating the job-training requirement created new ties with business and eventually the negotiated program—seeded by $5 million from DreamWorks—morphed into a larger $12 million effort called Workplace Hollywood.

In Gary, Indiana, an interfaith network started its community building efforts by launching marches designed to drive the illicit drug business from the abandoned housing where it had taken root. But participants soon realized that the drug trade would continue to be appealing so long as economic hopelessness reigned—and that addressing this despair required connecting residents with job opportunities, which were steadily drifting away from the central city. The usual strategy might have been to fight to bring the jobs back, spicing this demand with rhetoric about privileged suburbs. The network instead brought together congregations from both black and white neighborhoods, as well as from city and suburb, to fight together for an unlikely demand: expansion of regional transportation and establishment of a regional transit authority. Their argument: this strategy would both help suburbanites avoid long commutes *and* create better opportunities for central-city residents to access suburbanized employment.

In Atlanta, Georgia, the Atlanta Neighborhood Development Corporation came of age by financing, building, and rehabilitating affordable housing for low-income residents, but it eventually became aware that its very success in helping to revive the downtown was displacing low-income residents. The historical approach to such pressures is often to enhance tax credits and other measures to retain affordability in the central city, with a specific focus on building clusters of low-income units. But, convinced that concentrating poverty was a bad approach, the group instead focused on mixed-income housing with units set aside for lower-income residents—and simultaneously launched a regionwide effort to build mixed-income communities in Atlanta's suburbs as well. Their key allies: businesses that wanted to see housing throughout the region which would be accessible to all levels of their workforces.[4]

In Boston, Action for Regional Equity (Action!)—a coalition of community, church, environment, housing, civil rights, and environmental justice groups—has worked to ensure that equity criteria in state and

---

[4] Hattie Dorsey and Von Nikosi (2006). See also http://www.andpi.org/.

local policy protect low-income neighborhoods facing the swell of gentrification. In California, the Central Coast Alliance United for a Sustainable Economy (CAUSE) has helped pass five living-wage laws in the region, aided in establishing the Ventura County Health Initiative, and persuaded the city of Ventura to adopt Smart Growth strategies in its 2005 general plan—all to "improve the standard of living and quality of life of low and moderate income working people in the central coast region."[5] In Miami-Dade County, Florida, a nascent coalition of labor, community, and faith-based organizers have begun working together to fashion their own counterweight to the pressures of gentrification that are ravaging that region's poorest neighborhoods.

Can these and the other efforts we detail in this book continue to bubble up, informing—and perhaps contributing to—a broad-based and powerful revitalization of progressive politics and coalition-building in the United States? We understand the skepticism that might immediately greet such a question. How could actions so often under the media radar screen amount to something big? How can the disparate efforts of a wide range of grassroots groups, often with little in common directly or organizationally, shift a national politics that has gained traction to the right? Will the simple ideas that seem to motivate the regional equity actors—concentrated poverty is bad for everyone's economic health, regional policymakers can do something about it, and new and unexpected alliances are possible—wither under the further scrutiny of researchers and politicians?

These were exactly the sorts of dismissive statements that might have been made about the conservative movement as its leaders began their own long march through the fields of ideas, institutions, and ideology. Bear with us as we make our case—and, more important, bear with this emerging group of actors as they find their way to a new politics of hope and inclusion for America.

Who's in the Game?

The regional equity perspective has its analytical roots in three strands of research and action, each with its own particular set of emphases, messages, and strategies. The first strand is the "new regionalism," which

---

[5] CAUSE's mission statement is available at http://www.coastalalliance.com/we_are.html.

argues that the metropolitan region has emerged as the preeminent sphere for economic prosperity and that social equity is an important factor in regional competitiveness. The second is the "new community development," which suggests that older ways of focusing on the revitalization of poor neighborhoods need to be supplemented with an "outside game" that connects to regional opportunities. The third is the "new organizing," which looks to the region explicitly to understand and leverage power in the interests of lower-income and minority communities.

Economic Growth and the Region

Of these strands, the new regionalism—with its emphasis on the economy—has received the most attention from key actors in business and officialdom. This view stresses that in an increasingly global economy, the world is not "flat" (à la Friedman 2005) but spiked: software development is initiated and financed in the Silicon Valley, programmed and tested by computer scientists in Eastern Europe or Israel, sold along with hardware through a website maintained in Austin, Texas, and the inevitable hiccups experienced by end-users tidied up by call-center workers in Bangalore, India. National borders may be continuously crossed, but the connection seems to be team-to-team and region-to-region.

Such regional agglomerations are not limited to high-tech clusters. Consider the entertainment industry based in Los Angeles, the metalworking industries that sustain the Milwaukee metropolitan area, and even the business groupings that dot the rural landscape: the southern Kentucky houseboat industry, the carpet manufacturing complex in Dalton, Georgia, the wood-crafting firms in north central Minnesota (Rosenfeld 2001), for example. Partly because of this pattern, William Barnes and Larry Ledebur (1998) have labeled the United States less a national economy than a sort of "common market" of regions—and pointed to the increasing variation of economic performance between regions as evidence of the increasing need to think on a metropolitan scale.[6]

Although regions may matter economically, regional governance is virtually nonexistent in the United States. With some exceptions where

[6] For example, the coefficient of variation for employment growth—a measure of the dispersion from the mean and hence the heterogeneity of performance—rose by 10 percentage points between the 1980s and 1990s for the 100 largest metro areas in the United States, and there was an even larger rise in the coefficient of variation for median household income growth of 29 percentage points. Metro employment is taken from the State

cities and counties have been consolidated (such as Louisville, Kentucky), or metro governments have been created (such as Portland, Oregon), our only major metropolitan authorities are planning organizations or councils of governments plagued by limited resources, little power, and a system of voting that generally grants the smallest suburb the same voice as the largest central city (Wolf and Farquar 2005; Sanchez 2005; Altshuler et al. 1999). These public systems do not allow for much in the way of economic promotion, and this gap is increasingly being addressed by business-led, public-private collaboratives.

One of the most emblematic of these groups, Joint Venture: Silicon Valley Network, was born in the most regionalist of places, the Silicon Valley with its well-known information industries. But similar collaboratives have also sprung up in what some would have considered less fertile ground such as Kansas City, the San Joaquin Valley, and New York's Hudson Valley. And while these groups have kept their eye on the economic prize, they have also tended to go well beyond what are thought of as "business climate" issues—that is, access to low-cost labor and transportation, and pliant and supportive governments. They have addressed broader social infrastructure issues that affect the quality of life and the attractiveness of their regions to skilled and easily mobile workers—and in the process, they have often traipsed into the territory of social inclusion and widespread opportunity.

For example, in the fragmented terrain of the Chicago metropolitan area—a place where white and middle-class flight to suburbs has been a constant theme over several decades—a business group called the Commercial Club helped launch Chicago Metropolis 2020. Under the slogan "One Region, One Future," the organization persuaded 100 of the region's largest employers to sign a pledge to include the availability of housing and public transportation on the checklist used when deciding business locations—making it easier to attract workers by addressing congested freeways and the housing shortage, but doing so in a way that opened the doors of suburban housing and employment to those who had been shut out.

In northeastern Ohio, a region deeply affected by industrial decline, the Fund for Our Economic Future has brought together philanthropy

---

of the Cities Data Systems; see http://socds.huduser.org/index.html. Household income information is taken from U.S. Census 1980, 1990, and 2000.

and business in an attempt "to encourage and advance a common and highly focused regional economic development agenda that can lead to long-term economic transformation in ways that recognize the importance of core cities, inclusion/diversity, and quality of life."[7] One of its first efforts was a study of what drives growth for medium-size metropolitan regions like northeastern Ohio. Although the authors stressed the key factors one might traditionally associate with a business-sponsored project—skilled labor, entrepreneurial activity, and the age of the infrastructure—they also emphasized that factors like racial inclusion, openness to immigrants, and relative income equality were central to promoting growth (Eberts, Erickcek, and Kleinhenz 2006).[8]

You Can't Do It Alone: Communities and Regions

Stressing the intersection between metropolitan growth and social equity— between competiveness and cohesion at a regional level—can offer new entry points and alliances for advocates of social justice. At the same time, it is clear that the main thrust of the new regionalism is competitiveness, implying that this line of thinking is an important but insecure anchor for regional equity efforts. More in line with the equity perspective are those analysts and actors whose work is rooted in the field of community development.

Community development traces its modern roots to the antipoverty efforts of the 1960s, especially the federal War on Poverty, the philanthropic efforts of various national foundations, and the stubborn strength and activism of residents in areas of concentrated poverty. Rachel Bratt and William Rohe (2005) report that nearly 4,000 community development corporations (CDCs) are in operation, building and rebuilding housing, launching commercial developments, and running various programs in arenas as diverse as job training and parent education. Housing has been the main bread-and-butter of most CDCs, partly because it is a pressing community need but also because it is where financing and resources have been most available.

Although community developers can rightly point to communities they have helped turn around, including the South Bronx as well as a

[7] This quotation is taken from the Fund's mission statement; see http://www.future fundneo.org/page9066.cfm.

[8] See also a series of earlier studies on the growth-link, including Barnes and Ledebur 1998; Pastor et al. 2000; Pastor 2006; and Voith 1998.

slew of lower-income neighborhoods in Boston, Chicago, and elsewhere, statistical analysis by David Rusk (1999) suggests that there is very little difference, on average, between those distressed neighborhoods that were assisted by CDC efforts and those that were not. The gap between promise and performance arises in part because CDC activities are the equivalent of swimming against a raging stream—one in which the challenge is not water but a phalanx of policies and contexts that discourage investment in poor inner-city neighborhoods and encourage outward sprawl to suburbs and exurbs.[9] As a result, Rusk argues for an "outside game" to change the rules of metropolitan development, including urban land boundaries, deconcentration of low-income housing, and new systems of regional revenue sharing.

Such a perspective offers a complement to "Smart Growth"—that is, the notion that since sprawl is expensive and environmentally damaging, a focus on revitalizing town centers might lead to better-designed and more livable communities.[10] Smart Growth may not involve revenue sharing, but it does ask suburbs to pay the full cost of infrastructure development; it may not disperse all low-income housing, but it does insist on affordability and inclusion; and it may not result in strict growth boundaries, but it does encourage the development of existing urban areas. Recentering growth can thus have direct positive effects for low-income communities, and repackaging community development efforts under the rubric of Smart Growth has its own appeal, particularly as it leaves those on the other side appealing for—well, the alternative to being smart.[11]

Various community developers have recognized the opportunities possible when connecting to a region. Bethel New Life, a CDC based in the mostly African American neighborhood of Garfield Park in West Chicago, responded to a threatened shutdown of a light rail line running through the neighborhood by building alliances with suburban white residents to persuade the Chicago Transit Authority to keep the

[9] The concept of community development "swimming upstream" is also used by O'Connor (1999), who argues that the inability of municipal governments to address the scope and scale of housing and urban blight during the 1950s helped push a short-lived movement to reorganize governments along metropolitan lines.

[10] For a recent summary of Smart Growth principles and the challenges of implementing them, see Downs 2005; for a review of links between infrastructure costs and Smart Growth, see Muro and Puentes 2004.

[11] See Proscio (2003) on the relationship between Smart Growth and community development.

line open. The result: preservation of transit to downtown employment *and* an investment of $300 million in capital improvements that helped make the local station a hub for Bethel's own development strategy. In Oakland, California, a CDC in the largely Latino community of Fruitvale similarly leveraged the expansion of regional rail transit, first organizing the neighborhood to oppose the simple creation of more parking, and then putting together layer upon layer of financing to create a model transit village with affordable housing, public service, and retail.

Organizing for Regional Power

This "new community development"—less inward-focused, more market-oriented, and clearly linked to the region—has its advantages but also its risks. CDCs, after all, need to cultivate politicians and financial institutions to secure the funding needed to pursue development, and mixing deal-making with advocacy around metropolitan rules can involve a precarious balancing act. Moreover, CDCs often have a highly localized base and a highly specialized function (say, housing). Spreading itself too thin across regional space and regional issues can dilute the power and influence of a CDC.

Less conflicted about the region are those who engage in what we term the "new organizing." For these groups and individuals the focus is not on leveraging regional dynamics for project development but, instead, on how the region itself might become fertile ground for an entirely new scale of power-building, complete with broader implications for policy and political change. And they are often quite conscious of the real conflicts this strategy might pose, eschewing the "win-win" solutions of the new regionalism and the easy "common ground" of Smart Growth and the new community development.

Consider, for example, the work of author and activist, Myron Orfield. In a series of important essays and books, one of the most recent being the aptly named *American Metropolitics* (2002), Orfield has argued that problems once seemingly confined to inner cities are finding their way across jurisdictions and into older "first-ring" suburbs. But Orfield does not argue for city-suburb harmony, the parallel to the new-regionalist emphasis on merging economic and equity concerns; rather, he argues that central cities and older, poorer suburbs should form metropolitan coalitions that could strip resources from those wealthier suburbs—what he calls the "favored quarter"—to redistribute income to those most in need. Whatever one thinks of it, this is about as explicit a stab at reconfiguring metropolitan power as one can imagine.

Consider also the rise of labor organizing and policy advocacy at a regional level. In the 1930s, 1940s, and 1950s, the United Auto Workers, the United Steel Workers, and others organized firm by firm—a strategy conditioned by the fact that there were just a few important firms per major industry in oligopolistic America—and thereby managed to gain an important toehold for the protection of worker rights in both their industries and the nation (Silver 2003; Lichtenstein 2003). But with unionized manufacturing on a steep decline in recent decades, gains in union density have had to come from service-sector industries. Here, the company targets are more diffuse and may be more amenable to regionwide approaches. Thus, labor's celebrated victories in recent years have included a series of "Justice for Janitors" campaigns in which the Service Employees International Union (SEIU) took on the cleaning industry one metro area at a time, and the dramatic and ultimately successful attempt to unionize the hotels that serve the Las Vegas gaming industry.[12]

The shift to a regional scale for organizing has been accompanied by an enhanced role for some central labor councils (CLCs), institutions that have historically focused on the building trades, downtown construction, and local elections. In Seattle, for example, the King County Labor Council successfully coordinated affiliates in drives to organize both technology workers and port truck drivers, who had been working under contracts that provided them few benefits and no job security (Rosenblum 2001). In Milwaukee, a concerted and interrelated series of efforts guided by labor and community leaders have helped to lift wages, support innovative job training, and ensure benefits from new development. And in San Jose, the central labor council formed Working Partnerships USA (WPUSA), a think tank that has issued reports and helped steer policy on questions ranging from living-wage laws, to community benefits agreements, to affordable housing (Dean and Reynolds 2008).

A similar focus on regional organizing and policymaking characterizes the Gamaliel Foundation, an interfaith network rooted in the relational organizing techniques laid down by Saul Alinsky and also implemented

[12] For more on Las Vegas hotel workers' unions, see Meyerson 2004; on the recent Las Vegas hospital workers' strike, see German 2006.

in other networks such as ACORN, PICO, and the IAF. Gamaliel—with groups like MOSES (Metropolitan Organizing Strategy Enabling Strength) in Detroit, the New Jersey Regional Coalition in South Jersey, and BRIDGE (Baltimore Regional Initiative Developing Genuine Equality) in Maryland—may start with the typical one-by-one organizing and congregation-based networking long associated with Alinsky-style organizing.[13] But the very names of the organizations suggest that they see the path to community and neighborhood improvement lying through the region—and their organizers, actively informed by Rusk, Orfield, and john powell, a law professor from Ohio who has written eloquently on race and regionalism (powell 2000), fervently believe that metropolitan sprawl and its attendant costs in segregation, isolation, and despair threatens their communities and must be addressed.[14]

In short, although the traditional literature about urban planning and urban politics seems to consider organizing as simply a way to achieve objectives, these efforts are really about the organizing itself. The labor-based Los Angeles Alliance for New Economy (LAANE), for example, is widely acknowledged as pathbreaking in its forging of new land-use tools and strategies to secure community benefits from redevelopment. But talk to LAANE leaders and organizers, and you will not linger long on the arcane details of zoning restrictions, density bonuses, and first-source hiring; instead, you will find yourself quickly engaged in a conversation about what it means to reframe development, refashion coalitions, and build the power to transform fundamentally the way the economy works.

And in keeping with its focus on organizing, LAANE leaders—as well as those in Gamaliel and many other groups across the country—fully accept that although the region may be a lived reality, it is not necessarily

---

[13] ACORN stands for Association of Community Organizations for Reform Now; PICO, Pacific Institute for Community Organization; and IAF, Industrial Areas Foundation (all three are better known by their acronyms). For more on Alinsky, see Bailey 1972 and Horwitt 1989. For more on contemporary Alinsky-style organizing, see Santow 2007, Warren 2001, and Osterman 2002.

[14] Consider the mission statement of the Detroit-based affiliate of Gamaliel: "MOSES pushes for policies that promote regional equity, regional cooperation and connect people to opportunity. Through faith, fairness and action, we bring together Black, White, Latino, Baptist, Catholic, Apostolic, Lutheran, Church of God, Methodist, Church of God in Christ, Urban and suburban congregations to address racial and political activities and practices that continuously divide us as a region, as a community, as people of God." See http://www.mosesmi.org/.

the place where policies are determined and changed. Since there are, after all, few regional authorities, much of the action involves changing municipal and state laws. The argument of these groups is different: what they suggest is that the region can be an appropriate scale for forging coalitions and building power, which can then move policy as needed. From this perspective, the region is not just the new economic unit; it is a new political space.[15]

And it is within this evolving space that an entirely new movement has been incubating, one that may be able to scale up to the national level in ways that will fundamentally transform America. It is in what might be termed its "beta" phase: new ideas, new language, and new strategies are being tried and tested, and observers of these seedling efforts can catch a glimpse of what could be a more hopeful future.

Coming to Our Senses

This is not the book we meant to write. We originally intended a review of regional equity efforts across the country with an eye toward what was working, what was not, and what needed to be changed—a sort of practical guide to the field. We began our work partly out of a sense of responsibility or, perhaps, guilt: we three were among the early proponents of what we had termed "community-based regionalism"—that is, a regional approach that starts with a base in community organizations, CDCs, and central labor councils—and we felt we should chart the subsequent path of those groups that had listened.

One of us, for example, was the first research director for Working Partnerships USA and largely responsible for its early research efforts on the regional economy (Benner 1996, 1998a; Benner, Brownstein, and Dean 1999). Another of us was an organizer for Urban Habitat, an environmental justice group that pushed for regional tax-sharing in the late 1990s and helped to form the regionally focused Bay Area–wide Social Equity Caucus (Urban Habitat 1998). The third did interracial organizing around economic justice in Los Angeles and coauthored an influential

[15] There is an expanding literature on regions and political space in the field of political geography (see Brenner 2002; Soja 2000; Young 2000; Swyngedouw and Cox 1997). Our own approach is more rooted in the political and spatial framework suggested by Martin (2003), which posits "place frames" as important analytic and political structures used by community-based organizations and others to identify and locate grievances in social movement activities.

report that argued for "linking regional and community development" (Pastor et al. 1997).[16] In the years since these early efforts, we confess to having been perhaps as surprised as any outside observer when our various admonitions that "the region matters"—echoing the congruent messages of many others—were picked up by community organizers and community developers.

Of course, it is one thing to argue for new policies and strategies, and another to be involved in the tough work of implementation. Even though we had all gone on to academic careers, we kept our collective feet planted in community issues and struggles, and so we knew just how messy the real world could be. And in 2001, on the heels of the publication of the coauthored volume *Regions That Work* (Pastor et al. 2000), we were offered a unique opportunity: the chance to work with three community-based initiatives in the San Francisco Bay Area as they developed a regional aspect to their community revitalization opportunities.

We jumped at the chance and subsequently became involved in efforts in the traditionally African American community of West Oakland, the heavily immigrant Mayfair neighborhood in East San Jose, and the rapidly changing city of East Palo Alto. Over several years of work with these groups and encounters with many others (in areas that ranged from Chicago to Austin, Pittsburgh to Portland, Monterey to Miami), we had a ringside seat for many of the challenges that occur when others tried to put their money where our mouth had been. As it turned out, regionalist strategies could be abstract and distant from "real" community issues; addressing metropolitan policy requires that groups develop new and different sorts of technical capacities; and shifting policy and political aim from the neighborhood to the region requires a leap of faith that can be difficult to sustain (Pastor, Benner, and Matsuoka 2006).

It's hard out here for a regionalist, we thought, and so we decided to put together a volume focused on the fact that when community-based regionalism hits the ground, it sometimes succeeds but also sometimes stumbles. Learning why and when could be useful knowledge, we felt, and so off we went in search of literature, interviews, and site visits with those we thought to be the leaders in the field. Along the way, we recognized something that had been seeping through our work: by whatever metrics one chooses, community-based efforts at regional equity

---

[16] That report was the basis for the subsequent book, *Regions That Work* (Pastor et al. 2000).

are more likely to succeed when their advocates have a firm analysis of power and an explicit strategy for organizing. It's not about development, we realized; it's about politics, movement-building, and social change.

The Mayfair neighborhood was a good example. Its embrace of regionalism did not come through the traditional issue areas of housing and transportation; instead, the regionalist epiphany arrived when community leaders partnered with the central labor council and a local interfaith effort to force Santa Clara County and the city of San Jose to use dollars received through a tobacco lawsuit settlement in the extension of health insurance to all children in the county, regardless of documentation status. It was a localized problem—neighborhood immigrant kids not being able to access affordable health care—but it was one solved by understanding the regional power structure, organizing with others for regional power, and then tapping collectively into regional resources. From there, Mayfair leaders jumped into other issues such as workforce development, immigrant rights, and housing and, in so doing, found themselves inevitably linked to regionalist groups, regional policy tables, and regional foundations.

And so it went. From region to region, organization to organization, we began to notice that the successful examples evidenced common themes of power analysis, leadership development, and community organizing. While we, like so many in the field, had placed the emerging regional equity experiments squarely in the literature and practice of urban planning and public policy, this was something more fundamental: it was the development of regionally based movements aspiring to make lasting change. The actors themselves were quite conscious of this fact. As Rev. Cheryl Rivera (2003), former executive director of the Gamaliel-affiliated Northwest Indiana Interfaith Federation, has insisted, "Metropolitan organizing is about changing the rules of the game so that those who have not, will have.... Metropolitan organizing is the new civil rights movement."

Is it? To answer that question requires viewing the developments in regional equity through a prism that is as shaped by the literature on social movements as it is by the literature on concentrated poverty, housing desegregation, and transit development. It means asking a different set of questions about how power is obtained, created, and maintained and about why this particular scale has emerged as salient for social change and not just the economy. And it means seriously querying whether the wildly varying efforts at regional equity really stand the chance of transforming themselves into something big.

This is not the book we intended to write, but it is the one we are offering. Our conclusions may seem provocative and just one step past our base of evidence—a reaction we also faced when we unveiled earlier predictions that regional equity might actually catch on beyond a small group of academics and urban actors desperate for new alliances. But we think that there are both analytical and political reasons to consider the ways in which regional equity organizing might be one powerful stream of an emerging progressive national movement.

On the analytical side, we believe that there is a problematic mismatch of political and economic transactions. If the economy is organized regionally, at least some parts of governance will need to be so, as well—and many business groups have sought to fill the gap with regional collaboratives and public-private partnerships that have varying commitments to notions of Smart Growth and social inclusion. The race is on for our politics to catch up with our economy—and unlike so many arenas in which progressives arrive just as the party is ending (think: black urban political gains after sprawl had emptied out central city resources), this is one arena where there are still some chances to make a mark.

On the political side, we have become convinced that the regional equity movement, like the labor and civil rights movements of earlier decades, can offer a language with forward-looking and universal appeal. Mary Gonzales, an organizer with the Gamaliel Foundation who was originally based in the Mexican American neighborhood of Pilsen in Chicago, has talked about rejecting the frame of "scarcity and fear" so often associated with contemporary zero-sum politics in favor of a language of "hope and abundance."[17] Organizing for regional equity offers a way to do that: it starts from a premise that the current metropolitan form is causing strains for both older suburbs and central cities. It points to the possibility for wedding economic prosperity and fairness, and it relies on building relationships to solve our society's problems face to face, race to race, and place to place.

That's a recipe for regions, but it's also a recipe for America. In a society where social justice and economic vitality are often seen as opposites,

---

[17] Fear-hope, individual-community, and scarcity-abundance constitute a framework contributed by Mary Gonzales to the Conversation on Regional Equity (CORE) discussion on regionalism in Los Angeles, June 2005. For more, see CORE 2006.

we need a new unifying vision. In a polity where discussion is polarized and winning margins are razor thin, we need to bring constituencies together. And in a world where constituents are looking for answers and not just slogans, we need an effective strategy for governance. Regional equity might just be part of the ticket.

A Way Forward

Of course, such bold pronouncements also merit caveats. The most important for us is to spend little time actually making the case that high-performance regions and low-income communities should be better linked; in our view, that point has already been well made (see, among others, Blackwell and Fox 2004; Dreier, Mollenkogh, and Swanstrom 2001; Katz 2000; Orfield 2002; Pastor et al. 2000; Rusk 1999). And although the regional equity perspective has come under attack by some doubters (see, for example, Bruegmann 2005; O'Toole 2001; Conte 2000), we believe that the basic argument has been largely won by those who contend that regions matter for the fates of poor communities. Of course, the degree to which they matter and the degree to which this argument has gained ground with various constituencies is debatable, and we take up such issues throughout this volume.

Our second caveat is that partly because we are trying to portray a field in motion, we do not pretend to offer an exhaustive review of all those engaged in regional equity efforts. We do provide a brief history of the evolution of the idea and discuss the most important groups playing in this field, but there is simply no agreed-upon census or list of organizations, and we are surely missing or skimming over many important groups. We therefore choose examples that we think highlight key analytical points and trends—and encourage readers to provide their own continuous updating of organizations and efforts as a way of keeping track of the action.

Our third caveat is straightforward: because our focus in this book is on the issue of power and movement-building, we cannot do justice to a series of important complementary efforts—especially intermediaries such as the Brookings Institution's Metropolitan Policy Program or Oakland-based PolicyLink—which provide important research for equity activists, or those business efforts that understand social equity as important to economic health. Nor do we consider governmental structures per se—we have decided to forgo the almost obligatory regionalist chapter about Portland's Metro Council and instead fill a hole in the literature with regard to social analysis and community organizing.

Fourth on the list of caveats is paying attention to tone: while we explore theoretical debates about social movements, we strive to keep the analytics clear and make the book accessible to those who come from the policy, political, and organizing circles that have generated what we are studying. This effort is in keeping with Michael Burawoy's call for a "public sociology" in which the information gathered is open to an extra-academic audience, and a research piece can be "a vehicle of public discussion" (2005).[18] Being trained in economics, geography, and urban planning, we hadn't quite realized we were public sociologists—but apparently we are. We have consistently sought to bridge academic and activist worlds in our lives and work, and this book is no exception.

Which brings us to our last point: the need to acknowledge our own position in the field—and by this, we mean not the field of study but the field being studied. As early proponents of what we once termed community-based regionalism, we have had the opportunity not only to meet and observe the groups we discuss here but occasionally to provide them with research, support, and guidance. Does our active involvement with these social movement organizations bias our perspectives? Perhaps, and readers can judge for themselves. But even if that is the case, we believe that any danger of bias is far outweighed by the value of the deeper experience and knowledge we have gained in building and sustaining relationships with these organizations.

At the same time, we know the value of distance and critical examination. Thus, writing this book involved formal case study research rather than a reliance only on our own accumulated experiences. We generated a set of research questions that focused on particular regional issues and challenges, organizational strategies, and organizational development. We then developed a standard interview tool, and in each region profiled we conducted a series of visits and interviews with key regional leadership and staff members of the organizations. We are confident of the results, but we do not pretend to the usual academic objectivity: we are both interested observers and enthusiastic fans of the regional equity movement.

[18] Sociologist Herbert Gans was credited with the term "public sociology" in 1988 (Calhoun 2005; see also Gans 1989); Michael Burawoy elevated the term in his 2004 address to the American Sociology Association, later published in the *American Sociological Review* (Burawoy 2005).

Our portrayal of the movement develops as follows. In chapter 2 we offer a brief history of the idea of regional equity, tracing both the key research efforts that have informed regional equity analysis and policy and the intersection of this research with organizing in the field. We suggest that some of the early efforts embodied a sort of "optimal level of fog"—they were deliberately fuzzy enough to enjoy intersections with business and environmental efforts, but this came at the cost of sometimes obscuring the specific contributions and focuses of the equity perspective.

One of these specifics is a theory of change that implicitly (and sometimes explicitly) relies on community organizing to move the agenda. We specifically argue that under the regional equity tent there have emerged three variants: a community development regionalism that is of interest to CDCs seeking more effective urban revitalization, a policy reform regionalism that is moved by "policy entrepreneurs" seeking shifts in rules, regulations, and policymakers' attitudes, and a social movement regionalism that has been of interest to those seeking to build a new basis for progressive politics in the United States. These three variants—one focused on projects, one on policy, and one on power—are not always neatly separated in real-world practice. But the analytical distinction is crucial and helps us understand the transformative potential of regional equity organizing.

This theoretical discussion sets the ground for the series of case studies provided in chapters 3 and 4. Chapter 3 examines the experience in several different regions, paying special attention to the San Francisco Bay Area, Milwaukee, Detroit, and Chicago/Gary. We try to understand how key actors in each region came to add a regionalist frame to their work, what they gained from doing so, and whether they actually see themselves as part of a social movement. The answer varies: many actors seem to see regional equity as a tactical tool to achieve long-held goals, whereas others see the regional scale as a strategic element in movement-making.

Chapter 4 looks at one place where regional scale has become especially important and social movements most explicit: Los Angeles. We pick up the story after the civil unrest of 1992, tracking the evolution and transformation of three organizations: the Los Angeles Alliance for a New Economy (LAANE), Action for Grassroots Empowerment and Neighborhood Development Alternatives (AGENDA), and Strategic Actions for a Just Economy (SAJE). We tell their stories separately but also explain how the organizations interwove to create a power base in the region that intersected with parallel efforts and has helped to transform Los Angeles into a now celebrated location for new organizing.[19]

In chapter 5 we step back to consider the challenges of regional equity organizing *within* metropolitan areas. We first consider the circumstances that seem to create fertile ground for a regional equity perspective, focusing on the nature of governance, the state of the market, and the racial composition of the region. We then consider the key tensions that arise when organizing for regional equity. Foremost among these is race: some argue that an approach stressing commonality is the way to build regional power; others suggest that moving race up front is necessary if it is ever to be left behind in both organizing and policy. This debate is common to progressive movements, but it is particularly fierce in the arena of regional equity: after all, the metropolitan landscapes many are trying to transform were fashioned by the dynamics of racism and racial segregation. Moreover, many minority communities worry that their voices will be drowned out in a regionalist choir and think that place-based approaches, particularly ones that secure political power bases, may be best.

As if that weren't enough of a conundrum, organizations seeking to promote regional equity need to balance their desire to agitate for justice with their desire to attract private capital to invest. They need to worry about how to stop older or first-ring suburbs from defining themselves apart from the central city. They need to "keep it real" so that the abstractions of transit justice are translated into improvements in bus service and transit-oriented development. And the list goes on...It is not an easy set of balancing acts, but organizations are juggling these issues every day as they try to interest new constituencies in the principles and policies of regional equity.

Chapter 6 steps back further to consider the possibilities of social movement regionalism *across* America's regions. Drawing on Theda Skocpol's analysis, we argue that regional equity efforts rise up to the national level by addressing a "missing middle" in the infrastructure for change (2000). We point to a few sets of organizations that do have a vision of how region-by-region organizing for equity could eventually lead to a force for national change; most significantly, these include the interfaith organizations coming together under Gamaliel, and a

---

[19] For other accounts, see Waldinger et al. 1996; Pastor et al. 2000; Soja 2000; Gottlieb et al. 2005.

set of labor-affiliated organizations under the·umbrella of Partnership for Working Families. We also lift up allies, those networks that focus on equity and operate regionally but do not necessarily put themselves under the rubric of regional equity. And we consider both the range of policy strategies and the support from funders and intermediaries which will be necessary to make regional equity a reality.

We offer our own recommendations in these arenas with the full realization that as the movement evolves, any set of capacities and strategies will be a moving target. The vision, however, should become more stable: an optimistic perspective that values both economic prosperity and social inclusion, that stresses how democratic and sustained conversation can build stronger regions and healthier communities, and that meets a peculiarly American test—the offering of a pragmatic policy package that is doable in the near future.

A forward-looking and practical vision can have a real impact on America's regions. But it might also be of more general help to a country that finds itself at a perilous political crossroads. We can continue the polarization of the last several decades—Red state against Blue state, city against suburb, rich against poor—or we can try to find a new language and a new common ground.

We wrote this book before the presidential campaign of Illinois Senator Barack Obama captured the imagination of a nation with exactly this sense of a new dialogue, one that is more inspiring, more inclusive, and more pragmatic. However, we actually ended our first complete draft of this manuscript—in January 2007—with reference to Obama. We argued, based largely on his 2004 address to the Democratic convention and the "buzz" that surrounded him at that time, that he was a uniquely unifying figure—and suggested that his ability to cross the boundaries of race, space, and class was partly because he had found his voice through community organizing with a group deeply rooted in the regional equity framework.

Like others, we have tracked his progress ever since, partly because it has meant that we have had to keep updating our end—and in the wake of the November 2008 elections, we will all need to update our future. We firmly believe that the regional equity perspective offers some guidance to the broader national conversation and common purpose Obama has come to symbolize, and we hope that this volume contributes to a better understanding of the analytical and political tasks ahead.

CHAPTER TWO

Unpacking Regional Equity

In November 2002, PolicyLink, a national intermediary focused on issues of community development and community building, worked with a group of funders and other organizations to develop and host a "National Summit" on "Promoting Regional Equity." Held in Los Angeles, a place traditionally viewed as anathema to regional collaboration or coordination, the organizers quietly prayed that at least 300 people would gather to discuss the ideas regarding regional organizing and policy which had been bubbling up around the country. The low expectations were reasonable: many of the people and organizations PolicyLink sought to include in the big tent of regional equity thought of themselves as community developers, labor union leaders, Smart Growth advocates, community organizers, urban planners, faith-based activists, or environmental justice proponents—almost anything but equity-oriented regionalists.

What happens if you throw a party and nobody comes? Fortunately, PolicyLink didn't have to find out: some 600 individuals arrived, swamping the facility that had been designated for the conference. Enthusiastic and spirited conversations marked the event—but also struggle as participants tried to come to grips with whether their groups really did intersect and how. Most striking was the honest admission by many attendees that tackling those large regional forces which had created the contemporary metropolitan mess was going to require a whole series of partnerships and capacities, and maybe even the elements of a new movement for social justice.

Flash forward two and a half years to May 2005 and the Second National Summit, this time in Philadelphia and this time labeled "Advancing

Regional Equity." More than 1,300 people showed up, again roughly twice the goal set by the event organizers. Though there were some notable gaps in geographic representation, especially the South and the Mountain West, participants hailed from all around the country (see figure 2.1). Once again, debate was vigorous: in one particularly heated session, residents from nearby Camden, New Jersey, decried "regional equity" as an outside imposition that was producing gentrification and shifting resources away from the city to inner-ring suburbs, all in the name of making a regional connection.

Big crowds and vibrant conversations—something has indeed been going on. In this chapter, we examine the evolution of the regional equity perspective. Although we note earlier efforts by key academic analysts

Total attendees, 2002 and 2005 combined
- · 1 - 2
- · 2 - 5
- ● 5 - 10
- ● 10 - 20
- ● 20 - 40
- ● 40 - 60
- ● 60 - 100
- ● More than 100

Scale Equals: 1 to 21,000,000

Figure 2.1. National interest in regional equity. Number of attendees at Regional Equity Summits by metropolitan statistical area (or zip code if not in a metro area).
Source: Data on attendees provided by PolicyLink and geo-coded by the authors.

and some community development intermediaries to think about poor communities in a metropolitan context, we suggest that it was in the mid-1990s that the dam broke: an influential series of books, reports, and articles laid the analytical ground for the field, even as a series of initiatives such as living-wage laws, regional job-training programs, and new leadership development and policy institutions began to arrive on the scene. By the time the National Summits came around, the movement had at least a loosely outlined intellectual base, some degree of infrastructure, and a coalescing gel of different perspectives.

To frame this evolution, we briefly outline the other regional movements emerging at the time, including business-sponsored public-private collaborations and a more planning-oriented and environment-oriented emphasis on Smart Growth. We next suggest that the regional equity perspective consists of three variants: (1) community development regionalism, in which the main interest is using regional levers to promote a new form of community revitalization; (2) policy change regionalism, in which the primary emphasis is on shifting government rules to better distribute metropolitan resources; and (3) social movement regionalism, in which the principal goal is to build on a sense of grievance in order to mobilize communities for mass collective action at a regional level.

The last of these is bound to cause conflict—indeed, it is intended to do so. Social movement regionalism may deem as worthy the projects generated by community developers, and it may agree with targeting particular regional policies and policy makers. Its fundamental feature, however, is the belief that the nitty-gritty of constituency mobilization and regional coalition-building is not merely a method to achieve those objectives; such power-building is, rather, an end unto itself and can be a part of creating a national progressive movement.

What Is Regional Equity?

A report prepared by the Conversation on Regional Equity (CORE)—a collection of ten early thinkers and doers in the field—offers a succinct definition of regional equity:

> Achieving regional equity means considering both people and place. A competitive and inclusive region is one in which members of all racial, ethnic, and income groups have opportunities to live and work in all parts of the region, have access to living wage jobs and are included in the

mainstream of regional life. It is also one in which all neighborhoods are supported to be vibrant places with choices for affordable housing, good schools, access to open space, decent transit that connects people to jobs, and healthy and sustainable environments. (CORE 2006, 5)

Most metropolitan regions fall far short of this ideal. Housing is segregated, albeit less so than in previous decades; issues of spatial mismatch still limit opportunities to access viable employment. Some neighborhoods are clearly places of choice; others are saddled with high levels of toxic contamination, dilapidated housing, poor schools, and crime. In years past, many Americans thought that geographic disparity was fine—at least as long as they were on the favorable side of the divide— but the lines are blurring: the "first" suburbs of an earlier era have sustained increases in concentrated poverty even as poverty levels fell in the country as a whole (Puentes and Warren 2006).

Of course, those left behind in the first waves of sprawl—inner- and central-city residents—felt the sting of abandonment earlier. Community activists, community developers, and urban mayors have been actively trying to raise the profile of distressed areas and secure outside support. But especially since the administration of President Ronald Reagan in the early 1980s, national attention and federal resources for cities, particularly for poor neighborhoods, have been in short supply (Oliver et al. 1993; Delgado 1994; Halpern 1995).

One of the reactions to this urban aid fatigue was an attempt to reposition cities within an emerging regional framework. Swanstrom (1996) marks as a critical turning point, a summit of mayors from the country's largest twenty nine cities, held in New York in 1990; he suggests that the tone there represented a tentative shift from a plea for federal assistance and national sympathy to a "new regionalist" approach that insisted on construing central cities as the vital hearts of metropolitan economies. As the decade progressed, the argument developed further; new policy advocacy groups stepped up, and new organizing strategies began taking the regional scale seriously.

The Evolving Literature

The intellectual and political ferment around spatial inequality is not new. Researchers such as Kain (1968) and Wilson (1987) had long stressed the geographic gap between employment and residence for minority communities, and activists often relied on this academic work about "spatial mismatch" to make arguments for locating employment closer to needy neighborhoods. The spatial character of uneven urban development was also a common topic of discussion and action: in the 1980s, for example, many activists promoted the idea of "linked development," the notion that downtown improvements should be connected to housing and retail development in lower-income neighborhoods through the use of parcel-to-parcel development requirements or "linkage fees" (Keating 1986; Sanyika 1986). Although the scope of these strategies was generally citywide rather than regionwide (partly reflecting the political base that was thought ready to pursue them), the idea of connecting the poor to poles of growth was present.[1]

Regional equity represented an effort to assemble these earlier spatial strands and to connect them beyond city boundaries, both intellectually and politically. The emphasis on regional inclusion also intersected conveniently with a broader resurgence of regionalism, particularly the emerging view that "new economy" competitiveness was necessarily forged at the regional or metropolitan level. Indeed, some social equity proponents seemed to embrace regional thinking partly because it was in tune with emerging economic trends and policy opportunities (see Pastor et al. 2000; Benner 2002). But it was not just opportunism driving the shift in scale; changing the regional rules of the game, some suggested, was central to the fate of the urban poor.

David Rusk, for example, published the highly influential *Cities without Suburbs* in 1993, the same year that a popular version of the "new economy" argument for regionalism was laid out in journalist Neal Peirce's *Citistates*. Rusk, a former mayor of Albuquerque, New Mexico, argued that the more "elastic" cities—those able to annex adjoining suburbs—were more likely to avoid an outward drain of residents and resources, to minimize racial and economic segregation, and to improve the prospects for low-income residents. And though Rusk stressed regional revenue sharing and city-county consolidation, he went beyond the technical policy recommendations, concluding his book by advising

---

[1] These perspectives, of course, had earlier roots, particularly in the work of William Julius Wilson (1987) and his notion of an urban underclass stranded in places of little hope by the processes of residential suburbanization, outward employment flight, and resulting spatial mismatch with jobs. Wilson and others, especially Jargowsky (1997), also studied the effects of concentrated poverty on social networks and ways to connect the disadvantaged to broader economic opportunity.

that "sustained change will require a grassroots movement like the civil rights movement or the environmental movement" (1993, 125).

By 1997, Myron Orfield's *Metropolitics* offered one route for building this political momentum. Orfield, at the time a Minnesota state legislator and later head of the Institute on Race and Poverty at the University of Minnesota, noted the flight of whites and middle-class residents from central cities. But he also tried to "unpack" the suburban communities to which they had fled, noting the increasing minority presence in the inner-ring and older suburbs and highlighting the potential of shared alliances to combat the sprawl that was shortchanging residents there as well as in central-city neighborhoods.

Orfield's political strategies were hard-nosed. He argued that much of the new regionalism was based on an amorphous vision of "the common good" (1997, 103). This vague consensus, he suggested, could not overcome deep-rooted patterns of racial and economic segregation. In his own words:

> Regional reform is struggle.... We must achieve the broadest possible level of good feeling, gather to our cause as many allies as we can from all walks of life and from all points of the compass. We must educate and persuade. However, if there are those who stand in our path utterly—who will permit no forward movement—we must fight.... In the end the goal is regional reform, not regional consensus. (Orfield 1997, 34)

Based on his own efforts working with leaders in distressed suburbs in the Minneapolis–St. Paul area, Orfield argued for an alliance of central-city and inner-ring residents who could fight against the exurbs for regional tax-sharing, affordable housing, and other measures.

In other work (Pastor, Benner, and Matsuoka 2006), we have labeled this approach municipal-based regionalism: the main actors are municipal officials; the main tools are interjurisdictional public policy; and the main goal is reducing regional disparity measured city by city (or, perhaps better put, older suburb to newer suburb). The challenge is that the immediate incentives for such regional collaboration can be scant—residents in older suburbs are as likely to contemplate their next life in the exurbs as they are to identify with and work with disadvantaged communities. And Orfield's suggested remedy for many regional ills—sharing regional tax revenues—has gained little ground in the rest of the country.

Regional equity as a political strategy was also a central focus of *Place Matters* by Peter Dreier, John Mollenkopf, and Todd Swanstrom (2001). These authors shed light upon the alliances that could be formed not only between cities and suburbs but also between labor unions, community groups, and political officials at a metropolitan level. The real innovation in *Place Matters,* however, was to cast the regionalist argument in national terms—as a way to create a new political balance that would split the suburbs from the Republican Party and secure a Democratic victory that could move national politics toward a more progressive agenda. Indeed, Dreier, Mollenkopf, and Swanstrom stress that little can be accomplished unless the federal pressures that have generated sprawl and inequality—subsidies to home ownership, investments in the highway system, and stinginess in the allocation of community development funds—are reversed. So why hasn't this happened?

The reasons are complex and multifaceted, but one explanation is that although place matters greatly, so does race. As john powell, a law professor based at Ohio State University, notes, it's not just the suburbs that want to stand apart: he introduced an influential article (powell 2000) by recounting a discussion with an African American city official who agreed that regional dynamics were important but who also distrusted regional solutions because they seemed to rely on white suburbanites who had only recently moved away. Arguing for a sort of "federated regionalism" that can preserve local power, particularly for minority communities, powell (2000) has also stressed "in place" or community development strategies that might have great appeal for these constituencies. Unfortunately, his formula is complicated and underspecified: instead of the federated regionalism he advocates, we have too often seen a perpetuation of division by geography and ethnicity.

Of course, this brief listing of key books and articles cannot do justice to the full range of research into the intersection of communities and regions. Consider, for example, the various evaluations of the Moving to Opportunity (MTO) program, an experiment that provided vouchers to public housing residents to make the move from areas of concentrated poverty to more affluent suburban areas.[2] Bear in mind the vibrant debates about Portland's metropolitan government and whether its limits on outward growth have produced new opportunities or simply solidified

---

[2] For an overview of the MTO program and some of its results, see Goering 2005.

a gentrification process that is displacing lower-income residents.[3] Take into account the sharp disagreements about whether the consolidation of metropolitan governments—as in Louisville, Kentucky—have hindered or highlighted issues important to lower-income African Americans.[4]

That said, our task here is not to cover the wide swath and broad coverage of this literature but rather to highlight those authors who have focused less on policy per se and more on the dimensions of movement-building—and, with that project at least partially accomplished, we now examine the ongoing intersection of this research and the movements themselves.

Into the Mix: A Dash of Research and a Pinch of Practice

The usual trope in academic books is to begin roughly, as above, with a review of key pieces of literature that can provide the reader with a sense of the intellectual landscape. Whether or not that is a suitable strategy in general is questionable, but it is a particularly poor fit in describing the evolution of regional equity thinking. The field has been constructed in recent years not simply through a steady and sober discussion of data, regressions, and analysis but also through constant interaction with practitioners. Indeed, this is one arena in which practice, both new policy experiments and innovative organizing strategies, has often run ahead of research and in which key policy actors have helped set the stage with their own research activities.

To chart the evolution of this practice, the year 1990 is a useful demarcation, partly because it coincides with the mayors' summit that Swanstrom (1996) marks as the beginning of the research and policy wings of the field. It was also the year that the National Economic Development and Law Center, a development and policy intermediary based in Oakland, generated one of the first community-based regional analyses: a report on low-income neighborhoods in the Bay Area and their relationship to regional employment and transportation systems (see Sanyika and Head 1990 and also 1991). The report, hinting at the larger regional case, proved extraordinarily useful to Bay Area community advocates looking for a new handle on local problems. It also attracted the

---

[3] See Lang and Hornburg 1997, and the debate spurred by Abbot 1997.

[4] On the city-county consolidation of Louisville and Jefferson County, Kentucky, esp. the political influence issues that arose, see Savitch and Vogel 2004.

attention of activists in Los Angeles seeking to develop new "linkage" strategies to connect downtown and neighborhood development (Pastor and Hayling 1990).

In 1991, Congress passed the Intermodal Surface Transportation Efficiency Act (ISTEA), which set a bold new standard by granting greater power to metropolitan planning associations, introducing new mechanisms for community participation, and creating incentives for regional collaboration on transit. Perhaps as important as the policy gains themselves was the way in which they came into being: many of ISTEA's more equity-oriented features were lobbied into existence by the Surface Transportation Policy Project (STPP), a coalition of 100 groups founded in the previous year to focus on using regional transportation opportunities to create more "livable communities."[5] Coalition-building between unlikely allies, language that associated equity with broader environmental and economic goals, and a strong commitment to rapid policy implementation set a new style that regional equity advocates were soon to adopt as their own (Kruglik and Stolz 1999; PolicyLink 2002b; Bullard, Johnson, and Torres 2004).

The following year saw the formation of two innovative regional job-training programs: Project Quest in San Antonio and the Wisconsin Regional Training Partnership (WRTP) in Milwaukee. Each had its roots in organizing rather than in technocratic policy. Project Quest was lobbied into place by faith-based Alinsky-style groups in Texas; WRTP was union-initiated and union-designed.[6] The year 1992 also brought civil unrest in Los Angeles and, in its wake, the formation of two groups that would eventually cast the die of regional organizing into that city: the Tourism Industry Development Council, a union-based effort that eventually morphed into the Los Angeles Alliance for a New Economy (LAANE), and Action for Grassroots Empowerment and Neighborhood Development Alternatives (AGENDA), the latter an effort based initially in the devastated areas of South L.A. which would become a leader in forging cross-racial alliances to transform regional economic policies.

During the next few years, regional equity efforts accelerated. In Los Angeles the newly formed Bus Riders Union argued that suburban-serving light rail was being funded at the expense of the bus system used by the

---

[5] On the STPP, see http://www.transact.org/report.asp?id=22.

[6] On Project Quest, see Osterman 2002; on the WRTP, see Benner, Leete, and Pastor 2007.

region's working poor; in 1994 the organization filed a lawsuit against
the metropolitan transit authority which eventually led to a 1996 ruling
reversing a hike in bus fares and mandating a $1 billion investment to
increase bus service (Gottlieb et al. 2005, 106). Living-wage ordinances,
initiated in Baltimore in 1994 and then passed in twelve other U.S. cities
by the end of 1997, were soon proposed throughout the country—and
most often they won, signaling the strength of new community-labor alliances (Pollin and Luce 1998; Luce and Nelson 2004). In 1995 the Urban
Habitat Program, a San Francisco–based group traditionally associated
with environmental justice, published a regional analysis (in collaboration with the University of California–Berkeley's Institute for Urban and
Regional Development), of the impacts (and possible opportunities) of
a military base closure on low-income communities of color in the region's "flatlands" (Urban Habitat Program 1995). And in 1995 the San
Jose–based South Bay Central Labor Council, long a quiescent institution
dominated by the building trades unions, created Working Partnerships,
a labor-affiliated research center that was soon issuing analyses of the
regional economy (Brownstein 2000; Dean and Reynolds 2008).

Our point is simple: much of the intellectual and organizing ammu-
nition was already out there even as analyses by Rusk, Orfield, and others
began to hit the public square. Moreover, these and other authors were
intimately involved in some of the emerging practice and politics. For
example, one of the earliest midwestern adoptions of the regional equity perspective was the Interfaith Federation of Northwest Indiana. The
organization started with questions of environmental justice, particularly
the struggle to ensure that a county landfill be located away from the
central city of Gary, but it soon moved on to a transportation fairness
agenda that was deeply connected to a set of speeches and trainings provided to the organization's leadership in the mid-1990s by Rusk and Orfield (Rast 2006, 255–56).

The interweaving of theory and practice was also present in Los Angeles. UCLA economist Paul Ong headed a 1989 project, *The Widening Divide: Income Inequality and Poverty in Los Angeles* (Ong et al. 1989),
research that triggered a flurry of interest in new urban policies and
inspired significant university-community discussions about the future
of the city. Building on this momentum, Manuel Pastor, Peter Dreier,
Eugene Grigsby, and Marta Lopez-Garza teamed in the mid-1990s to explore the connection between regional restructuring and community
outcomes in L.A.'s shattered economy, largely inspired by their work

with organizing groups based in the region's minority communities. The resulting report, *Growing Together: Linking Regional and Community Development in a Changing Economy* (1997), was then utilized by the very same groups as a justification for strategies that varied from enhancing unionization to tying development subsidies to local job creation.

At the national level, the mid-1990s witnessed an ever widening circle of thinkers, researchers, and practitioners exploring the emerging regional equity paradigm. Among the most important of these was Scott Bernstein, president and founder of the Center for Neighborhood Technology (CNT) in Chicago. One of the founders of the STPP, Bernstein, with CNT, helped conceive and develop the location-efficient mortgage, a lending instrument that reduced costs in central cities by allowing the lower monthly costs associated with living near public transit to be factored into lender guidelines. Bernstein also seems to have coined the term "community-based regionalism," in an article for the CNT's magazine, *Neighborhood Works* (Bernstein 1997), and he worked with Bruce Katz of the Brookings Institution to produce a 1998 report on the "new metropolitan agenda."[7]

In 1999 a new national intermediary, PolicyLink, was established in Oakland with the seemingly amorphous mission of "lifting up what works"; it turned out that what worked was persuading the community development and community building fields to adopt a more regional approach. One of PolicyLink's first acts was convening California practitioners in the summer of 1999—including the founders of Working Partnerships, AGENDA, and LAANE—specifically under the rubric of the community-based regionalism that Bernstein had coined. By December 1999, PolicyLink staff had drafted and published the first "translation paper" for the Funders' Network on Smart Growth and Livable Communities, itself formed only two months earlier (Blackwell and McCulloch 1999).[8] The paper set forth a national agenda for funder support of emerging community-based regionalists; in retrospect, the document is long on hope but short on evidence, citing only three real examples of regional organizing in support of social equity.

Since then, however, the cases and the evidence have proliferated. The Gamaliel Foundation and its affiliates, including the Interfaith

[7] For more on the CNT, visit http://www.cnt.org/.

[8] For the translation paper, see http://www.policylink.org/pdfs/OpportunitiesFor Smarter Growth.pdf.

Federation, became increasingly explicit in their embrace of a regional equity framework, including the 2001 "Statement on Regional Organizing," which declared that "the power and significance of a neighborhood group has diminished. The Gamaliel Foundation encourages and assists in the creation of large metropolitan organizations that bridge divisions of race, class and political boundaries."[9] Working Partnerships in San Jose became even more focused on regional planning issues, debating the ways in which the Coyote Valley, undeveloped land south of San Jose, should mix jobs and housing. And state actors began to get into the game by, among other things, passing an initiative in Pennsylvania to bring supermarkets to distressed neighborhoods and adopting planning strategies in Maryland and elsewhere that used Smart Growth principles to steer development toward older communities.

In 2004, when PolicyLink redrafted its initial 1999 translation paper for the Funders' Network—a sort of version 2.0 for the regional equity framework—examples were jumping off the page, including new coalitions working for regionwide affordable housing, more equitable transportation, and better land use in Boston, the Bay Area, and elsewhere. Meanwhile, an entire host of organizations had taken up the banner of community benefits agreements as one way of securing local benefits from regional investments (Blackwell and Fox 2004). Something had definitely begun to click.

An Optimal Level of Fog?

As the idea of regional equity began to gain ground, it was sometimes hard to define exactly what set it apart from other regionalist efforts, including environmentalist strategies to curb sprawl and business efforts to promote regional competitiveness. This sort of "fog" was not surprising—it partly reflected the natural step-by-step evolution of an idea in which early proponents cast their intellectual and organizing net widely, drawing broadly (and sometimes inexactly) on multiple traditions, strands of evidence, and constituencies. But this early fuzziness also reflected an attempt by both researchers and activists to articulate their interactions with the economic and environmental perspectives, partly to hitch their stars to these other regionalist wagons. Such seeming

[9] Quoted in Kleidman 2004, 409.

vagueness is not something peculiar to the regional equity proponents; as Taylor (2000, 517) notes, the builders of social movements sometimes "submerge" frames and tension, thus preventing fragmentation among possible allies and allowing for greater movement growth.

One such set of fuzzy ties lay between those working on community development and those interested in the debates and strategies around Smart Growth and regional planning.[10] While various academics and activists pointed to the suburbanization of housing and jobs as one reason for inner-city decline and the social and physical isolation of the poor (Richmond 1997; Geddes 1997; Orfield 1997), others took a more environmental approach, noting that sprawl development consumed green space, threatened farmlands, and encouraged auto dependence (Cieslewicz 2002). The goals may have been different, but the tools were the same: Smart Growth principles such as making exurbs pay their full share of infrastructure expansion, encouraging infill approaches and compact development, and improving access to mass transit were as likely to improve the lives of those in distressed neighborhoods as they were to save the earth.

Of course, the potential confluence of interests also masked some underlying tensions. Steering people back to the central city, after all, was as likely to generate gentrification pressures as to provide new opportunities for longtime residents. The associated "New Urbanist" design of mixed uses and walkable neighborhoods didn't seem that new to inner-city residents. Many were worried that its first applications were in newly fashioned cities such as Seaside, Florida (famously the site for the movie *The Truman Show*), rather than in the tired neighborhoods whose existing grid already fit the vision.[11] In places such as the San Francisco Bay Area, where mainstream environmentalists had long fought to conserve open space near whiter suburbs while paying less attention to toxic contamination in the minority "flatlands," an underlying suspicion of Smart Growth and its trailing supporters was long-standing. Still, the emerging green-brown alliance gave hope for new metropolitan thinking and policy (PolicyLink 2002), and over time, Smart Growth principles have increasingly taken into account social as well as environmental sustainability.

[10] See Weaver 1984; Friedmann and Weaver 1979; Pincetl, Jonas, and Wilson 1999.

[11] Andres Duany and Elizabeth Plater-Zyberk, and their firm Duany and Plater-Zyberk, designed Seaside's town plan in the early 1980s and, as cofounders of Congress for the New Urbanism, have led a movement of New Urbanism in the United States and worldwide. See http://www.cnu.org/.

A more challenging linkage—and thus a higher level of fog—occurred between those advocates focused on pursuing equality and those economic regionalists stressing growth or competitiveness. The traditional argument, after all, was that efficiency and equity involved trade-offs—a bit more fairness, a bit less growth. But there are reasons to think such constraints are not binding: regions characterized by high levels of inequality may also tend to underinvest in human capital, even as they get involved in distributional conflicts that can derail a focus on economic growth (Pastor 2007a). And in the late 1990s a series of researchers—including Barnes and Ledebur (1998), Pastor et al. (2000), Voith (1998), and others—set out to prove the point with a series of statistical exercises demonstrating that, in fact, regional economic growth and a more equitable distribution of income at the metropolitan level tended to go hand in hand.

Both the research and the frame around the compatibility of equity and growth made inroads into some areas of the business community: in 1999, Joint Venture: Silicon Valley Network (JV:SVN), the paradigmatic business organization for a new regionalism based on the new economy, spun off the Silicon Valley Civic Action Network, an organization that included representatives from community groups as well as business leaders. JV:SVN's annual index of indicators for the Silicon Valley soon grew to include measures such as the degree of concentrated poverty and the difference between algebra scores for Anglo and Latino schoolchildren, and the yearly document made specific mention of the need, as part of a regional prosperity agenda, to reduce such disparities.

It was not a marriage of interests confined to the relatively liberal San Francisco Bay Area. The national Alliance for Regional Stewardship, formed in 2000 with a membership drawn largely from business and civic leadership groups, in the early 2000s stressed social inclusion as well as economic innovation and collaborative governance, and it promoted these principles among members covering twenty-seven states and the District of Columbia.[12] In a study of forty-five business-civic organizations in twenty-nine regions, a consulting firm named FutureWorks suggested that "a new agenda has emerged for metropolitan regions...where business leaders see clearly the link between how well their firms compete in global markets and how well their region promotes sustainable growth and economic opportunity for its citizens" (FutureWorks 2004, 3). As evidence,

[12] The membership coverage is drawn from http://www.regionalstewardship.org/members.html (as accessed on August 5, 2006).

FutureWorks cited a wide range of policy efforts, including targeted resources for poorer neighborhoods, efforts to bridge the gaps between urban and suburban school districts, and more indirect equity-enhancing efforts such as workforce development and affordable housing.

Of course, business did not always have an especially deep commitment to social equity: only one-third of the organizations FutureWorks profiled ranked social equity as a "very important" concern. And about the same percentage ranked their organizations as "effective" or "very effective" in promoting social-equity strategies—in stark contrast to the organizations' self-reported effectiveness on other issues. Between 58 and 79 percent saw themselves as effective in dealing with such issues as sector-based economic development, regional governance, building and retaining talent, and pursuing transportation and other infrastructure (Future-Works 2004, 9, 14).

Given this lackluster attitude by business, some equity advocates are worried about supporting a competitiveness agenda: corporate leaders, they argue, are uncertain allies, and competiveness will surely eclipse the focus on justice. An initial case along these lines was put forward by Ben Harrison in a piece written shortly before his death in 1999 and subsequently published in 2000, brilliantly titled "It Takes A Region (or Does It?)." Harrison wrote skeptically about the studies that showed a complementarity between growth and equity—not because he did not wish it to be true but, rather, because he thought the case remained unproven and was not likely, even if true, to have a big effect on moving business in a more progressive direction. Even though newer methods and better controls have led to higher confidence in the statistical argument, Harrison's point about political reality was well taken.

Still, some equity advocates continue to labor in the field of business. The Metropolitan Policy Program at the Brookings Institution, headed by Bruce Katz, has emphasized the importance of central cities to America's economic future and has highlighted the issues facing poor communities, including those in America's older suburbs. Katz and his colleagues have produced some of the country's highest-quality research on concentrated poverty, housing affordability, and the extent of income inequality by space and race in U.S. metro areas. They have also constantly couched the issues in terms of regional competitiveness, hoping to interest business and civic leaders in working together on appropriate policy.

One example: a Brookings report arguing that if a more compact style of development were implemented over the period 2000–2025, it could reduce road-building costs at the national level by nearly 12 percent, shave water and sewer spending by 6 percent, and save 4 percent on annual spending for operations and service (Muro and Puentes 2004). A better argument for "fix it first" is hard to come by, and Michigan's Governor Jennifer Granholm soon adopted the fiscal rationale in explaining why she sought to steer the state's infrastructure dollars to central Detroit and its older suburbs.

But a critical factor in moving Governor Granholm to the seemingly rational argument was an interfaith organizing effort based in Detroit and its suburbs which had made redirecting transportation dollars part of its agenda—so much so that it was willing to sue the local metropolitan planning organization to change the voting structure so that Detroiters could exercise more influence. Our point: while there is a business case for equity—and we ourselves have often made it (Pastor 2007a; Pastor and Benner 2008)—there also needs to be a set of constituencies and institutions with "skin in the game"—folks who have a critical stake in keeping equity on the regional agenda and who see the regional agenda as a new way to fulfill long-standing demands for fairness in American society.

To understand who's doing that and why, we need to lift the fog and draw the demarcations that separate equity-oriented regionalism from other efforts. And in order to do so, we need to understand the emerging strands within the regional equity perspective itself.

Regional Equity and Its Variants

There are many ways to slice and dice any social phenomenon or policy perspective. One could look at philosophical or ideological views, drawing distinctions between those rooted in more or less radical approaches to analysis or organizing. One could examine issue areas, clumping together those who take on transportation, those who tackle housing, and those who focus on environmental disparities. One could perform a breakdown of constituent bases, analyzing whether the main supporters for any particular variant of the regional equity perspective stem from labor, community groups, community developers, urban officials, or struggling suburban mayors.[13]

[13] This constituency-based approach was taken in Pastor et al. 2000, and Dreier, Mollenkopf, and Swanstrom 2001.

Below, we take a different tack, one related to an analytical frame that we find more compelling: the distinction between projects, policies, and politics. We suggest that *community development regionalism* has as its focus the use of regional tools to achieve particular *projects*—in this view, regionalism offers a set of new strategies to achieve the traditional objectives associated with CDCs and related local efforts. We postulate that *policy reform regionalism* goes well beyond a neighborhood to focus on changes in *policy*—this perspective, often not associated with any particular constituency, tends to be more focused on technical issues and collaboration with, and persuasion of, existing policymakers. Finally, we argue that *social movement regionalism* is being built by a set of advocates who have seen regionalism as a vehicle for doing *politics*—that is, for building power in the interests of forging a broader coalition for social and economic justice.

Community Development Regionalism

Community developers are among urban America's unsung heroes. They build housing where private developers have failed. They create job-training programs where both skills and opportunities are in short supply. They offer family-support programs where households are often nontraditional and under considerable economic, social, and environmental stress. Where and when they succeed, it seems a testimony to their will and faith, a miracle of achievement against the toughest odds.

But the dramatic success stories—symbolized, for example, by the remarkable history of the Dudley Street Neighborhood Initiative in Boston—have often been accompanied by a record of only modest economic and social differences wrought by the hundreds and thousands of less able community development efforts.[14] Part of the reason, Rusk and other regionalists argue, is that they are struggling against a set of policies and practices designed to drain resources from the communities in which they are based.

In *Inside Game, Outside Game* (1999) David Rusk analyzed the impact of thirty-four "exemplary" CDCs (selected on the recommendation of two leading national associations of community development professionals)

[14] For an early account of the Dudley Street Neighborhood Initiative (DSNI), see Medoff and Sklar 1994; for more recent updates, see Weber and Smith 2003; the account in Simon 2001; and the DSNI website: http://www.dsni.org.

over the 1970s and 1980s. He found that, on average, poverty rates actually rose faster in the neighborhoods in which these CDCs were operating than in the metropolitan areas where they existed. There were, of course, some successes—and one can also argue that the neighborhoods might have fared worse in the absence of CDC activity—yet the failure to make much progress prompts concern and implies that another approach to tackling concentrated poverty might be in order. Rusk suggests that one such approach is the "outside game": organizing to change rules in regions so as to share tax resources and constrain outward sprawl, and working to deconcentrate the poor by promoting affordable housing in existing suburbs.

Some have argued that Rusk's frame disparages local capabilities; critics such as Imbroscio submitting that the CDCs' failure to move the needle on poverty is mostly due to a shift to market-oriented development and a consequent depoliticization of the community development movement (2006, 230). Others have argued that Rusk is essentially recommending a dispersal strategy—that encouraging the exodus of successful residents is "destroying the 'hood' in order to save it." Nonetheless, the regional perspective fit well with a shift in the CDC world in the 1990s from a bricks-and-mortar approach to a focus on community building and comprehensive community initiatives (CCIs) (Walsh 1997). This new emphasis on social fabric and "social capital" was easily extended to a notion that both challenging regional decisions and forming alliances with local and regional leaders could leverage new resources and opportunities for distressed communities.

The much-told tale of the Transit Village in the Fruitvale neighborhood of Oakland may be a case in point. Long a diverse lower-income area neglected by the region—as of the 2000 census, Fruitvale was about 63 percent Latino, 12 percent African American, 15 percent Asian and Pacific Islander, and 53 percent foreign-born—community leaders rose up in opposition when the Bay Area's transit authority decided in 1991 to revamp the part of the neighborhood that adjoined a local rail station in order to facilitate commuting into San Francisco for employment.[15] At first blush, the project sounded positively regional, offering local

---

[15] Of the variety of definitions of the Fruitvale area, we have chosen a slightly tighter definition than have many authors, one focusing on four census tracts, including the Fruitvale Village; the tracts excluded are whiter and wealthier. For a longer-term history of Fruitvale, see Younis 1998.

residents better access to a high-opportunity city, but in reality the improvements were aimed at constructing a parking garage so that suburbanites would have yet another place to board the Bay Area Rapid Transit (BART). Worse yet, the garage was designed to be built between Fruitvale's main commercial street and the station, virtually ensuring little spillover of commuter purchases from local businesses.

The community, led by a local CDC called the Spanish Speaking Unity Council, challenged BART in the project's environmental review. The initial plan for the garage was stopped, and the transit authority was forced to negotiate with the community on a whole new development scheme—one that placed the garage in a different location and allowed for the creation of a walkway from the commercial district to the train station. The planning and development process was laborious, as was putting together the layered financing necessary for such mixed-use development. As a result, the Fruitvale Transit Village took years and required many partners and financiers, but the plan and emerging development created space for nonprofits, neighborhood child care, a health clinic, retail shops, and both affordable and market-rate housing (Hughes 2004).

This story sounds like the best of what might be termed community development regionalism: a local CDC sees a regional opportunity gone astray, uses organizing to shift an adverse decision, leverages regional resources to promote better development, and generates a concrete project as a result. The experience also resonates with the field's original view that "poor communities need to break the isolation that left them without powerful allies and resources in mainstream society" (Anglin and Montezemolo 2004, 57). But although CDCs may find this brand of regionalism a new way to influence development, it is not clear that such organizations can be the leaders in a broader movement.

After all, CDCs have to maintain productive relations with investors, city officials, foundations, and all the other entities that help them create jobs, housing, and social services; "rocking the boat" to change regional rules can raise challenges for the basic mission of building housing and developing workforce training programs. Moreover, both the power and the accountability of CDCs are inevitably local; straying too far from that base represents a form of mission drift. Thus, in a sense, some CDCs have embraced regionalism as instrumental rather than fundamental, tactical rather than strategic. They have not discovered a whole new form of community development business; they have discovered another and perhaps more effective way to do the same business.

Policy Reform Regionalism

In trying to understand policy innovation and diffusion, political scientists have identified the concept and role of "policy entrepreneurs." The basic notion is that in various issue fields there exist a series of actors who may work outside the formal government structure—often as independent, nonprofit intermediaries. They seek to identify problems, build networks with politicians and other decision-makers interested in the problems, provide these decision-makers with appropriate research, strategies, and "frames" for understanding and solving the problem, and, through this complex combination, influence policy change in a preferred direction.[16]

Like market entrepreneurs, policy entrepreneurs are often boosters of their "product"; their recommended policy solutions are frequently a bit ahead of the research that might actually back them up. In a way, this modus operandi is no surprise: a policy innovation is driven by a sense that what is currently implemented is not working and a hunch (albeit informed by some familiarity with the issues) that a new approach could do better. Living-wage proponents, for example, early on argued that requiring companies contracting with municipal authorities to pay higher salaries would help the poor and have only minimal impact on employment; luckily enough, they were right, but it is also the case that they were basing their initial arguments on indirect research about the effects of the minimum wage.[17]

---

[16] See Roberts and King 1991, and Mintrom 1997 for discussions of the literature on policy entrepreneurs. We do not delve into the nuances here, as our main point is simply to identify this as one strand of the regional equity movement. We do, however, follow Roberts and King in limiting our attention to extragovernmental actors; some of the policy entrepreneurship literature includes public-sector officials and elected officials, but we concur that this simply muddles the analytical waters (and does not fit our case very well either).

[17] David Card and Alan Kreuger published a series of important papers in the early 1990s (summarized in Card and Kreuger 1997) challenging the conventional view that higher minimum wages reduce jobs. Living-wage advocates often explicitly based their arguments on this research. But not all the examples of policy advice outpacing research have turned out so well. Fans of charter schools, for example, have offered scant guidance (for one recent careful study which found that charters actually underperformed compared with

The field of regional equity has certainly seen its share of policy entrepreneurs—and practice has indeed often outrun theory and sometimes evidence. This phenomenon is not limited to the equity side of regionalism. In the mid-1990s, for example, the consulting firm Collaborative Economics helped develop JV:SVN, using a set of emerging ideas about the importance of regional industrial clusters, particularly in high-tech metro areas. Though nascent in the theoretical and empirical literature, Collaborative Economics worked to spin a theory and strategy that gained hold in Silicon Valley and soon elsewhere. It then helped found the Alliance for Regional Stewardship and popularized the notion that new "civic entrepreneurs" could lead economic and social change— a placeholder that both guaranteed a role for businesses and gave them a higher moral calling than what might otherwise have seemed like self-serving efforts to promote their companies (see Henton, Melville, and Walesh 1997, 2004). Along the way, the firm helped make policy and history as well as money.

On the equity side, policy entrepreneurship has been important as well. For example, building on ideas developed while working with Secretary Henry Cisneros at the U.S. Department of Housing and Urban Development (HUD), Bruce Katz created the Metropolitan Policy Program at the Brookings Institution in Washington in 1996. The program provides studies ranging from examinations of the growing foreign-born presence in America's regions to evaluations of the role of convention centers in downtown revivals, to considerations of the impact of sprawl on jobs and inner-city prospects. Its mission: to provide policy to support "inclusive, competitive, and sustainable" growth, with inclusivity often slipped in under the banner of restoring competitiveness.

How does the Brookings Metropolitan Policy Program do its work? In classic policy-entrepreneur form, it goes to where key politicians may be open to its ideas and then creates an information base that can engage those policymakers. In 2003, for example, researchers from the program began working with the then newly inaugurated Pennsylvania governor (and former Philadelphia mayor) Ed Rendell to develop a set of new

---

traditional schools, controlling for school demographics and other variables, see Braun, Jenkins, and Grigg 2006). This has not stopped charter school proponents: it is always possible to say that the experiment is ongoing, that the methodology of critics is flawed, and that the golden age lies just around the corner. As boosters of regional equity, we hope that our evidence is firmer and that the evolving performance will be demonstrable.

strategies for the state. In its December 2003 release, *Back to Prosperity: A Competitive Agenda for Renewing Pennsylvania,* the Brookings researchers argued that sprawl was "hollowing out" Pennsylvania and weakening its attractiveness to the younger creative workers that drive economies—and that the remedy consisted of reinvestment in older cities and suburbs, a move sure also to close the equity gap even as it restored competitiveness and fiscal health. To support the report, the release was accompanied by a series of presentations throughout the state and a spate of supportive news stories.

This was Policy Entrepreneurship 101: find an already sympathetic public official, craft research and a message that resonates with dominant concerns, and develop a set of relationships with "influentials" who can move the ideas forward. It is a style not limited to Brookings. The Surface Transportation Policy Project, discussed above, utilized a very small staff and a very long list of coalition members to shift federal transportation dollars in ways that encouraged transit-oriented development. Metropolitan mapper Myron Orfield has barnstormed throughout the country to sell the idea of regional tax-sharing (and now school desegregation); his success in the actual tax arena has been limited, but he has helped reframe the way officials see themselves in the regional tapestry. Smart Growth America has enlisted the support of local and state officials in the interest of more compact development, and the Funders' Network for Smart Growth and Livable Communities has, along with PolicyLink, organized a series of National Summits to spread the specific ideas associated with regional equity.

What are the limits to this approach? The first is that at least some of these policy entrepreneurs sidestep hard issues in the interest of a mainstream "framing" that can capture the attention of current policymakers. Using a competitiveness rationale to support central-city revitalization or stressing Smart Growth rules to quietly redirect dollars to distressed neighborhoods amounts to a sort of "stealth equity"—it does not address the ongoing challenges of race and de facto segregation, and some worry that these issues drop off the agenda whenever the going gets tough (or if competitiveness, say, can be restored without reducing concentrated poverty).[18]

The second limitation is more fundamental. Implicit in the policy entrepreneur approach, and not just in this field, is the sense that the real

[18] See the discussion in CORE 2006.

task is to bring intelligent analysis to those who need it, that well-framed, smart ideas can win the day. This view is part of the logic behind Smart Growth: who would support its direct opposite, and who can resist its allure once they realize the elegance of new urban design? Of course, the world is more complicated and policy entrepreneurs also get engaged in coalition-building—but as Roberts and King (1991) note, this outreach is often limited to cultivating bureaucratic insiders, high-profile elites, and select elected officials. Policy entrepreneurs, in short, generally lean toward "elite persuasion" rather than the development and building of broad constituencies.

Why is constituency development so critical for achieving regional equity? Although some imagine a win-win-win world—in which the goals of improving the economy, enhancing equity, and restoring the environment always go together—the current configuration of outward sprawl and inner-city underdevelopment does have winners and losers. The winners are naturally invested in the status quo, and they unfortunately tend to constitute the elites that policy entrepreneurs need to move. Indeed, this helps to explain why equity issues are sometimes slipped in through the back door of competitiveness: since elites stand to lose ground in any direct redistribution, they will be more persuaded by strategies that aid the economy directly—and oh, by the way, will also help the poor.

It is not clear, however, that our metropolitan policyscape can be changed without a base that can consistently challenge and not just mollify elite decision-makers. One lesson from the administration of President Bill Clinton was that a leader with good ideas and liberal principles can go only as far as he or she is supported—or pushed. Critics blamed the president when he accepted "don't ask, don't tell" rather than insisting on unlimited rights for gays in the military. But the political price he would have paid for the latter was high, and gays and their allies could not at the time mobilize the troops (so to speak) to shift the electoral calculus. The same analysis may be used for welfare reform, affirmative action, and a series of other policy arenas where more centrist ideas took hold in the Clinton era—there was no mass movement strong enough to keep the president "honest," and the imperative of political survival dictated a strategy of moderation rather than quixotic stands.[19]

---

[19] Another aspect of this calculus had to do with visibility. Many policy reforms that did make a difference often slipped in under the radar—one thinks of the HOPE VI program that helped alter the fact of public housing by providing opportunities to deconcentrate

We acknowledge that our lines between policy entrepreneurship and constituency mobilization are too starkly drawn. Myron Orfield, for example, may sell his ideas to elites, but he knows that the real market for his research is among officials in older and less glamorous suburbs, and he hits his real stride with the faith-based movements that often bring him to talk in church basements and town halls. PolicyLink may try to bend the ears of policymakers, but its Regional Equity Summits have brought together community developers, public officials, and social activists alike. Nevertheless, our analytical point is straightforward: if policy reforms are to stick—particularly reforms that can be controversial—mobilization and popular education must be part of the equation.

Social Movement Regionalism

Two of the coauthors of this book (Pastor and Matsuoka) first met in a church in South Central Los Angeles in 1997. One of us was a grad student and community advocate; the other was an academic who had recently collaborated on a report titled *Growing Together: Linking Regional and Community Development in a Changing Economy* (Pastor et al. 1997). The report's message was simple: the Los Angeles region would do better if it paid attention to the poor; the poor would do better if they paid attention to the region. And while such a set of links were yet to be forged, there were examples in the rest of the country suggesting that it was possible.

Being possible and being real are two different things, and the meeting in South Central was intended to mobilize a broad range of community and faith leaders to challenge the city of Los Angeles to produce a workforce development program that would accompany subsidies to regionally rooted industries, especially entertainment. After nearly 300 people had listened to a parade of speakers, a preacher stood up to close the evening gathering. He waved a copy of *Growing Together* at the crowd—and rather than wandering through the regressions and graphs, invoked in a lilting cadence the simple moral message that "people are tired of drifting apart, they want to be growing together!"

It was a heady moment for the academics among us—a bit of writing had actually been useful, something not usually noted in a tenure case

---

poverty and gain ownership. It should also be noted that Clinton did, in fact, support many of the centrist strategies. Our point here is merely that mobilization of constituencies is critical if more fundamental and progressive change is to take place.

but surely more consequential on a more fateful judgment day. Yet the preacher's shift from the details of data to the imperative of social connection signaled, especially in the context of a sweltering church, that what regional equity could speak to was far more than urban planning, community redevelopment, and transportation efficiency. It had the power to bring forth a message of cohesion for which many seemed to be longing—and it provided a way to bring to the fore progressive ideas about power, voice, and common destiny.

For many in the regional equity field, building a progressive movement is exactly the heartfelt point of their work. Many organizations and individuals are swayed by regional analysis and regional policies per se—the set of faith-based groups that constitute the Gamaliel Foundation's network do fundamentally believe that we need to think and to make policy at a metropolitan level. But network head Greg Galluzzo does not speak much about growth management—instead, he worries about inequality and lack of connectivity in American society. For Gamaliel's leaders, the region is more than the scale of the problem; it is the level at which congregations separated by geography, race, and class can come together and change the balance of power in America.

You find the same broader vision in many labor-based efforts as well. The labor-affiliated think tank Working Partnerships in San Jose, has taken the regional scale seriously in its various analyses: it has issued studies on the region's key industries, highlighted the need for affordable housing in a high-tech economy, and participated in urban planning efforts aimed at livability.[20] But its hallmark has been training a cadre of interconnected community leaders in understanding the economy and developing a systematic analysis of power in Silicon Valley. Talk to the current head of the effort, Phaedra Ellis-Lamkins (2008), and you may hear a few words on zoning; listen longer, and you are far more likely to hear how all these studies and programs add up to an enhanced labor and community voice in a wide range of policy decisions; listen even longer, and you will hear how she is working with central labor councils from Atlanta, San Diego, Miami, and New York in order to reassert

[20] Its parallel organization in San Diego, the Center on Policy Initiatives, is perhaps even more analytically regional: one of its most well-known studies uses sophisticated cluster analysis to show how the region's high-growth industries actually contributed to rising inequality (Marcelli and Joassart 1998; Marcelli, Baru, and Cohen 2000).

labor's voice in the national debate over our nation's economic direction (Dean and Reynolds 2008).

One of the most explicit versions of this approach is seen in the work of SCOPE in Los Angeles. Founded by Anthony Thigpenn, a former member of the Black Panther Party and a longtime architect of precinct-based organizing and get-out-the-vote campaigns for progressive coalitions, SCOPE is a multidimensional social justice organization centered in South Los Angeles—and it was the host of the church-based meeting at which two of us first met. For many organizations such as Gamaliel, Working Partnerships, and others, the region is important on an *objective* level: it is the scale on which inequalities are created. For SCOPE organizers, the region is also important on a *subjective* level: it is the scale at which broader patterns of inequality are actually experienced even if they are created by national policies. As such, adopting a regional perspective is an intermediate step between a more narrow consciousness of community, neighborhood, and family and a broader consciousness of society. And SCOPE, entirely self-conscious that it is movement-building, has even developed a diagram to illustrate its view and distinguish it from traditional community organizing (see figure 2.2).

Our point is simple: for these various groups, the region is not only a new level for understanding problems and proposing solutions; it is also a new, fundamental, and strategic arena for building a broad-based social movement for justice.

What's a Social Movement?

Labeling anything a social movement gives it more immediate cachet—it certainly sounds more important, more community-oriented, and more capable of achieving fundamental social restructuring. But such labeling also lands any analyst in a long-standing and still unsettled theoretical stew about what exactly constitutes a social movement. In our particular case, the focus on regional equity also places us squarely in the midst of an academic squabble about which scale or geographic level is best suited for both building and understanding such movements.

Although it comes in many variants, social movement theory fundamentally attempts to provide a framework for examining collective action by organizations that are committed to some form of social change. In the theory, results are less important than aims: many of the efforts of such groups are not necessarily successful in either making movements

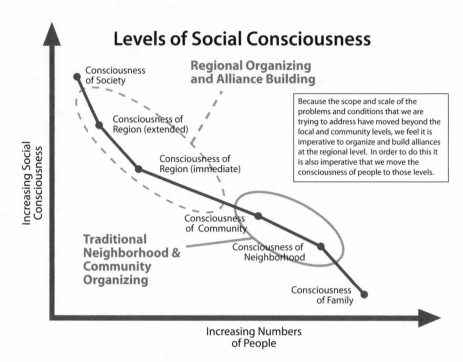

Figure 2.2. Scale and consciousness.
Source: Diagram courtesy of Strategic Concepts in Organizing and Policy Education (SCOPE), originally published in SCOPE 2003.

or shifting policy, but the *intention* of such groups is to create a social movement large enough or powerful enough to achieve their goals for social change. According to Kreisi (1996), one of the explicit strategies of these organizations is to build a base of "people power," meaning a large constituency of politically educated and empowered people with a common goal.

Social movement theories—analytical frameworks that attempt to connect people, organizations, and social change into one unified understanding—generally fall into six categories: classical social movement theory, Marxist theories on social movements, resource mobilization theory, political process and opportunity theory, new social movement theory, and "framing" theory.

According to the "classical" approach, social protest movements occur when rising expectations are not met with tangible results (Gurr 1968;

Davies 1962); the resulting tension is often exacerbated when major societal changes—depression, industrialization, urbanization—fracture the ties that bind people to the institutions and associations that exert control over the political behavior of individuals, leading to a relaxation of norms and a rise in social protest (Kornhauser 1959).

Marxist theories also tend to focus on deprivation, usually in terms of class. Here, the deprivation is not temporary but structural; however, the timing is connected to economic crises and other hardships that signal a "far more profound conflict which cannot be resolved within the existing social formation" (Piven and Cloward 1979, 8). And although in this view it is the structural features, such as class, that tend to define self-interest and collective interest, at least some in the Marxist framework suggest that collective interests are also defined in the process of movement-making.[21]

Resource mobilization theory emerged in the 1970s and tends to see social movements not as acts of deviance or even necessarily defiance but rather as deliberate, patterned collective actions directly related to the flow of social resources (McCarthy and Zald 1977). Such theorists argue that in periods of economic growth, people find the time and resources to participate in, or contribute to, social organizations—and so social movements emerge not from levels of grievance, beliefs, or other psychological conditions of participants but from the opportunities, benefits, and costs perceived by members to flow from collective action. In this sense, social movements are "integral elements of social and political life and not the product of social or psychological pathology" (Darnovsky, Epstein, and Flacks 1995, xii). Looked at in this way, the role of charitable and philanthropic involvement in funding efforts for social change suddenly becomes key.[22]

Political process and opportunity theory argues that shifts in political power and structure create shifts in the costs of challenging authorities, changing the incentives and disincentives for social protest and organizing. This changing cost-benefit calculus is critical: even though resources

---

[21] See, for example, Thompson 1978. Tilly (1979) leans to a more structural view of collective interest based on congruent self-interest.

[22] This is precisely the argument made by Jonas and Pincetl (2006), who show how investments by the Irvine Foundation seeded and grew the numerous business-led regional civic leadership efforts throughout California. Founded in 1998 and modeled after the business-led collaborative of JV:SVN, the California Community for Regional Leadership Initiative had funded twenty similar regional collaborations by 2003.

may be available (or provided by philanthropy) to launch a social movement, the nature of political conditions and structures may be so repressive that the costs of collective action are too high (McAdam 1982).[23] The emergence of social movements thus depends on how vulnerable to change the political structure is—and the relationship of social movements and political structure determines how social movements evolve and how their repertoires of collective action change over time. In his analysis of the civil rights movement, for example, McAdam (1982) argues that a slow loosening of traditional social controls in the South gave African Americans greater political leverage, creating a momentum that resulted in the *Brown v. Board of Education* ruling (1954) and the Montgomery bus boycott.[24]

The new social movement theory emerged from the explosion of social protest that characterized the 1960s. Scholars such as Alain Touraine (1971) and Manuel Castells (1983) argued that culture and identity, in addition to class, were informing political struggles in the state and economy. According to this perspective, the working class is in decline as a political actor in the postindustrial world, even as new "agents" such as women, minorities, gays, and even environmentalists, consumer advocates, and other issue-focused groupings, are rising to take their place. The resulting efforts are community-based, meaning they arise around communities of interest and geography rather than at the site of production or against the owners of capital; they are "transclass groupings of constituencies and cultural identities, where labor becomes one of, not *the* constituency group"; they tend collectively to emphasize a neopopulist vision of democracy and representation; and they tend to focus on community self-help and empowerment, often seeking independence from the state rather than state power (Fisher 1994, 217).

A final approach to social movement theory involves "framing" or social constructionist theory. This perspective suggests that social movements provide ways for individuals to make sense of their experience, particularly the interpretation and expression of grievances. These "frames" help to identify an injustice, communicate a sense of agency, and create a "we" identity that is then counterposed to those who are seen as doing the harm (Taylor 2000, 511). Dorceta Taylor notes that frames come in

---

[23] See also Tilly 1979 and Tarrow 1991.

[24] For an overview and discussion of social movement theory as the context for the emergence of women's and multiracial organizations, see Minkoff 1995.

both restricted and elaborated forms: "Black Power" lets in just a few potential allies, whereas "civil rights" casts a broader umbrella, even though both may be used by actors seeking primarily to further the interests of African Americans. Of course, the risk is that the elaborated frame can be too fuzzy—consider how former University of California Regent Ward Connerly and other conservative advocates have tried to package anti-affirmative action initiatives as part of a fight for "civil rights."

Regional equity has been compared to the civil rights movement, and we argue below that it runs the same risk—by being all things to all people, it can become nothing to everyone. But that is a subject for our conclusion. The point here is that the framing approach to building social movements lifts up the important element of consciousness-building; detaches it from specific class, ethnic, or sexual preference locations; and stresses the activity of creating a new shared identity through storytelling, collective action, and camaraderie. It brings in resource mobilization and other practical elements, but it shines a light on the struggle of ideas in which many of the regional equity proponents seem currently engaged.

Exploring the Fit

Although we do not intend to privilege frames as the master narrative of social movements, we do find the other explanations to be less appropriate to understanding regional equity. The idea of "relative deprivation" in classical theory, for example, is applicable to the kind of regional organizing that highlights the contradiction between suburban prosperity and inner-city despair. The idea that mobilization emerges from grievances, which is articulated in both classical and Marxist theory, is found in the organizing efforts of community groups that decry the lack of transportation to employment opportunities or the inadequate affordable housing in their communities.

But the classical theory seems to offer little insight about the proper scale for social movements, a key issue for our analysis. The Marxist view also has an overemphasis on class. With some exceptions, few of the regional equity proponents focus on class per se; even the labor-based initiatives broaden their scope to include other important social and residentially based groupings. This may be because class is often a difficult motivator in a world in which one's racial background, neighborhood character, and city-suburb location are also critical to economic mobility, to one's sense of identity, and to opportunities for political action.

Moreover, unlike the Marxist view that some problems cannot be resolved in the current capitalist system, social movement regionalists tend to be more willing to work toward state reform and to build relationships with state actors. This fit, in short, falls short.

Resource mobilization theory, on the other hand, accurately captures the important role that charitable investments have played in shifting some social movement organizations toward a more regional agenda—indeed, some seem to believe that philanthropic organizations, such as the Ford Foundation, have played too large a role.[25] The political opportunity theory—focusing, as it does, on the costs and benefits of engaging in social protest—would seem useful in explaining the "timing" of the regional equity movement. It has, after all, surged just as the region became important to business and civic actors, just as some suburbanites seemed eager to confront both the leakage of city poverty and the soullessness of the suburban built environment, and just as environmentalists began to realize that the route to preserving open space lay through constraints on resource-draining sprawl. With opportunities for new forums and new allies, equity proponents have jumped into the fray.

But explaining the timing does not help explain this impulse, and resource mobilization and political opportunity models do not offer a deeper analysis of the nature of the metropolitan landscape and its meaning to the actors involved. Resource mobilization theory and political opportunity theories do emphasize how special interests that mobilize assets or seize opportunities often fail to amass a broad transformational movement for systemic change. This is a useful warning—but it is against this cacophony of pluralism that regional equity proponents often rail. They are, after all, in search of a new metropolitan and national identity and not simply a specific transit-oriented development package.

The new social movements and framing approaches are helpful in this regard: though they also worry about whether multiple and fragmented identities—including the racial identities stressed by some in the regional movement—can be fashioned into a broad collective, they

---

[25] Our experience in Camden, N.J., for example, suggests that some activists see the regional equity overlay as a sort of foundation-driven imposition ill suited to their circumstances. On the other hand, the role of foundations is not limited to the equity side of the regionalist ledger: the business-oriented regional collaboratives in California, Ohio, Illinois, Pennsylvania, and elsewhere have received significant support from foundations, and some suggest that the support to the business side of regionalism seems to dwarf what is available to equity advocates.

simultaneously stress those community-based efforts and trans-class alliances that have emerged.[26] These approaches also focus on how grievances and opportunities are mobilized through action, how these play out across multiple identities, and how they come together in a single narrative or frame (see Kleidman 2004). The latter point is striking: it helps us understand why the regional equity tale turns out to a constant interplay of research, storytelling, and activism.

Social Movements and Scale

But even these perspectives on new identities and collective framing leave open a big question: why would such equity-oriented social movements operate at a regional scale? Since the late 1990s, the role that scale (or the size of geographic space) plays in social movements and in the strategies of social movement organizations has become a topic of interest for many researchers. Robert Wilton and Cynthia Cranford (2002) argue that "a full understanding of the political potential of social movements requires recognition of their inherently spatial nature." Similarly, Deborah Martin presents the idea of "place frames" as important analytic views from which collective action rearticulates spatial understanding and action. She writes:

> Place-based collective action involves definitions of problems, goals and strategies with explicit reference and attention to the site and subject of the activism through place-frames. It continues the "geographical project" [Herod 1991] of specifying how place informs social action, and provides a conceptual tool for imagining and understanding alternative scales and forms of place-based organizing. (2003, 747)

In their own contribution to the debate, Martin Jones and Gordon MacLeod (2004) distinguish between "regional spaces" and "spaces of regionalism," suggesting that the former are more economic and objective in their origin, whereas the latter are more a matter of created territory for political mobilization and even cultural expression. While echoing social movement theorists' notions of grievances and shifts in political

[26] Indeed, according to Castells (1997), these social movements are no longer primarily interested in contending for power in the polity, but instead in "civil society" as a cultural power formation, a strategy more relevant in a network society.

opportunity structures, all these territorial debates make the argument explicitly geographic: they suggest that new forms of organizing and regional democracy arise with both the evolution of regional economies and the devolution of federal authority to states and local entities in the absence of necessary public fiscal supports (Jonas and Pincetl 2006).[27]

In our view, scale influences the nature of social movements in several ways. First, understanding the spatial dimension of the grievance can help to clarify how the social problem arose. Consider, for example, a group of individuals who contend that their elected representatives do not represent their political priorities. Although there are multiple reasons why this might be so, one explanation might be that certain communities with common political priorities, such as minority or working-class neighborhoods, are divided by voting-district lines. Challenging districting, then, can enhance power and voice.

Second, the spatial geography of a social problem can reveal new opportunities for solutions and hence mobilization around a positive alternative. For example, many activists in inner cities are frustrated by the lack of public funds available for school, housing, or transportation improvements. Myron Orfield and David Rusk have identified regional tax base–sharing as the long-term solution to underfunded public projects and programs. Others have identified increased control over metropolitan transit authorities and the resources they allocate.[28] Still others have raised the allocation of affordable housing and how it concentrates poverty.[29] Whichever is the best strategy, the fact is that looking at the spatial dimension of the problem—that resources exist in the region but that the resources are unevenly distributed—suggests new approaches to old and seemingly intractable problems.

Third, shifting scale can also change the balance of power. In recent years, several analysts (Cox 1995 and Amin 1999, among others) have

---

[27] Jones and MacLeod (2004) define *regional spaces* as those regional economic territories theorized by economic geographers and regional planners (e.g., Storper 1997; Amin and Thrift 1995), and *spaces of regionalism* as a territorial concept in the political science, cultural geography, and cultural studies literatures which focuses on the territorial shifting of citizenship. See also Agnew 2000 and Boudreau 2000.

[28] In addition to early organizing by the Labor/Community Strategy Center and the formation of the Bus Riders Union, examples of activists challenging transit authorities include the Interfaith Federation in northwestern Indiana, and MOSES in Detroit (see chapter 3).

[29] For a critique and policy alternatives that could prevent such concentration via altering the low-income-housing tax credit, see powell et al. 2007.

argued that businesses may actually be "sticky" rather than "footloose" because of regionally based workers, markets, expertise, and business relationships.[30] This point is made eloquently by Cox, who insists that

> strong competition results in spatial embedding, a territorialisation of economic activity, or what was referred to earlier as local dependence. In other words, firms become anchored down, locally embedded by the conditions which give them the unique edge that allows them to appropriate superprofits.... In turn, this combination of superprofits and spatial entrapment opens up the possibility of a resolution of the distributional question that is more responsive to the "community": on the one hand, superprofits mean that there is something to be redistributed without threatening business viability; and, on the other hand, spatial entrapment may leave the firm with little alternative but to bargain away some of its gains. (1995, 218)

If businesses are indeed at least thus partially rooted in regional networks, it becomes possible to implement change locally in ways that might be impeded by power relations at a national scale. Thus, we saw a wave of local living-wage laws and statewide hikes in the minimum wage prior to any such movement on the national front—change is coming from the region up rather than the nation down, and smart organizers are noticing the new causal route.

Fourth, and most crucial to our analysis, by "shifting scale," organizers can identify unexpected actors who have a common interest in the social issue being addressed. The resulting alliances can bring together actors who are not necessarily unified by race, class, gender, or even a common employer (a commonality on which labor organizing sometimes depends). Thus, it is not simply lower-income blacks, whites, and Latinos working together; it is neighbors in the city and its adjoining suburbs who align to support (for example) a fairer distribution of transit dollars. Scale can also help groups cross the single-issue barriers noted by the political opportunity school: geographic alliances sometimes include a diverse assortment of actors with an array of resources and skills who would not work together on an issue had organizers not developed an awareness of the spatial dimension at play.

---

[30] These are the sorts of "untradeable interdependencies" to which regional theorist Michael Storper refers (1997, 18–22; see also Piore and Sabel 1984; Sabel 1988).

Jumping scale—from the local to the regional, from the region to the state, and from the state to the nation—is exactly the sort of stuff that builds a movement. We are not suggesting that this is the only approach to forging a new national consensus on social justice, but we do think that the identities of commonality being created at the metropolitan level can contribute to precisely that sort of unified national project.

Drawing Lines

Although we have separated regional equity proponents into three camps—*community development regionalism, policy reform regionalism,* and *social movement regionalism*—and associated each with one of a troika of *projects, policy,* and *power,* groups in the real world often drift from one role to another. Moreover, all three must come together to effect change: projects make us see the possible; policy helps make the possible standard practice; and power is what ultimately drives policy reform.

The distinctions, however, highlight some differences that we go on to explore in case studies. As we summarize in table 2.1, community development regionalists tend to have an instrumental or tactical view: the region is regarded as a way to connect new resources to achieve traditional goals of neighborhood revitalization; the constituents are local residents; and coalitions are seen as one way to leverage the outside power needed for success. Policy reform regionalists are a more amorphous bunch: they see the region as a fundamental determinant of the problems community developers wish to solve, and they believe that smart policies, appropriately researched, can be a tactical way to persuade politicians and policymakers who are eager either to address the issues or to secure new bases of support.

Both those groups are important to the social ecology of change; neither sees its role as mainly organizing the troops to make it happen. The social movement regionalists, by contrast, stress that the region is a fundamental source of social problems and a strategic arena for power-building. They too design policies and marshal research efforts (and even sometimes herd unruly academic researchers into collaborative arrangements to help them), but they ultimately believe that leadership development and community organizing are the keys to their success. They are all about the troops—and all about seeing whether they can build membership organizations, not just coalitions. Finally, some have the explicit

Table 2.1. Components of the regional equity movement

	Community Development Regionalism	Policy Reform Regionalism	Social Movement Regionalism
Concept of region	TACTICAL arena to secure resources and supporters; arena to expand scope of services and development	TACTICAL key scale to focus federal, state, and local policy intervention; interested elites at regional level who might accept changes resisted at state and national levels	STRATEGIC strategic arena for organizing to build power to influence economic and development decision-making and develop alternative institutions; attempt to use this to build up to national scale
Primary goal	physical, economic and social revitalization of neighborhoods	policy reform to change the "rules of the game"	increased power and influence
Mix of strategies	project and program development; facilitation of private and public investment	advocacy of particular regional policies; use of research and influential reports	direct organizing; policy research (in-house and targeted at certain efforts); advocacy; leadership Development
Motive forces (who is being organized) and key constituency	recipients of housing and services; those benefiting from reinvestment in marginalized neighborhoods	opinion-makers, including press; decision-makers, especially elites	working people and their families; low-income communities of color; stressed middle class, particularly those in older suburbs
Form of organization	professional nonprofits; coalitions and partnerships	professional nonprofits	membership organizations (residents, community leaders, and workers); coalitions and alliances; nonprofit organizations

notion that the region is also an important strategic scale for raising a broader consciousness and securing national power.

How this view is playing out on the ground—how the various regional equity strands are interacting—is key to whether such broad national ambitions can actually be realized. And it is to the field—its activists and their stories—that we now turn.

CHAPTER THREE

The Landscape of Social Movement Regionalism

The launching point of the civil rights movement is often portrayed as the Montgomery bus boycott of 1955–56. The popular version recounts how an unassuming black seamstress named Rosa Parks, exhausted after a long day of work, refused to give up her seat in the front of the bus to a white man. Her simple act of defiance then inspired others to rally to the cause—a spark that ignited two decades of social movement protest that transformed American society.

The full story is much more complicated. Parks's "spontaneous" act in December 1955 was rooted in her personal history as an NAACP worker, as well as in the extensive training she had received on race relations and civil protest at the Highlander Folk School. The launch of the Montgomery bus boycott was built on years of growing mobilization around racial discrimination in the city and throughout the South—indeed the first bus boycott in the region was held in Baton Rouge, Louisiana, in 1953; and as early as 1954, at least twenty-five different local organizations had been discussing plans to launch a boycott of buses in Montgomery (Kennedy 1989). The specific strategies that proved successful in sustaining the year-long boycott—originally, few people thought it would last more than several days—emerged from often intense, frequently rancorous discussions among leaders of the Montgomery Improvement Association. Keeping up the struggle required the tireless, and often anonymous, efforts of thousands of Montgomery residents. These ordinary citizens were so motivated by the vision and possibility of racial equality that they were willing to brave dogs and guns, racial slurs and fire bombs, in order to fight the good fight—and the long fight—to obtain civil rights.

The sketch of regional equity organizing we have offered up to this point is perhaps a bit too similar to the popular story of Rosa Parks: a few individual visionaries, a few acts of courage, a few striking achievements. Yet as a fuller examination of the civil rights movement demonstrates, the devil (or perhaps the angel) is in the details. A vision for regional equity remains just that—a vision—unless it is also combined with experienced political leadership, sufficient resources, and the organizational capacity to mobilize large numbers of people to engage in political action and realize significant social change.

The tasks involved are sometimes mundane and quotidian—the questions more mechanical: what does it take to move from a narrow neighborhood base to broader regional organizing? Under what circumstances will central labor councils emerge as strong voices, not just for union members but for working families throughout their regions? How have faith-based organizers linked their visions of regional equity with people's spiritual beliefs to transform regional political dynamics? What are the dynamics between these efforts and the business, environmental, and other voices also taking part in the regional debate?

We tackle these questions by examining the efforts of labor, community, faith-based, and environmental justice organizations in five metropolitan areas of the country—the San Francisco Bay Area, Detroit, Milwaukee, the Chicago/Gary region, and Los Angeles (see table 3.1). We offer up these regional stories, but our focus is on whether the various groups view regional equity as a new way to *understand problems* of economic inequality, as a new level at which to *find solutions* to community challenges, and/ or as a new scale at which to *build power* for achieving social justice.

Why these regions? Why these cases? We think that they represent a useful diversity of contexts, experiences, and approaches. The five regions possess some economies that are rapidly growing and some that are declining or stagnant; they include both newer, multicultural regions of the West and older, predominantly black and white regions of the Midwest. The regional equity organizing efforts in each region are led by a different combination of labor, community, faith-based, and environmental justice organizations. Even though these five cases do not cover the full range of regions that have experienced regional equity organizing efforts (we lift up other examples in our concluding analysis) they do span a broad and illustrative spectrum.

In Chicago, for example, the organization profiled—Bethel New Life—falls chiefly in the arena of community development regionalism.

Table 3.1. Regional case studies

Region	Regional Equity Initiative
San Francisco Bay Area	Working Partnerships USA (WPUSA) Urban Habitat (UH) Mayfair Improvement Initiative (San Jose) (MII) 7th Street/McClymonds Corridor (West Oakland) One East Palo Alto (OEPA)
Detroit	Local Initiative Support Corporation (LISC) MOSES (Gamaliel affiliate)
Milwaukee	Campaign for a Sustainable Milwaukee (CSM) Milwaukee Jobs Initiative (MJI) Wisconsin Regional Training Partnership (WRTP)
Chicago and Northwestern Indiana	Bethel New Life, Inc. Northwest Indiana Interfaith Federation (Gamaliel affiliate)
Los Angeles	Los Angeles Alliance for a New Economy (LAANE) Agenda for Grassroots Empowerment and Neighborhood Development Alternatives (AGENDA) Strategic Actions for a Just Economy (SAJE)

Bethel understands the regional framework as a way to obtain new resources, and although its work has a social movement component, it does
not see that aspect as connected to the regional level as much as does,
say, the interfaith organization in nearby Gary, Indiana. In Detroit, we
profile two groups taking very different approaches to the same regional
equity framework, one focused on community development, the other
on organizing and policy change. Traveling to Milwaukee, we demonstrate how a regional strategy around workforce development inspired
change but was ultimately bogged down in implementation. In the Bay
Area, we stress how community-based and labor organizations took advantage of an emerging business regionalism to triangulate their way
to metropolitan power. And finally, arriving in Los Angeles (reviewed
separately in chapter 4), we observe that all the strands of regional equity
seem to have flowed into supporting a major transformation of politics
and possibilities.

In each case of our region-by-region analysis, we provide some details
on the regional context and then examine the specific organizing efforts
in some depth. Along the way, we try to draw some lessons, tightening
our scrutiny of how organizations came to see the regional scale as critical for their goals, how they experienced organizing at that scale, and

how their various efforts may or may not relate to the more ambitious agenda of social movement regionalism.

Behind in the Boom:
Regional Equity and the Bay Area

The San Francisco Bay Area is well known as a hotbed of progressive social movements. From the streets of Oakland—where the Black Panthers cried out for Black Power and set up free breakfast programs for the poor; to the Berkeley and San Francisco State campuses, where shouts for civil rights, women's rights, ethnic studies, and free speech transformed the nature of higher education and national politics; and even to the former prison in the Bay, Alcatraz, where the American Indian Movement staked its claim for land and justice. Indeed, the roots of social justice struggle run deep in the San Francisco Bay Area.

It has also proved to be fertile soil for regionalism, with much of the impetus for a regional framework stemming from the business side of the equation (Jonas and Pincetl 2006). By the early 1990s, such organizations as the Bay Area Council, the Silicon Valley Manufacturing Group, and the Joint Venture: Silicon Valley Network were all on the rise—and with business regionalism in the air, community-based groups were soon to respond. In the heart of the Silicon Valley, Working Partnerships USA, a think-and-do tank launched by San Jose's central labor council, challenged "development as usual" and fought for living wages, localized community benefits, and control over new projects. In Oakland and San Francisco the Urban Habitat Program, originally focused on issues of environmental inequity, took on transportation, community investment, and even regional tax-sharing, forming a new regionwide Social Equity Caucus to carry the ball. Even resolutely neighborhood-focused efforts such as the Mayfair Neighborhood Initiative in East San Jose included regional organizing in their toolbelts.

Why did regional organizing catch on with these groups? Partly it was a reaction to the changing opportunity structure: with business in the regional game, communities needed to jump in as well. But another part of the answer lies in spatial topography: poor communities are concentrated in the flatlands that surround the Bay, and wealthier communities have spread across the green hills that ring the Bay; this configuration has created a shared experience of inequality and exclusion for poor communities in multiple jurisdictions.

The Regional Context

Historically, the Bay Area has centered on San Francisco itself, known simply as "the City" to locals in a way that symbolizes its centrality. San Francisco was previously the largest employment and population center of the region, home to many of the financial service firms and corporate headquarters that were important in its early development. Few people inside or outside the region paid much attention to San Francisco's gritty cousins in the East Bay, including the industrial working-class cities of Oakland and Richmond. San Jose in the South Bay was considered to be a sprawling backwater, essentially Los Angeles without the charm—and in the Bay Area, L.A. was never regarded as especially charming.

The 1990s brought a dramatic realignment of power and prestige. Propelled by the Internet boom, the South Bay/Silicon Valley became the Bay Area's economic engine; San Jose rose in both power and sophistication; and "the City" became the site for back office operations and Web design. But even as the Silicon Valley boomed—by the late 1990s, the San Jose metropolitan area had passed New York and Detroit as the single largest exporting region in the United States and was playing host to ten of the top thirty information technology companies in all of North America[1]—its economy was marked by striking inequalities (Siegel 1994). Highly paid engineers, programmers, technicians, and professional staff reflected the scientific and knowledge-intensive nature of production. Relatively low-paid workers in the service industries, including clerical, building services (janitorial, landscaping), cafeteria, laundry, and security staff, kept the economic machine running. But middle-level positions were few and far between.[2] Conditions for these workers and their families were exacerbated by the scorching housing

[1] U.S. Census, Exporter Location Series, 1997, as prepared by the Office of Trade and Economic Analysis, International Trade Administration, U.S. Department of Commerce. The Exporter Location Series was discontinued by the Census Bureau in 2002 and replaced by the Origin of Movement (OM) series. Current data on exports by metropolitan area is still available from the Office of Trade and Industry Information of the Department of Commerce: http://ita.doc.gov/td/industry/otea/metro/index.html. Following the economic downturn of the early 2000s, and with changes in the data-gathering system, San Jose had dropped to the seventh largest metropolitan area when measured by value of exports in 2006.

[2] In 1996, just as regionalism seemed to be bursting onto the scene and the Valley was becoming a much-celebrated paradigmatic case, an estimated 55 percent of jobs in the Valley paid less than $15.72 an hour—the threshold of pay in full-time work needed to sustain a family of four without public support (Rosner and Benner 1997).

market, which drove displacement and gentrification in many low-income neighborhoods.[3]

Regional equity organizing in the Bay Area, rooted in these conditions of economic inequality and insecurity, was also a response to political dynamics, particularly to the growing collaboration among business and government leaders throughout the region. In 1990, regional business and civic leaders developed a comprehensive regional governance proposal called Bay Vision 2020. This plan would have melded three existing regional agencies (the Association of Bay Area Governments, the Metropolitan Transportation Commission, and the Bay Area Air Quality Management Board) into a single, powerful regional planning and policy body. The proposal ultimately failed to pass muster in the state legislature; nevertheless, the discussions about creating such an entity contributed to increased civic and business collaboration throughout the region.[4]

That experience, in turn, led to the creation of a more informal regional body to deal with economic and social challenges in Silicon Valley, and in 1993, the Joint Venture: Silicon Valley Network was born. JV:SVN marked a turning point in business collaboration for regional economic development. Along with the Silicon Valley Manufacturing Group (another regional business organization, founded in 1977 by David Packard, which included representatives of thirty-two other key employers), it played an important role in ensuring that the region emerged successfully from the defense-industry-induced downturn of the early 1990s (JV:SVN 1995). But for our purposes, the key point here is that the new regional organization of business meant that social equity advocates had to decide whether to respond—and, if so, how.

The Labor Movement and the Region

The most visible response took the form of new labor groups organizing for social change and regional power. This phenomenon may come

---

[3] Between January 1996 and January 2001, the median house price in Santa Clara County, the core of Silicon Valley, more than doubled, rising from $251,000 to $577,500. By 2006 the median-priced home in the Valley was selling for an astonishing $775,000, the highest for any metropolitan region in the nation and more than three times the national median price. All housing price data is from the National Association of Realtors, available at http://www.realtor.org/Research.nsf/Pages/MetroPrice.

[4] For more information about Bay Vision 2020, see http://www.spur.org/documents/990901_article_02.shtm.

as a surprise to some observers, since most studies of the Silicon Valley economy pay little attention to unions (Kenney 2000; Lee et al. 2000; Saxenian 1994; Winslow 1995). Adding to the perception of labor as lackluster, efforts in the 1980s to organize workers in the Valley's dominant high-tech firms were defeated through a combination of intense antiunion tactics and the growing use of outsourcing and offshoring (Benner 1998b). Yet in spite of these setbacks, organizing in other key industries and occupations did gain ground and created a template for community-labor collaborations.

In 1990, for example, Service Employees International Union Local 1877, began organizing janitors at Shine Maintenance Company, a contractor hired by Apple Computer Corporation. When Shine management discovered that its largely immigrant workforce was trying to unionize, employees were suddenly required to provide evidence of their legal residence status; and those who could not document legal status were fired. SEIU 1877 then took the struggle to the community—uniting with the broader Latino population in the Valley, as well as prominent church and political figures, to publicize the plight of immigrant workers in the region's labor market. By 1992 this labor-community coalition, which named itself the Cleaning Up Silicon Valley Coalition, succeeded in persuading Apple to hire a unionized cleaning services firm. Within two years, more than 1,500 janitors working at high-tech firms throughout the Valley had become union members.[5]

A new role for labor as a regional player was signaled with the 1994 election of Amy Dean as executive officer of the South Bay Central Labor Council (SBCLC), which represents more than ninety local unions and some 150,000 workers. Dean argued that for labor to advance in the new economy, it must address the unprecedented changes in corporate structures and in market institutions that were taking place in the new information economy. She also stressed that for labor to succeed in meeting its goals, other constituencies in the Valley needed to find common ground with labor's initiatives; thus, labor's core program had to expand to include a broader notion of social equity and a concern for the needs of all working families (Brownstein 2000).

To help further its new agenda, the SBCLC established a separate nonprofit policy and research institute called Working Partnerships

<hr>

[5] Bacon n.d., http://dbacon.igc.org/Unions/04hitec0.htm (accessed March 21, 2007). See also Zlolniski 2006.

USA. The SBCLC and WPUSA began to pursue a series of specific policy objectives and coalition-organizing efforts designed to change the very rules of the game for economic development in the Valley:

> *Subsidy Accountability:* Based on the principle that corporations receiving public-sector economic development subsidies were accountable to the public, Working Partnerships developed a specific set of guidelines requiring firms that received property tax rebates to provide jobs with health insurance and a minimum wage of $10.00 an hour. This policy also required firms to refund the rebate if they failed to generate the number of jobs promised. The Labor Council organized a broad coalition in support of these provisions, and, despite the opposition of the Silicon Valley Manufacturing Group, the Santa Clara County Board of Supervisors unanimously approved the new requirements (Brownstein 2000).
>
> *Living-Wage Ordinance:* Working Partnership's and the Labor Council led a successful fight to have the city of San Jose pass a living-wage ordinance in 1997. At the time it was passed, San Jose had the highest wage level in the country—$9.50 an hour with health benefits, or $10.75 without. The ordinance also contained a worker retention clause designed to protect employees of contracted service firms and a "labor peace" clause that allowed the city to consider the potential consequences of unstable labor relations, including nonunionized firms, when it evaluated individual bidders for contracts. Despite fervent opposition from the Chamber of Commerce, the ordinance passed the city council with a handy 8-to-3 margin (Brownstein 2000).
>
> *Children's Health Initiative:* In 1999, Working Partnerships, in cooperation with People Acting in Community Together (PACT—an organization made up of thirteen local faith-based congregations), began promoting a countywide Children's Health Initiative that had the goal of providing universal health insurance coverage to all children under the age of five. By the end of 2000, WPUSA and PACT had mobilized thousands of supporters throughout the Valley. Together, they eventually convinced both Santa Clara County and the City of San Jose to dedicate their tobacco lawsuit settlement funds to this initiative, and they also managed to mobilize philanthropic monies to meet the rest of the demand for services (Long 2001).
>
> *Reforming Urban Development:* In late 2002, Working Partnerships led an initiative to ensure benefits to the local community from publicly subsidized development projects. The initial target was a $200 million downtown

development agreement between the City of San Jose, the San Jose Re-development Agency, and the CIM Group, a large developer. The resulting community benefits agreement, negotiated in early 2003, included affordable housing additions, small business outreach, subsidized leases for child care, living-wage standards for parking lot operators, and a good-faith commitment by the developer to negotiate living-wage and union-neutrality provisions with hotels and grocery stores (Folmar 2003). The SBCLC and Working Partnerships then launched a vigorous campaign with community partners for a citywide policy requiring the completion of a community impact report (CIR) for major development projects involving public subsidies (see Muller et al. 2003; Rhee and Sadler 2007).

As significant as the policy victories was the process of organizing them. These campaigns increasingly grew out of an active engagement with a range of community, faith-based, political, and business stakeholders throughout the region. Indeed, some of the struggles, particularly the Children's Health Initiative, also contributed to establishing labor as the voice for working families in general, rather than just union families. To craft this broad coalition, WPUSA worked with multiple constituencies to design a Community Economic Blueprint, a policy agenda with wide-ranging economic development goals that would ensure equitable growth for all residents in the Valley (Bhargava et al. 2001).

Working Partnerships also created an ongoing series of "Leadership Institutes," which are eight- to twelve-week courses that provide a shared analysis of the economic changes and political institutions helping to shape the region's development. Participants, who by 2007 totaled over 450, are strategically recruited to represent five key constituencies in the region: labor leaders, community organizations, leaders of faith-based communities, public-sector staff and elected officials, and leaders from the small business community and ethnic business associations (Ellis-Lamkin 2008). Leadership Institute participants are also invited to join an ongoing Leadership Network, which meets throughout the year to discuss regional issues.[6]

---

[6] The SBCLC and WPUSA also supported direct representation of workers, including three components designed to help temporary employees: (1) the creation of a best-practices temp agency in an effort to set high standards for the industry, (2) the formation of a temporary workers' membership association to lobby for change and base standards for

This was the stuff of movement-building, not just policy development. Taken together, these efforts provided a frame for identifying the regional processes that constituted significant stumbling blocks facing working families. These groups promised forums for addressing regional problems and created a new, powerful voice for building coalitions and mobilizing constituencies. Working Partnerships, in turn, increasingly positioned itself as the alternative regional voice to that of Joint Venture—and despite their early run-ins with the Silicon Valley Manufacturing Group over subsidy accountability, labor and the SBCLC began an active process of triangulation, often collaborating with the Manufacturing Group on transportation, housing, and other initiatives of mutual interest.

From a handful of staff in 1994, Working Partnerships grew to nearly thirty people in 2001. When Dean resigned from her post in 2004, she was succeeded at both WPUSA and the central labor council by Phaedra Ellis-Lamkins, a forceful, energetic young African American leader who has kept the organization engaged in regional politics, including recent efforts to influence development in the Coyote Valley, south of downtown San Jose, and a new set of reports on life for working families in the Silicon Valley (Auerhahn 2007). Meanwhile, the San Jose City Council, central to labor's regional concerns, shifted to a strong pro-labor majority, despite active carping from the local pro-business newspaper.[7] From initially being viewed as a marginal player in regional politics, representing the interests of only its own members, the labor movement had transformed itself into a unified power block on the regional level—and it began to be seen as speaking not just for the interests of union members but for all working families.

---

the industry, and (3) improved access to training for workers who were clients of the staffing service and the membership association, with a longer-term goal of creating recognizable skill ladders through standardizing certifications. Ultimately, Working Partnerships decided that the temp agency itself was not effective in transforming regional employment practices, but the membership association continued (see Benner, Leete, and Pastor 2007).

[7] One setback for labor's political power in San Jose came when the council's former political director and then city council member Cindy Chavez ran for mayor in 2006. She came in a close second, damaged by her association with the former mayor, Ron Gonzalez, who was accused of conflicts of interest, and by a vigorous campaign conducted against her by the Chamber of Commerce. The outcome was not optimal from labor's viewpoint, but labor did manage to retain a council majority.

From Environmental Justice to Regional Equity

One of the more dramatic examples of the response of social justice advocates to the new business interest in regionalism came from Urban Habitat (UH), a community-based intermediary whose principal mission was responding to issues of environmental (in)justice in the Bay Area.

Founded in 1989, UH had long utilized an underlying regional analysis that contrasted the environmental plight of the minority flatlands of the San Francisco Bay Area with the situation of the whiter hills and suburbs. In the view of UH leaders, mainstream Bay Area environmentalists had generally worked to preserve green space along the hilly areas by helping to create an impressive regional parks system, but they had ignored the flatland areas that were the sites of the region's major industrial enterprises and transportation corridors—concentrated pollution hotspots and toxic sites. This flatlands framework—in which a spatial justice agenda was essentially filling in for a racial (or, more appropriate, multiracial) agenda—was also applied when the proposed closure of four major military installations in low-lying communities threatened community economic well-being; in response, UH sought to work with advocates and community leaders to mobilize political will for the redevelopment of former federal facilities and the restoration and redevelopment of nearby contaminated and underutilized private property (so-called brownfields).

UH took a further step in this new spatial focus on geographic disparities in a regional context when it teamed up with Myron Orfield in 1997–98 to generate a document titled "What If We Shared?" (Urban Habitat 1998). The document rightly noted that everyday inequities faced by low-income residents and communities of color (housing, wages, transportation access, educational quality, public safety, etc.) were driven by tax structures that privileged suburban and exurban development. These same tax laws left inner-core neighborhoods without adequate resources to address social, economic, and environmental conditions. Following Orfield's lead, UH recommended regional tax-sharing; while, theoretically, they had prescribed the right medicine, it was a difficult fit, given the fragmented governance structure of the region (the Bay Area consists of nine counties and 101 cities) and the property tax limits in California (WPUSA 2006).

Still, the base closure effort and the growing trend toward regionalism persuaded Urban Habitat to inject its racial and spatial justice perspective into the ongoing regional dialogue. It thus joined the Bay Area Alliance for Sustainable Development, a regional coalition of business, civic, philanthropic, faith, and environmental organizations. The Bay Area Alliance, formed in 1997 to pursue shared regional goals, was perceived as closely tied to the business-oriented Bay Area Council, which UH purported to serve as its social equity voice. But believing that scarce resources should be committed to grassroots organizing and base-building—not to staffing seats at a distant regional table—some of UH's allies in the environmental justice movement criticized this move.

The growing tension was evident in a pivotal meeting that UH and its founding director, Carl Anthony, hosted in October 1998 and billed as an opportunity to develop a shared framework around "community-based regionalism." Forty-one people, representing a broad spectrum of community interests, attended the day-long event. The mood of the meeting was mixed: some organizers were animated by the possibility of "thinking and linking" to the region; others, particularly those with strong neighborhood bases, were worried that their issues would be submerged in the tide of regionalism. Urban Habitat persisted, however, and went on to found the Social Equity Caucus (SEC), a regional coalition with the goal of building an advocacy base for its regional justice agenda.

The SEC was initially a sort of shell organization: through it, Urban Habitat was able to claim that it represented a wide array of groups when it attended meetings of the Bay Area Alliance. UH served as the cochair of the newly unveiled Community Capital Investment Initiative (CCII), a regional public-private effort to revitalize low-income areas through investments in transit oriented development, brownfields cleanup, and small business development. But the actual community base of the SEC was thin, uncertain, and sometimes wary, and so UH, under the leadership of its new director, Juliet Ellis, began to shore up its organizational underpinnings through a series of quarterly meetings. These were followed by a key conference in April 2003 called "Bridging the Bay." At that meeting, nearly 100 activists—including two of this book's authors, Pastor and Matsuoka—came together to forge an explicit set of regional equity strategies and priorities.

In short order, the Social Equity Caucus developed a stronger backbone. In 2004, for example, its Transportation Justice Work Group began a campaign to have an environmental justice framework adopted by the Metropolitan Transportation Commission (MTC)—which agreed, in March 2006, to these demands for increased public participation. The

MTC committed itself to data collection and analysis that would help identify the extent of inequities in transportation funding.

Next, the SEC also became a key player in the 2007 revision of the general plan for the city of Richmond—one of the flatlands areas plagued by toxic contamination from refineries and depressed by high rates of unemployment. Along the way, it organized a series of ongoing leadership institutes, similar to the ones developed by Working Partnerships. The SEC now boasts seventy-five active member organizations throughout the region, and its current partners in developing a statewide policy agenda include Working Partnerships USA, SCOPE, ACORN, and the Community Coalition in Los Angeles.

The trajectory is striking. UH's analysis of environmental disparities had long contained an implicit theme of regional equity, but it was not until business's pursuit of regionalism in the Bay Area opened the door that UH found its footing. In forming the Social Equity Caucus, it was able to position itself as the "equity voice" in larger regional groups, all the while scrambling to bring affected constituencies on board. That it did so—rather than simply serving as a sort of Potemkin village of protest—suggests that it knew that the real muscle for change comes not in policy advocacy alone but in social-movement-building.

Communities and the Region

Urban Habitat's scramble to develop a regional approach that intersected compatibly with business and local-interest organizations suggests an important fact: being effective on a regional scale requires developing new skills and new capacities, engaging with unfamiliar organizations, and taking risks in challenging regional disparities. Both the opportunities and the obstacles faced by community-based organizations adopting a regional approach became clear to us in working hands-on with the Neighborhood Improvement Initiative (NII)—a set of multiyear, multisite capacity building projects funded by the William and Flora Hewlett Foundation in three Bay Area target neighborhoods: West Oakland, East Palo Alto, and Mayfair in San Jose (see figure 3.1).

The initiatives started without a regional frame, being based instead on the emerging notions of comprehensive community initiatives, or CCIs. Largely based in the community development field, CCIs in general and the NIIs in particular tended initially to look inward to community assets. One of the biggest innovations of CCIs, however, was their

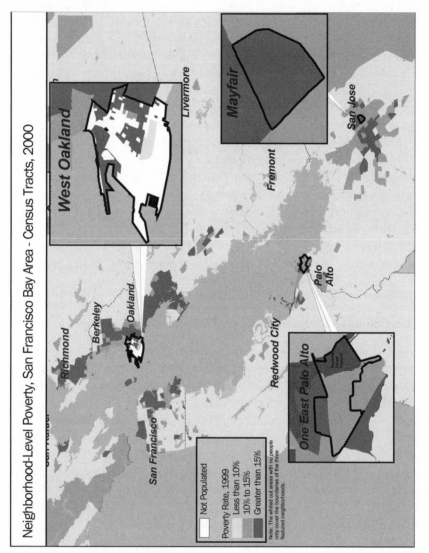

Figure 3.1. Neighborhood improvement initiatives and neighborhood poverty in the Bay Area.

focus on leadership and organizational capacity in community-based organizations.

How did a regional lens come into the picture? Just as the NIIs were launching (Mayfair in 1996, West Oakland in 1998, and East Palo Alto in 1999), the Hewlett Foundation took note of the intense regional activity in the Bay Area and decided to couple a regional training component with its technical assistance package. The three authors of this tome were asked to work with the neighborhoods as they tried to make the jump to regional action and politics. Eager to take a front-row seat as groups grappled with regional opportunities, we quickly said yes—and soon learned that linking communities and regions was much easier in theory than in practice.[8]

In Mayfair, regionalism did become a central part of the organizing efforts. In West Oakland, initial forays into regional organizing were undermined by internal organizational dynamics and tensions; however, the perspectives and the social networks of individuals involved in the initiative eventually prevailed. In East Palo Alto, organizers missed several key opportunities to focus a regional lens on their work, partly because of a sense of isolation and partly because of the state of organizational development.[9]

MAYFAIR

Why was Mayfair so seemingly open to a regional approach? One explanation is that the neighborhood has long been an immigrant entry point and thus a springboard to other locales in the region: nearly 60 percent of the population is foreign-born, half having relocated in the 1990s (U.S. Census 2000, Summary File 3). Estimates based on a survey of workers that we helped to administer suggest that at least half the adult workforce may be undocumented (Empowerment Research 2004). This sense of mobility, we think, contributed to receptivity regarding the interconnectedness of the neighborhood, the larger economy, and society. Moreover, leaders of the initiative had strong personal and historical ties to regional government entities, and early on, the organization created an advisory group of external policymakers.

[8] For background on the Hewlett NII and a critical analysis of gains and shortfalls, see Brown and Fiester 2007.

[9] Our discussion of the three cases reflects the knowledge gained from direct work with each site. For a more detailed analysis, see Pastor, Benner, and Matsuoka 2006.

Its real regionalist epiphany occurred not around housing, jobs, or transit—the usual menu of regional equity issues—but around children's health. The Mayfair Improvement Initiative (MII) initially tried to approach this question in a typical neighborhood way: leaders concentrated on training local health *promotoras,* who assisted local residents in gaining access to health services. But this method would not work without insurance, particularly for children who were not in the country legally, and so Mayfair teamed up with labor and other groups under the Children's Health Initiative mentioned earlier in persuading Santa Clara County and the City of San Jose to use tobacco settlement funds to underwrite health coverage for all the county's low-income children— regardless of immigration status. Local problem, regional lever, positive results: this experience set the stage for MII to utilize regional resources and organizing in order to better serve local needs.

Having dipped their toes in the waters of regionalism, Mayfair leaders grew interested in seeing what else might float. The initiative soon sought to develop a new employment strategy as an effort to improve job prospects for neighborhood residents. Through partnerships with the National Economic Development and Law Center (NEDLC) and the State Employment Development Department, Mayfair identified regional industries such as health services, manufacturing, and special construction trades as their top three critical employment sectors.[10] But in the process of "ground-truthing" their partners' research findings, Mayfair leaders quickly realized that no such sectoral approach could overcome the structural obstacles faced by undocumented workers. Thus, they developed an Adult Learning Center designed to work with the city's Workforce Investment Board (WIB) in addressing the gaps in job training and the absence of employment networks experienced by Mayfair residents. In this case, the regionalist analysis, flavored with local understanding, led to a more effective approach.

Along the way, the MII redefined its organizational mission from acting as a local social services agency to being an intermediary that consciously attracted and managed outside resources and initiatives to

[10] Of males in the neighborhood, 30.1 percent are in production, transportation, and material-handling moving occupations; 23 percent are in service occupations; 19.2 percent in construction trades. Of women, 28.4 percent are in production, transportation, and material-moving occupations; 24.4 percent in service occupations, 20.6 percent in office and administrative support occupations. All data are from U.S. Census 2000, Summary File 3.

meet neighborhood needs. Rechristened in 2007 *Somos Mayfair,* it has explicitly adopted a social movement frame, describing itself as "one of many Mayfairs"—that is, as one member of many similar communities throughout the Bay Area which might link together to create a larger, more powerful network, better able to organize for change, particularly around immigrant rights and neighborhood development. This commitment to change is consistent with Mayfair's history—it is the place where Cesar Chavez (1966) emerged as a neighborhood leader and then an urban organizer before turning to the activities that made him famous— but not all neighborhoods with such a glorious tradition actually stick with it. The regional perspective, we would suggest, helped Somos Mayfair steer its time-honored course.

WEST OAKLAND

The largest of all the NII sites was in West Oakland, a predominantly African American neighborhood of 14,000 residents in which 36.2 percent of the population live below the official poverty line, and 60.8 percent below 200 percent of the official poverty line—a more reasonable measure of self-sufficiency in the high-cost Bay Area.[11] It is a neighborhood physically divided from central Oakland by a freeway and socially isolated by high rates of joblessness. It is also the home of numerous activists involved in regional issues such as the reuse of the closed Oakland Army Base, the regulation of pollution from the nearby Port of Oakland, the aforementioned Community Capital Investment Initiative, and various planning processes, such as the Smart Growth Strategy/ Livability Footprint Project launched by the Association of Bay Area Governments (ABAG).

The West Oakland Initiative's original community plan seemed to reflect this sort of regionalist thinking (Bay Area Economics 1999). For example, it laid the blame for unaffordable housing on the region's rising prices and local government's unwillingness to take action. It also advocated for investments from the CCII and the Project Labor Fund (established through the Project Labor Agreement signed between the Port of Oakland and labor and community groups). Although the staff members chose to center much of their policy work on the City of Oakland, including the city's Redevelopment Agency, the West Oakland

---

[11] Ibid., block group level. For more on the footprint of the three sites, see Pastor, Benner, and Matsuoka 2006.

Initiative also took into account regional institutions and efforts such as the Business/Economic Development Caucus of the Bay Area Alliance for Sustainable Development (now called the Bay Area Alliance for Sustainable Communities) and multiagency brownfields policy and planning efforts.[12] Ironically, regionalism came naturally to West Oakland, an area long neglected by the region but filled with activists who saw a broader picture.

Unfortunately, the West Oakland Initiative was shut down at the end of 2002. The immediate cause of its demise was disagreements with its funder: the Hewlett Foundation thought that basic issues of capacity-building had been neglected and pulled the financial plug, whereas local leaders thought the foundation was being too forceful in its organizational directives. Only a small part of the disagreement was directly related to regional efforts, but the experience did indicate a need to fortify one's neighborhood and institutional base before "going regional." Mayfair, which started two years before West Oakland, had a longer period in which to build its neighborhood power and establish itself as an organization; thus it was able to take on regional work in a more selective and disciplined way.

Regional efforts begun by the West Oakland Initiative have not entirely disappeared, and community leaders have carried the lessons they've learned into other arenas. Rhonnel Sotelo (2003), former program officer from the San Francisco Foundation, notes that the "tools, skills and questions learned from regionalism discussions are visible in policy discussions. There's an increased training and knowledge base now...less quantifiable (than the usual community improvement measures) but still powerful." For example, residents and leaders affiliated with the initiative have been involved in the Social Equity Caucus, and former staff member Margaret Gordon went on to help establish the Bay Area Ditching Dirty Diesel Collaborative, a regional effort to address the negative environmental impact on neighborhoods of ports and goods-movement activities. Still, the fact that the West Oakland Initiative no longer exists as an initiative teaches a valuable lesson: regional analyses and relationships are important, but community developers and organizers must also tend to their own gardens.

---

[12] For more information on the Bay Area Alliance for Sustainable Communities see http://www.bayareaalliance.org/

EAST PALO ALTO

The third NII, One East Palo Alto (OEPA), was located in East Palo Alto, a small city of only 2.5 square miles which has remained an island of concentrated poverty in the sea of prosperity that is the Silicon Valley.[13] In the portion of the city that was part of the OPEA effort, African Americans, who had been a solid majority in the 1980s, represented just 25 percent of neighborhood residents in 2000; Latinos constituted nearly 62 percent of the population and tended to be younger, to have more recently migrated, and to be more likely to participate in the labor market.

Regionalism appeared to be a good match for East Palo Alto, partly because market-driven opportunities were abundant. After years of what might be termed "drive-by development"—serving as a traffic-clogged thoroughfare for those heading off to high-wage employment in the Valley—East Palo Alto found developers interested in building new commercial and office space. The city thus decided to bring in both a Home Depot and eventually an IKEA—both of which were sure to attract regional tax dollars to local coffers and could be prime levers for promoting community benefits agreements to ensure living wages, greater local hiring, job training, and other possible project-related developments (e.g., space for child-care centers that would ease access to work for local residents).

But the case of IKEA, a major home-furnishing chain that was seeking to locate somewhere in the peninsula, suggested that a regional frame was not fully in place. After years of having been neglected by the region, residents were suspicious and worried that the downside of increased traffic congestion would outweigh any benefits from additional jobs and tax revenue. A vigorous resistance to IKEA led to a March 2002 election in which voters decided on Measure C, an effort to rezone an area near the freeway and bring IKEA to East Palo Alto. With political actors pressing community organizations for their views, it was an opportunity for One East Palo Alto to step up and suggest a community benefits agreement—and they did not.

The measure passed (by fewer than 150 votes) anyway,—IKEA came, community benefits were limited, and OEPA missed out on the potential momentum. Even though one could argue that the organization was still

---

[13] Indeed, in one Brookings Institution report, East Palo Alto was listed as number 26 on a list of the nation's 100 poorest suburban places, ranked by ratio of per capita income to regional per capita income (Swanstrom et al. 2004).

in development and that taking a stand one way or another could have challenged a community process built on consensus, it was an opportunity lost. The experience suggested that shifting to a broader regional equity frame, and offering popular education to bring people along, was still a bit beyond OEPA's reach.

One East Palo Alto did eventually sample the regional waters with an employment program. Reaching out to the county's Workforce Investment Board, it sought to connect East Palo Alto residents with jobs in the region's biotechnology sector and also worked with local training partners such as the Opportunities Industrial Center West (OICW) and Cañada Community College to create a vocational ESL (English as a second language) program in health care. Unfortunately, just as OEPA was positioning itself to take on jobs, a downshift in the regional economy, as well as changes in the Hewlett Foundation's program goals, led OEPA to focus its attention on other, less regionally oriented, program areas (Berger, Sale, and Galin 2006).

This shift included an inward-looking turn to educational achievement gaps and the lack of resident community involvement in local schools. With support from Cañada Community College and coaching from the National Community Development Institute (NCDI), a capacity-building intermediary, OEPA incubated and supported a new parent educational and organizing group, Nuestra Casa. Noting that many Latino parents have a difficult time communicating with predominantly monolingual English-speaking teachers, Nuestra Casa began partnering with Cañada College (and, later, faculty from Stanford University) to teach ESL classes for parents. OEPA also built on relationships with the local school district and the New Teacher Center at the University of California–Santa Cruz to launch an after-school program focused on literacy development, referral and tracking, and parent education (Berger, Sale, and Galin 2006).

Interestingly, this experience actually had elements of regional outreach, particularly the inclusion of outside educational institutions.[14]

---

[14] A similar mix of regional connections and local strategies was taken with regard to crime prevention and community safety when OEPA first joined an East Palo Alto Crime Reduction Task Force and was then tapped by a county supervisor to become the convener of the Task Force. OEPA emerged as a trusted adviser and partner to city and county leaders, including the police chief in East Palo Alto, and it was then able to bring together staff from thirteen community-based organizations to design a summer employment strategy

Still, the overall experience suggests that timing is critical. OEPA's strongest *potential* regionalist moment came during the IKEA debate when benefits from linking to the regional economy were both evident and available. The problem was that the community was not ready to accept such an argument, and OEPA was too young to do the work of persuasion. Instead, it turned to securing its neighborhood base—perhaps appropriately, since there is no regionalism before its time, and that time is set by community (not outside) dynamics. In general, OEPA's experience highlights the challenge nearly any locally based effort will face in jumping the scale to regional equity.

Make the Road by Organizing: Labor and Community in Milwaukee

In the San Francisco Bay Area, business interest in regionalism, a history of progressive organizing, and the metro's spatial topography created a fertile environment for regional equity strategies. Milwaukee actually exhibits a parallel process in the economic roots of its regionalism, albeit in the grittier confines of manufacturing; firms throughout the region faced a set of common challenges that were due to deindustrialization in the 1980s, and a prominent elite regional leadership organization was interested in facilitating regional collaboration to confront them. This occurred, however, in the context of a strong labor and socialist tradition, which meant that conservative pro-market approaches were likely to prompt tough resistance. The path to revitalization went through incorporating, not rebuffing, lower-income constituencies.

Milwaukee's spatial structure, however, is chiefly a classic central-city/suburb arrangement, with the City of Milwaukee still providing a dominant hub for the region. Partly as a result, regional equity took two forms: a Wisconsin Regional Training Partnership (WRTP) that sought to improve the skills of workers in order to retain basic industries; and a set of labor-community organizing efforts around jobs and development focused primarily on the City of Milwaukee itself. This mix of players led to a sometimes uneasy combination of advocacy and service activities.

---

for youth. In 2005, thirty young people participated in the summer program; in 2006 the program expanded to serve 200 (Phone interview with Kris Palmer, Program Officer, Hewlett Foundation, July 27, 2006).

The Regional Context

The national economic shift from manufacturing to a service-based economy deeply affected the industrial city of Milwaukee and the southeastern Wisconsin region.[15] Between 1977 and 1987, manufacturing employment in the region declined by 19.6 percent (Levine and Callaghan 1998). The City of Milwaukee was hardest hit, losing one-third of its manufacturing jobs between 1979 and 1987 (Zeidenberg 2004).[16] Partly as a result, concentrated poverty grew: in 1979, 10.2 percent of census tracts in Milwaukee County were high-poverty tracts (those in which more than 40 percent of the residents lived below the poverty line), but by 1989 this figure had increased to 47.4 percent (Levine and Callaghan 1998). Although concentrated poverty subsequently dropped to 24.4 percent of the county tracts in 1999, the dramatic increase of the earlier years foreshadowed the challenges facing the Milwaukee-based labor movement as it began its own march through regionalist thinking (Zeidenberg 2004).

Race and place mattered. In 2000, African Americans constituted 24 percent of the county's total population with about 77 percent of those living in high-poverty tracts. Much of this disparity had to do with the relative lack of access to jobs, particularly in the inner city and inner suburbs, where the majority of African Americans in the region live (Zeidenberg 2004). Employment in Milwaukee's inner city was essentially stagnant (a loss of 0.7 percent) between 1994 and 2003, whereas the metro region as a whole gained 7.3 percent, and the outer suburban counties saw an increase of more than 20 percent. In the hardest-hit neighborhoods of the inner city, the number of jobs declined by nearly 30 percent from 1994 to 2003 (University of Wisconsin–Milwaukee 2006). Employment also dropped significantly in the older, inner-ring suburbs, a phenomenon much in keeping with Orfield's vision of changing metropolitan space. Between 1986 and 1996, eleven inner-ring suburban communities underwent declines in jobs per capita, including Pewaukee (–14.8 percent), Cudahy (–18.5 percent), and West Milwaukee (–49.3 percent); meanwhile, cities west of Milwaukee, primarily in Waukesha County, continued to lead the rest of the region in number of jobs per capita, with the developing

[15] The southeastern Wisconsin region comprises of four counties: Milwaukee, Ozaukee, Waukesha, and Washington.

[16] For more information, see http://www.ssc.wisc.edu/~wright/dresser.pdf Manuscript 2000.

northern suburbs (in southern Ozaukee and Washington Counties) gaining jobs at the fastest rate (Wood, Orfield, and Rogers 2000).

Milwaukee, in short, seemed to fit a sort of regional equity paradigm to a T: an older industrial base, high levels of concentrated poverty, and unequal opportunities based on race and space. But two additional factors are important for understanding the region's unique response to these conditions. The first is its strong history of labor union organizing and its linkage with a generally progressive political environment. The second is the fact that the process of economic restructuring threatened but did not completely undermine the traditional bases of trade union power in the region.

Milwaukee's history of progressive leadership and trade union presence goes back to the early part of the twentieth century. The city has had more than forty years of being governed by socialist mayors (including the nation's first, Emil Seidel, elected in 1910): the longest continuous socialist administration in U.S. history, with Daniel Hoan, from 1916 to 1940, and Frank Zeidler, from 1940 to 1960, arguably the last socialist mayor of a major U.S. city. Linked with this strong socialist tradition was a strong labor tradition—indeed, the nation's first modern trade union, Local 125 of the Molders Union, was formed in Milwaukee in 1865.[17] Building on this history, Wisconsin became one of the most unionized of states in the nation (on a percentage basis): in 1986, 25.1 percent of the Milwaukee region's workforce was still covered by a union contract, including 31.4 percent in manufacturing, 48 percent in construction, and 60.7 percent in the public sector.[18]

The importance of unions in the region, however, is not adequately captured by numbers; for example, in 1986, nearly 20 percent of metro areas in the country had higher total unionization rates.[19] More important, in Milwaukee, unions have been accepted as a key part of the political terrain in a way that provides crucial political openings for labor-based initiatives, including those in the business sector. In the words of

[17] More information is available at http://www.wisconsinlaborhistory.org/milestones.html.

[18] Current Population Survey data for Milwaukee-Racine Consolidated Metropolitan Statistical Area (CMSA) accessed from www.unionstats.com; see also Hirsch and Macpherson (2003).

[19] Data for Milwaukee Primary Metropolitan Statistical Area (PMSA), compared to other PMSAs and Metropolitan Statistcal Area (MSAs), as accessed from www.unionstats.com; see also Hirsch and Macpherson (2003).

Julia Taylor, the current president of the Greater Milwaukee Committee (a private-sector, predominantly business-led civic organization set up in the 1940s to promote development in the region):

> The GMC has always had a strong labor component in our membership probably from the beginning. The GMC started back in the '40s, but really got going in the '50s and '60s. I think the business leadership had a pretty good relationship with labor leaders at that time. This is a big manufacturing town, and labor was always at the table. I think both on the county executive side, as well as the business community side, they worked pretty well with the various labor leaders at that time. Our membership over the years has included key labor leadership.... I've never really heard of problems working with unions as an issue in our work. (Taylor 2006)

It's a surprising statement from a business leader and one that reflects the simple fact of union power: businesses have had to get along with labor in order to get their way.

Training and the "High Road"

Of course, the immediate challenges for unions were the economic difficulties facing their core membership in manufacturing. With the specter looming of a "low road" of declining wages and shrinking employment, unions stumbled onto a regional cluster-industry approach that could ensure the competitiveness of local firms with unionized labor forces— that is, a formula that could generate a new "high road" to regional success.

One expression of this formula was the Wisconsin Regional Training Partnership (WRTP), founded in 1992 after a detailed study of skill needs and training strategies for area manufacturing firms was conducted by the Center on Wisconsin Strategies (COWS) at the University of Wisconsin–Madison. Twelve firms primarily in the metalworking industry agreed to benchmark their emerging skill needs in advanced manufacturing, conform their internal promotion and their external hiring decisions to demonstrated worker competencies, and administer their growing investments in training through joint labor-management committees. The primary unions involved were the UAW (autoworkers), the IAM (machinists), the USWA (steelworkers), and the UPIU (paperworkers) (Bernhardt, Dresser, and Rogers 2004).

In some ways, the WRTP is simply an innovative, multiunion/multi-employment labor-management partnership. In this context, its constituency is already-unionized firms and existing union members. Their goal is to promote expanded training, technological investment, and high-road competitive strategies in an effort to preserve and expand good unionized jobs. The fact that they have already accomplished this goal is a major achievement in itself, with significant demonstrated effects (including an estimated 6,000 additional jobs among member firms between 1994 and 2000). But if their activities were confined to this, they would probably be more appropriately analyzed in the context of labor revival strategies, rather than regional equity strategies.[20]

Since its founding, however, the WRTP (and the Milwaukee labor movement more broadly) has added additional components to its training and placement work that are specifically devoted to nonunion members—particularly disadvantaged inner-city residents—and built a close relationship with a series of labor-community alliances. One of the most significant of these was the Campaign for a Sustainable Milwaukee (CSM), a broad-based community effort to articulate, define, and implement an alternative economic plan for the Milwaukee metropolitan area (Weir 2001).

Founded in 1994, CSM soon released a detailed plan called *Rebuilding Milwaukee from the Ground Up* and began to focus on passing a living-wage law and improving transit for the poor. In 1997, with technical support from COWS and working closely with the WRTP, CSM helped found the Milwaukee Jobs Initiative (MJI). An eight-year project with major funding by the Annie E. Casey Foundation and matching funding from state and local sources, the initiative had the goal of pairing central-city residents with good jobs. By 2002, MJI had placed 1,405 participants in full-time jobs at an average starting wage of $10.55 an hour plus family benefits. The overwhelming majority of placed participants were people of color: 68 percent African American, and 20 percent Latino. Retention was strong by the usual standards: of all MJI placements, 73 percent were still working after a year, and 41 percent making the same or better wages (Milwaukee Jobs Initiative 2002).

The improvements in job prospects constituted a reasonable feather in CSM's hat—but the Milwaukee Jobs Initiative no longer exists. CSM was primarily an advocacy-oriented effort rooted in a tradition of political

---

[20] For that sort of analytical approach, see Benner, Leete, and Pastor 2007.

mobilization and community organizing; MJI, on the other hand, was essentially a workforce development initiative that included the business-oriented Greater Milwaukee Committee in its governance structure and also focused on training, placement, and support services. Locating both activities in the same organization, along with MJI's partnership governance structure, created significant organizational tension. Funding for the Jobs Initiative itself came to overshadow other resources, even as the leadership of CSM remained dedicated to its advocacy and activist agenda. Ultimately, this tension was not successfully managed: CSM eventually disbanded, and the activities of MJI were transferred to the WTRP.

Shifting Goals, Securing Benefits

That experience seems to illustrate how hard it is to blend activism and program implementation in the same organization, and in 2003 a more purely activist group emerged from many of the same organizers who had built relationships in CSM. Dubbed the Good Jobs and Livable Neighborhoods Coalition, it positioned itself strategically to influence the rise of redevelopment priorities within the city. Led by the Milwaukee County Central Labor Council, the Institute for Wisconsin's Future, and a church-based organizing group called Milwaukee Inner-City Congregations Allied for Hope (MICAH—a Gamaliel Foundation affiliate), the coalition included a wide range of groups such as the Sierra Club, the Milwaukee Minority Chamber of Commerce, and 9 to 5, National Association of Working Women.

The initial focus of the Good Jobs and Livable Neighborhoods Coalition was on the City of Milwaukee's Park East project, a major redevelopment initiative. The project entailed tearing down a portion of the Park East freeway just north of the city center, thereby freeing up twenty-six acres of prime real estate for development between a low-income, predominantly African American neighborhood and existing downtown development projects. The coalition's demands included a 20 percent composition of affordable housing units, a requirement that 75 percent of permanent jobs pay a living wage, a guarantee that construction contracts would go to locally owned firms paying prevailing wages, a first-source hiring program mandating that 50 percent of permanent jobs be awarded to local residents, and a project design that would benefit the adjacent community. Faced with intense opposition from the city, the coalition turned its focus to the Milwaukee County Board, the owner of sixteen of the twenty acres of land where the project was located.

At the county board level, the coalition was successful. The resulting community benefits agreement, the Park East Redevelopment Compact (PERC), is to remain in effect for the entire twenty-seven-year life of the tax increment finance district created for the project. It requires the developers to comply with the prevailing wage, follow the Disadvantaged Business Enterprise policies, set goals for local and minority hiring, fund an apprenticeship and training program, and construct affordable housing.[21] The ability to capture such community benefits is notable because it took place in a weak market region where such requirements are usually tossed aside in favor of further development. The experience also illustrates the morphing of a labor-led effort from a more traditional sectoral (sector-by-sector) employment approach to the place-based strategies typical of regional equity proponents.

The labor and community alliances that have emerged in Milwaukee and the partnerships they have forged with allied groups across the country reflect an acknowledgment of the regional economy and its influence in defining local development priorities. Many of the activities, however, have been confined to the City of Milwaukee and, to a lesser extent, Milwaukee County. The Campaign for Sustainable Milwaukee once represented a more explicit regional scale of organizing, and the efforts of WRTP do include some member firms that are in the broader metropolitan region, but the Milwaukee Jobs Initiative focused its attention within the City of Milwaukee. The Good Jobs Livable Neighborhoods Coalition combines the potency of labor and community organizing to win community benefits from local redevelopment projects—a principle that applies throughout the region—but their focus has been on development in Milwaukee city and county themselves.

Getting to regional scale, then, can involve a multilevel process in which opportunities at a local or city level are used to illustrate regional contradictions and challenges. This seems to be a thread in the Los Angeles case as well (see Chapter 4). Regardless of level, one important point from the Milwaukee case seems to be the importance of a historic legacy of labor organizing and progressive politics; though not a sine

---

[21] Details of the campaign and components of the agreement available at http://www.goodjobsfirst.org/accountable_development/community_benefit_vic.cfm (accessed January 12, 2008).

qua non, such a legacy can create the basis for concerns about regional equity to fall more squarely in the social movement regionalism that we highlight in this volume.

Race, Sprawl, and Abandonment: Equity and Collaboration in Detroit

When we first decided to visit Detroit as a case study, one of us contacted a community developer to ask for an interview. She responded suspiciously, something that we, as community-friendly academic researchers, found disconcerting. So we talked about our own histories, our own interests, and a few mutual friendships and soon discovered the reason for her wariness: too many people, she said, come to visit Detroit to profile it as the disaster of the Midwest, as the place you definitely do not want to become.

We offer here a different story. Once a thriving hub of the nation's automobile industry, the City of Detroit certainly has experienced dramatic deindustrialization and disinvestment, with large numbers of vacant lots or boarded-up buildings leading to the feel of a war zone in various parts of the city. It also seems to be a classic case of regional inequity: its central city has been defined by racial segregation and abandonment; the sprawling northern suburbs have been the iconic beneficiaries of white flight and intraregional business relocation; the fragmentation of governance structures and a history of racial conflict have made regional collaboration seemingly elusive.

But against this bleak background have risen up some of the most remarkable efforts we know of to link city and suburb in terms of political strategies and physical development: the establishment of Metropolitan Organizing Strategy Enabling Strength, a faith-based organizing affiliate of the Gamaliel Foundation, and the projects of the Local Initiative Support Corporation, a community development intermediary.

The Regional Context

Detroit's economy has become almost synonymous with the automobile industry, and at its peak, manufacturing accounted for over 40 percent of the region's workforce, with transportation manufacturing alone making up nearly 20 percent (Hyung 2002, 10). Once employing over 600,000 people, by the year 2000, manufacturing had shrunk to less than 340,000 (Neil 1991; Hyung 2002). The region as a whole still has a higher proportion of the population employed in manufacturing than the national average, but it has struggled to diversify from its dependence on the declining auto industry.

The regional decline has been spatially uneven. As the City of Detroit has slipped, the suburbs have grown dramatically, with whites (and, increasingly, others) fleeing the high tax rates and deteriorating infrastructure of the inner city to seek a better life in the surrounding areas. Between 1991 and 2001, for example, the city experienced a 7 percent decline in employment, whereas employment in the suburbs grew by 25 percent; total population in the city declined by 7 percent in the 1990s, while it grew by 8 percent in the suburbs. These patterns of flight and isolation have been accompanied by a tremendous disinvestment in the city, including abandonment of housing and properties. Detroit has almost ten abandoned buildings for every thousand residents, the second highest ratio of vacant buildings to population of all U.S. cities of more than a million residents. The city is estimated to have over 10,000 abandoned buildings, and some 45,000 land parcels have reverted to city ownership because of tax delinquency (Fox and Treuhaft 2005).

Race relations, often antagonistic, permeate nearly all aspects of political and economic life in the region (Thomas 1997). Detroit is the most segregated metropolitan area in the country, at least as measured by the black-white segregation index. In 2004, the city was 85 percent African American, compared with only 7 percent of the rest of the Detroit metropolitan area.[22] Problems of disinvestment and urban decline in the Detroit region, however, are not as simple as a city-suburb divide might imply. In fact, many older suburbs in the region have also experienced deteriorating infrastructure and declining population. Between 1990 and 2000, 57 percent of Detroit's eighty-nine suburbs experienced declining population, and 13 percent declined faster than the central city (Fox and Treuhaft 2005).

Business and public-sector leadership in the region have responded in various ways to this crisis, but a broad regional governing coalition has never been formed. The Big Three automakers retain headquarters in the

[22] The dissimilarity index for whites and blacks was 84.7 in 2000, making Detroit the most segregated Metropolitan Statistical Area (MSA) in the country (the equivalent value for Los Angeles is 67.5, and for San Jose 40.5): nearly 85 percent of whites in the metropolitan area would have to move to different census tracts in order for every census tract to reflect the same racial composition as the metro region as a whole. See http://mumford1.dyndns. org/cen2000/WholePop/WPsort/sort_d1.html.

region, but their focus has been more on restructuring within the auto industry than on significant engagement in urban redevelopment and regional economic restructuring. Other elites—based in banking, utility, and real estate—have some involvement in regional planning efforts, but as service-sector offices have moved to the Detroit suburbs, these business leaders have all too easily abandoned the city and instead focused on their suburban economic base. After the riots of 1967, business leaders did create some regional organizations such as New Detroit, Detroit Renaissance, and the Detroit Economic Development Corporation, but none of these has formed an effective overarching regional leadership coalition or vision (Orr and Stoker 1994). According to one analysis,

> Detroit Renaissance and the Detroit Regional Chamber represent the white corporate community. Among these organizations, the Big Three automobile companies and others of the old corporate "nobility" have mainly influenced Detroit Renaissance. On the other hand, banks, utilities, and the rising service-based industries have mainly influenced the Detroit Regional Chamber. New Detroit and the Detroit Economic Development Corporation are seen as the structures for the articulation of black elite preferences and, in the latter case particularly, for the mayor....These business organizations have tried to realize their own economic interests, but do not share a common vision for the region. (Hyung 2002, 16)

This, then, is not the Bay Area: there was no concerted business-sponsored regionalism to which regional equity proponents might respond, triangulate, and maneuver. Instead, organizations needed to create their own vision and strategies both to respond to disinvestment in the city and to bridge city and suburban concerns. Into this space stepped Metropolitan Organizing Strategy Enabling Strength (MOSES) and the Detroit chapter of the Local Initiative Support Corporation (LISC). And although the political goals of MOSES would seem to clash with the physical development goals of LISC, we find that in Detroit the two approaches have successfully collaborated and complemented each other through a shared regional framework.

Space, Race, and Faith

As a regional affiliate of the national Gamaliel network, MOSES was formed in 1997 with the explicit goal of becoming a regionalist social movement organization. The network is actually rooted in an earlier set of neighborhood revitalization efforts led by three congregation-based, non-profit organizations that made up the new network's core.[23] When leaders of these neighborhood revitalization projects realized that their efforts were being swamped by broader development patterns of sprawl, MOSES was founded as an attempt to address this problem.

With more than sixty-five congregations and five institutions of higher learning involved, MOSES pays attention to neighborhood concerns such as community reinvestment and safety, but it also works to address systemic issues, including "urban sprawl, lack of affordable housing, lack of adequate transportation and education, infringement upon the civil rights of immigrants, land use, and blight."[24] Its campaigns seek to mobilize large numbers of urban and suburban residents, partly to change policy, partly to "teach" groups how to reach across the usual spatial and racial boundaries in order to deal with issues such as transportation, infrastructure improvements, and the development of a land bank to facilitate redevelopment of blighted areas.

Perhaps MOSES's greatest success was related to its "Fix-it First" proposals, which required the state of Michigan to prioritize repairing and maintaining existing roads, sewers, water systems, and schools ahead of building any new infrastructure. This Fix-it First approach was to be combined with its MI*VOICE (Michigan Interfaith Voice) initiative to provide state incentives for regions to engage in regional land-use planning. MOSES worked closely with Governor Jennifer Granholm's office in promoting these policies, and at a mass meeting of 4,500 people in September 2004, the governor publicly declared her support for the policies, stating (according to MOSES organizers) that "MOSES's policy is my policy."

MOSES views its transportation initiatives as an integral part of the regional Fix-it First efforts, focusing on expanding access to mass transit and better integration of transit in the region. Detroit has an extremely limited rail system (circulating only around the downtown) and a highly fragmented transit system, with different authorities for Detroit and the

[23] These three congregations were the West Detroit Inter-faith Community Organization (WDIFCO), the Jeremiah Project, and the Northeast Organization Allied for Hope (NOAH). For more on the history of MOSES, see http://www.mosesmi.org/index_files/Page1356.htm.

[24] See MOSES' scope of work at http://www.mosesmi.org/new%20website/history2.htm.

suburbs. This patchwork creates significant problems for many people who need to commute from the city to suburban job locations, as it requires transferring at the urban border, and city and suburban bus schedules are often not coordinated.

In 2003, MOSES was instrumental in pushing for the creation of DARTA, the Detroit Area Regional Transportation Authority, as part of an intergovernmental agreement among three public agencies: the City of Detroit, which runs city transit; the Suburban Mobility Authority for Regional Transportation (SMART), which runs suburban transit; and the Regional Transit Coordinating Council (RTCC). Though this was an important step in building regional cooperation, DARTA fell short of actually becoming a regional authority. It had the power and authority to plan, design, and coordinate operation of an effective and efficient regional transportation system, but it did not merge the Detroit Department of Transportation and SMART; nor did it have the authority to impose liabilities on local governments without their consent, or to levy taxes.[25] It was dealt a further blow when a powerful public-sector union, the American Federation of State, County and Municipal Employees (AFSCME), filed a $1 million lawsuit to block establishment of DARTA until promises were made to guarantee retention of the workers at the Detroit Department of Transportation. Though the agreement was initially upheld by a lower court, the Michigan Court of Appeals in July 2005 agreed with AFSCME and voided the agreement that created DARTA. The parties that established DARTA continue to express support for regional transit coordination, but it remains unclear as to how this task will be implemented.[26]

In an alternative regional play, MOSES signed on as a key plaintiff in a lawsuit against the Southeast Michigan Council of Governments (SEMCOG), which has responsibility for distributing federal transportation dollars in the region. The voting structure of SEMCOG is based on a one-jurisdiction, one-vote principle; as a result, Detroit's predominantly African American population gets the equivalent of one vote on SEMCOG's board for every 317,000 residents, whereas the predominantly white population of suburban Livingston County gets one vote for every 39,000 residents. After unsuccessfully requesting that SEMCOG change its voting structure, the plaintiffs in the suit (which included the inner-ring

[25] See http://www.darta.info/about.html#docs.
[26] For more on DARTA, see http://www.darta.info.

suburb of Ferndale, a SEMCOG member) argued that SEMCOG, originally conceived of as a voluntary organization, had grown into a powerful regional governing entity and that its voting structure amounted to
racial discrimination. The judge ruled against them, claiming that as
an appointed body the special-purpose government was not required
to have proportional representation, and that the plaintiffs had not
brought sufficient evidence that racial discrimination influenced SEM-
COG spending (Grengs 2005).[27]

MOSES, as can be seen, offers a broad approach to regional equity, and
its issues are the stuff of planners' dreams: how great to see a community-
based organization actually worried about regional infrastructure, transit, and governance! But although it has made significant inroads into
acquiring public support and endorsement from elected officials, it has
been hard pressed to change some of the rules that have frustrated its
constituencies. In the difficult terrain of Detroit's racialized landscape,
efforts at regional integration and cooperation face sharp and constant
challenges.

Bridging Race and Place One Brick at a Time

One way to facilitate bridging efforts is one neighborhood at a time—and
this has been one new thrust of the Detroit office of the national Local
Initiatives Support Corporation. Like all LISC branches, it works with
local community development corporations to revitalize neighborhoods,
focusing on commercial revitalization and affordable housing.[28] What
does differentiate the Detroit office from many other LISC branches has
been its new concentration on accomplishing revitalization not in the
inner city but on the boundaries between Detroit and its suburbs.

Until 2003, all of Detroit LISC's investments had been concentrated
in the city itself. It began to develop a regional program when the Ford
Foundation proposed a significant investment of its resources in regional
efforts as part of a new set of Regional Equity Demonstration projects.
After extensive discussions, Detroit LISC put out a call for proposals
under its newly created Metro Detroit Regional Investment Initiative

[27] On the local side, MOSES also sought to create a Land Bank to remedy the vacancy
problem in Detroit and promote central-city reinvestment. The landbanking strategy has
not yielded success, largely because of the competing proposals put forward by the city
council and the mayor.

[28] For more on LISC, see http://www.lisc.org/detroit/.

(MDRII), a multiyear funding initiative that would focus on revitalizing communities located on the border between Detroit and the inner-ring suburbs. Projects had to be developed collaboratively, with active participation of CDCs on both sides of the city boundary, and programs had to be comprehensive, addressing both physical revitalization and social equity.

MDRII awarded each of seven lead organizations a $25,000 planning grant to develop a three-year plan, and three proposals eventually received full funding to begin implementation in 2005: the Fort Visger Revitalization Initiative in the southeast corner of the city, including the cities of Ecorse, Lincoln Park, and River Rouge; the Van Dkye–8 Mile Gateway on the northern border of Detroit and the city of Warren; and the Detroit–Grosse Point Park collaborative on the city's eastern border. Each received a one-year grant of $130,000 to $200,000 to implement physical revitalization and social equity strategies, with additional funding available for related grants, loans, technical assistance, and tax credit equity through 2007. The MDRII grant recipients represent three distinct neighborhoods with different goals and strategies, but all included a range of public, nonprofit, and private-sector collaborative partners on both sides of the city border.

By themselves, the LISC projects are not truly *regional* initiatives; they are focused on particular neighborhoods. At the same time, the challenges that these initiatives face in trying to revive neighborhoods and corridors that cross city boundaries reflect the real difficulties in bridging multiple jurisdictions within a region and, as such, shed some light on pursuing a broader regional agenda.

The challenges are perhaps clearest in the case of the Detroit–Grosse Point Park collaborative. The stark contrast between the wealthy, predominantly white suburb of Grosse Point Park and the dilapidated, run-down, predominantly African American neighborhood on the Detroit side of the border is literally evident on opposite sides of the same street. Here, much of the focus has been on "building good neighbors," trying to bring together white and black families from opposite sides of the border through youth sports leagues and arts and recreation programs. This collaboration has been further enhanced through efforts to create a Mack Avenue Business Association that would unite locally owned businesses on both sides of Mack Avenue (in an effort to improve facades and the streetscape and to promote cleaning) and the greening of the street (in an effort to foster business development).

These may be modest goals, both in the Detroit–Grosse Point Park area and in the other focal neighborhoods, but to achieve them requires facing real challenges of bridging historical racial divides and bringing people together around joint projects. It is crossing the city-suburb divide at its actual boundary line, and it is the brick-by-brick building of a new kind of community development with a new, visceral set of understandings of our common regional fate.[29]

Rebuilding the Core: Faith and Equity in Chicago and Northwestern Indiana

The Chicago metropolitan area is a sprawling megalopolis, with nearly 10 million people spread over a full fourteen counties in three different states. It has also been home to numerous neighborhood and regional equity efforts, including the South Shore Bank, which helped to break the credit barrier facing low-income minority neighborhoods, and the pioneering activities of the Center for Neighborhood Technology (profiled in chapter 2). We do not intend a full study of Chicagoland's equity initiatives here; our modest focus is on two distinct organizing initiatives—one in Chicago itself, and one centered in nearby Gary, Indiana—in which spiritual values, development, and faith-based organizing have become intertwined with regional equity organizing efforts.

We specifically examine the efforts of Bethel New Life, a community development corporation in the West Garfield neighborhood of Chicago which has evolved from a church organizing project into a multifaceted development organization whose mission is to transform West Garfield into a regional "neighborhood of choice." We also lift up the experiences of the Northwest Indiana Interfaith Federation, an affiliate of the national Gamaliel organization which works across Gary and its inner-ring suburban towns, and other cities in northwestern Indiana. Like its sister affiliate MOSES in Detroit, the federation seized regionalism as a strategic arena for forging alliances and coalitions.

We suggest that Bethel New Life represents a sort of community development regionalism "plus"—it has definitely seen and used the region

---

[29] Detroit has also been the site of a unique collaboration between the local chapter of the National Association for the Advancement of Colored People and the Michigan Land Institute, with latter better known for its attention to issues of sprawl and land preservation. See Crowell (2005).

as a lever to improve neighborhood outcomes, and it has a social movement perspective. Yet that its leaders do not really see regional equity as constituting the basis for the movement offers important cautionary lessons for enthusiasts like ourselves. The Interfaith Federation, on the other hand, sees regional equity and movement-building in the same vista, and it has had more success than Detroit's MOSES in changing some important rules and institutions.

The Regional Context

Chicago is the nation's third largest city, home to nearly 3 million residents within a metropolitan area containing more than 9 million.[30] The region is defined largely by the economy of Chicago, a city whose historical development revolved around its role as a transcontinental railroad hub and a center for steel production. Chicago's regional economy transcends urban and suburban lines into the cities and communities of Gary, East Chicago, Hammond, and Merrillville, as well as areas along the shoreline of Lake Michigan in northwestern Indiana. Chicago is also an American poster child for sprawl: between 1990 and 1996, its urban land use expanded by 40 percent while the area's population rose just 9 percent (Sierra Club 1998).

In adjacent Lake County in the neighboring state of Indiana, Gary, a city once the hub of African American culture, economy, and politics, has struggled to get a grip on the changing economy. Its industrial base, made up of steel and heavy manufacturing, began to decline in the 1970s, and between 1990 and 2000 the city's population dropped 11.9 percent to 102,746 (the fewest Gary residents since the 1930s). Meanwhile, Merrillville, its suburban neighbor, grew 12.2 percent—from 27,257 to 30,560—in the same time period (U.S. Census 2000). The decline that began in the 1970s was all the more frustrating because in 1968 Gary was the first major U.S. city to elect an African American mayor, Richard Hatcher. Political success, it seemed, came just as businesses and whites were fleeing Gary and other urban areas—and, as white flight was followed by black middle-class flight, impoverished neighborhoods were left in its wake.

---

[30] U.S. Census 2000 for Chicago MSA (Chicago–Naperville–Joliet).

Regions and Rights

As one drives south on Broadway out of downtown Gary, the impacts of sprawl and abandonment are clear. Storefronts that once housed department stores, movie theaters, and local services are boarded up. Houses on either side of Broadway, once home to large numbers of steel and oil workers and their families, are now abandoned. The building once owned by the city's newspaper, the *Gary Post-Tribune*, stands vacant. Past the intersection of 53rd Avenue and into the adjacent suburb of Merrillville, however, the Broadway landscape changes dramatically. The road, now well-paved, leads past vibrant stores, shopping centers, and auto dealerships. Signs of new housing construction are everywhere. Within ten miles from Gary, large areas of woods and open fields seem to beckon new development.[31]

It was in one of these open fields that thousands of residents from the cities and towns of Gary, Hammond, and northwestern Indiana gathered to protest sprawl development (Eaken 2002). The site, a 400-acre cornfield at 93rd Avenue and Broadway in south Merrillville, was slated to become the new home for Purdue University–Calumet's $7 million high-tech business incubator. The project promised to bring jobs and important tax revenue to the region but was to be located on undeveloped land, and in order to provide access, a large public investment to build a $47 million highway interchange on agriculturally zoned land was planned.

The protest drew thousands. Led by the Northwest Indiana Interfaith Federation, residents throughout northern Lake County argued that the project should be located in Gary so that it might anchor revitalization in that city and help rein in regional sprawl and disinvestment. Organizers had originally planned to hold the rally at a local church, but the swell of attendees forced the congregants outside to a large tent (Jackson 2006). Standing together were activists and residents from white working-class suburbs and inner-city communities, both of whom saw their futures threatened by sprawl development. Although the proposed project did go forward, the campaign to stop it helped the federation build and galvanize a stronger base of clergy and alliances throughout the region. In particular, their highly visible campaign linked the issues of transportation with inner-city development and generated a large antisprawl and civil rights constituency.

[31] Site visit by authors, February 22, 2006.

The origins of the Interfaith Federation go back to the late Rev. Vincent McCutchen, whom former federation executive director Rev. Cheryl Rivera described as "the Father of Regionalism"—a catalytic and charismatic presence that moved community leaders to test, try, and embrace regionalism. In an interview, she commented: "Pastors in the local churches, including myself, were largely focused on meeting the needs of their congregations through social services. McCutchen dragged us all kicking and screaming to this regional work" (2006).

Some of the first concrete manifestations of a regional approach came in 1991 when local church officials in the small blue-collar, inner-ring suburb of Hammond formed the Interfaith Citizens Organization (ICO) to try to prevent a federal courthouse from relocating to newer suburbs. Arguing that for a declining inner-ring suburb like Hammond, the relocation of the courthouse would further reduce the number of local jobs and substantially inhibit the amount of downtown foot traffic that fed local businesses, ICO's campaign soon became linked with faith-based organizing efforts in inner-city Gary, a place quite familiar with disinvestment (Hertz 2002). The racial contrast between the cities was striking—in 1990, Gary was nearly 80 percent black, Hammond nearly 80 percent white—but working together across the lines of race and space, and bolstered by the support of Hammond's Republican mayor, Thomas McDermott, the interfaith coalition eventually won the courthouse fight.

The announcement of a federal Empowerment Zone program in 1993 provided another opportunity for local churches to come together collaboratively and across cities in order to develop a proposal that would encompass many of the needs—particularly social service needs—of their individual communities. McCutchen and other clergy helped rally a range of community-based organizations (CBOs) from four towns in Northwest Indiana—Hammond, East Chicago, Gary, and the white working-class town of Whiting—around a unified plan that ultimately secured $100 million in Empowerment Program funds for the region. Rivera notes, "Because the CBOs worked together, it forced the respective cities to also come together and work collaboratively across municipal lines."

In 1996 the Interfaith Federation of Northwestern Indiana was born, merging the ICO with organizations in Gary. As their collaboration began to deepen and expand across the region, the federation leaders sought guidance and insight from policy and academic experts. In mid-1996 they held their first regional summit, inviting noted regional equity experts john powell, David Rusk, and Myron Orfield. This triumvirate raised the energy and commitment to the region as a strategic arena for neighborhood action. The federation's first campaign, "Operation Holy Ground," was, however, decidedly local: congregations and residents organized to take public action in the form of marches and testimonies before local city councils and to direct action against drug dealers. Together, they successfully reduced the number of drug houses operating in their neighborhoods. In the wake of that win, however, the federation realized that no matter how many abandoned buildings and crack dealers were removed, the systemic causes of concentrated poverty that spurred both addiction and the drug trade remained (Rivera 2006). A bigger target was in order.

With the help of academic and research allies, the Interfaith Federation began to focus attention in 1999 on the patterns of regional development and investment. Its members quickly learned that less than 1 percent of the then $880 million regional transportation budget of the Northwestern Indiana Regional Planning Commission (NIRPC) was proposed for bus service, the essential mode of transit for many low-income workers and residents in Gary. The federation thus chose the issue of regional transit for its campaign because transit directly related to the everyday needs of many residents in Hammond, East Gary, and Whiting.

The Federation began to call for a regional transportation system that would link urban-core residents to regional opportunities. Though local governments responded quickly to create a regional transportation authority, the federation's members were locked out of planning and decision-making; the result was a transportation authority and plan that did little to address conditions in the urban core. Recognizing that the issues and voices of the predominantly white suburban communities were also ignored in the establishment of the transit authority, the Federation reframed its transportation issues and redesigned its organizing and advocacy strategy to work in coalition with suburban interests.

The Federation argued that an efficient regional transportation system was being hindered by the fragmentation of local transportation systems—which were often designed to make access to white suburban areas more difficult for central-city blacks—and insisted that the same fragmentation also inconvenienced city-bound suburban commuters. Following the lead of the Bus Riders Union in Los Angeles, the Federation cited Title VI of the 1964 Civil Rights Act and charged the Metropolitan Planning Organization with distributing funds in a racially discriminatory manner. The result: the establishment of a regional, community-based coalition with enough influence and power over elected officials to direct establishment of the Regional Transportation Authority (RTA), which meets the needs of the region—including, in particular, the urban core.

Invariably, a victory in one arena leads to a new set of challenges. Without a secure source of funding, the RTA was unable to implement the hard-won regional transportation investments brought forth by the Federation—which therefore pushed for a statewide tax on food and beverages consumed outside the home as a permanent funding stream of approximately $6 million for the RTA to spend in Lake County. This proposition met stiff resistance from business owners but ultimately passed with a 5 to 2 vote (Shields 2002). But the tax proposal stalled in the state legislature, and the politics were soon complicated by proposals put forth in late 2006 by the Lake County Convention and Visitors Bureau to use the 1 percent food and beverage tax to fund a regional sports complex.

The Interfaith Federation was also drawn into a campaign to locate a new airport development in Gary, rather than in a suburban location in southern Lake County. The Regional Development Authority (RDA), an agency established in May 2005, secured $10 million from state toll road funds to begin regional transportation investments in northwestern Indiana, starting with the Gary/Chicago International Airport (Benman 2005). In early 2006 the airport project received a big boost with the approval of $57 million in federal funding over ten years (Benman 2006). When completed, the Gary/Chicago International Airport, located in Gary, twenty-five miles from downtown Chicago, will become the region's third airport (along with Midway International and O'Hare International).

Though the future of the RTA, the RDA, and the region's transit infrastructure is still unknown, the power relations have shifted: there is now a strong and organized force for regional equity, a force that must be reckoned with by local and state politicians. From neighborhood organizing to regional power, the Northwest Indiana Interfaith Federation has transformed the landscape so that equity considerations are clearly part of the policy table.

A Neighborhood of Choice

Forty miles northwest of Gary in the City of Chicago, the small Bethel Lutheran Church began in 1979 to fight the poverty and hopelessness that characterized its neighborhood of West Garfield Park. Today, that small church group has evolved into a powerful and often cited community development corporation, Bethel New Life, responsible for the renovation of the acclaimed West Garfield Conservatory, for the development of a charter school focused on issues of environmental sustainability and community leadership, and for the creation of a transportation-oriented development project that features an innovative model for community banking, embraces the best of green building, and hosts a highly utilized community-run day-care center.

To develop Garfield Park into such a "community of choice," Bethel New Life and its founder and former president, Mary Nelson, embraced the asset approach advocated by John McKnight (Kretzmann and McKnight 1993; McKnight 1987). Bethel New Life, however, went beyond the usual inward-looking approach that identified neighborhood strengths; it sought as well to imagine the neighborhood as a regional asset and began developing strategies to "draw the suburbs into us" as a way to achieve the overall goal of neighborhood revitalization (Nelson 2006). Thus, when the organization began looking around at the neighborhood's neglected buildings and counting up its physical and social assets, Bethel New Life quickly identified the Garfield Park Conservatory, once nationally renowned but fallen into disrepair, as a potential project. Arguing that this local resource was an underutilized regional attraction, Bethel leadership and staff worked with the Chicago Park District to renovate the site and host a new exhibit that attracted more than 500,000 visitors in the first nine months. The conservatory is now a vibrant year-round site for cultural events and exhibits and brings significant numbers of visitors to the neighborhood.

The conservatory also plays an important anchoring role in the neighborhood, serving as an onsite laboratory for a newly formed charter school across the street. The charter school, named after civil rights leader Al Raby, was the result of a campaign led by Bethel New Life to emphasize education as a core to revitalization of the neighborhood and a regional draw for parents seeking a quality urban environmental education for their children. The school features a youth-led curriculum and programs that emphasize environmental sustainability and justice— including a focus on geographic information systems (GIS)—as well as the training of community organizers.

A more far-reaching example of Bethel's regional perspective emerged when a commuter rail line running through the neighborhood was threatened with closure in 1992. Bethel recognized that the closure would damage the ability of residents to get out to the suburban areas where lower-skill employment was growing. But Bethel's leaders also recognized that suburban residents farther out on the line had an interest in maintaining access to downtown employment. As a result, they were able to form an unusual alliance of city and suburban residents. The two groups eventually persuaded the Chicago Transit Authority to keep the line open and to lay out $300 million in capital improvements and upgraded services. The Lake-Pulaski station in the neighborhood has now become the hub of Bethel's transit-oriented development project, with a 23,000-square-foot commercial center that houses a day-care facility, a community bank, commercial enterprises, a clinic, employment services, and job training.

Although Bethel New Life positions itself squarely in the business of community development, its regionalism comes in the way its members frame the issue of development: specifically, "How can West Garfield be an attractive destination point within the region? How do we capture suburban growth?" In one sense, they embrace a strategy of competitive advantage, a concept advocated by Michael Porter (1995), who makes the case that inner-city neighborhoods possess the strategic location, the assets, and the infrastructure to compete within a regional economy; the twist is that Bethel has also played up the larger regional connections and possibilities. In a sense, then, Bethel New Life is an example of community development regionalism rather than social movement regionalism.[32]

This is not to say that it is not part of a social movement. Mary Nelson and other members of Bethel New Life have been active participants in national conferences on Smart Growth, regional equity, and related matters. Like the triangulators of the Bay Area and Milwaukee, Bethel has engaged tactically with business regionalists, finding common ground when appropriate with Chicago's business-led effort, Metro 2020. Bethel's leaders clearly see themselves as part of a broader regionalist and Smart Growth trend—and they are very much movement activists. During our visit there, former director Nelson and her successor Steven McCullough were proud to note that they had just been arrested in Washington for protesting federal budget priorities.

---

[32] Simple longevity has elevated Bethel New Life's influence in City Hall as well: with a bureaucracy that experiences rapid and high turnover, Bethel emerges as an important "institutional memory" regarding development and its staff have become the experts to which the city and the political body turn for counsel and leadership.

When asked if they thought that regional equity was a social move-ment, however, they were hesitant, seemingly eager not to disappoint researchers who clearly had this in mind but also wanting to speak the truth. In their view, regionalism offers policy handles but not yet a moral vision—and what sustains movements, they argued, is a deep and abid-ing sense of values and vision. The answer suggests shortfalls in the devel-opment of the movement and directions for the road ahead.

The Terrain of Social Movement Regionalism

This quick march through the regions suggests a range of approaches to regional equity. In the Bay Area, social movement regionalism is thriv-ing, having been built both by a self-conscious labor movement and by organizations responding to business interests and regional opportuni-ties. In Milwaukee, the labor movement also played a key role, but a more community-oriented base has now stepped in; the case also illus-trates the difficulty of combining advocacy and implementation within the same organization. In Detroit, where a vigorous interfaith movement has forged allies but has often found itself stymied when trying to move policy, a community development intermediary has made progress by focusing on linking the region one neighborhood at a time. In Chicago, social movement regionalism has gained ground in terms of both poli-tics and policy, while one of the city's most successful community devel-opment efforts has embraced regionalism as a lever for resources but not as a level for social-movement-building.

Is there a common thread in these efforts? And how might they con-tribute to a broader social movement for progressive social change? To get at these questions, it may be useful to examine how the groups have used the framework of regional equity to (1) recognize the region as a new way to *understand problems* of inequity, (2) see the region as a new level at which to *find solutions* to inequity, and (3) consider the region as a larger scale at which to *build power* and fight for social justice.

Using a Regional Lens to Understand Problems

For labor-led efforts like those in Milwaukee, regional political economic analyses formed the basis for understanding inequity. A stagnating manufacturing sector and the need for regional planning that focused on high-road economic development drove the Wisconsin Regional

Training Partnership to engage with community allies in forging the Campaign for a Sustainable Milwaukee. This was also, to some degree, the pattern whereby Working Partnerships in San Jose identified many of the problems facing workers and community members in the area as being irrevocably connected to the changing regional economy, particularly the pressures in Silicon Valley generated by both the high cost of housing and rising worker insecurity.

For community-based organizations the regional perspective reveals unchecked sprawl and development patterns that have caused negative neighborhood conditions such as disinvestment, lack of affordable housing and jobs, and inadequate transportation access. Both the Interfaith Federation and Urban Habitat, for example, see the problems facing Gary, Indiana, and the flatlands of the Bay Area as directly tied to the pattern of regional sprawl and disinvestment from urban core neighborhoods of color. They also stress the dynamics of racism as it plays out in inequitable regional development—although in the spirit of coalition-building they often tend to focus more on space than on race.

Community development corporations have reframed neighborhood conditions in a broader regional context, revealing the critical and increasing gaps in the overall physical, economic, and social structure of neighborhoods. The Mayfair Improvement Initiative in East San Jose has insisted it not be left behind as the region grows, and Bethel New Life has clearly made the connection between the patterns of disinvestment in its community and the larger processes of suburbanization. But analysis does not necessarily lead to action: as the case of One East Palo Alto illustrates, even understanding the need to attract regional dollars does not automatically lead to support for the development of a region-serving furniture store—although on the other hand, OEPA has successfully used regional connections to address local issues such as education.

Looking to the Region for Solutions

On the solutions side, the regional framework prompted Detroit LISC to invest in community development collaboratives that encompassed inner-city as well as suburban issues. MOSES saw the opportunity to influence state and regional transportation policy by fusing inner-city and suburban residents into a mass base of power to win regional transportation investments. Bethel New Life recognized regionwide interest in the conservatory as a first step to neighborhood improvement, and it used suburban alliances as the regional solution to win funding to re-instate a commuter rail line in West Garfield. And Mayfair was able to stake the seemingly local issue of children's health on a broader regional campaign for city and county resources to provide insurance regardless of documentation status.

Recognizing the regional explanations for problems of inequity, how-ever, does not always lead to regional solutions or strategies. In some cases, regional-scale organizing and coalition-building were attempted at specific points in campaigns but then dropped when attention turned to more localized project development and program implementation work. In Milwaukee, the Campaign for a Sustainable Milwaukee tried to forge a broad-based effort that could change regional economic development strategies (Weir 2001). Tensions arose, however, when two divergent sets of activities—running an advocacy campaign and running a job-training program—began to clash. These tensions were exacerbated by the shrinking funding available for organizing and the increase of resources available for workforce development. Although a progressive vision for the region is still reflected in WRTP's sectoral analysis of manufacturing for workforce development opportunities, the organizing and long-term vision for community-labor infrastructure building fell by the wayside until a series of redevelopment possibilities rekindled the flame.

Similarly in Chicago, Bethel New Life found a regional solution when it reached across the region to organize local West Garfield residents and link them with suburban commuters in order to build the coalition it needed to influence decision-making by the Regional Transit Authority. The coalition came together under the common goal of saving regional transit for suburban commuters who needed the line to access their jobs downtown, as well as Garfield Park residents who needed the line to access employment opportunities in the suburbs. Once the line was reinstated, Bethel New Life turned its attention toward development of the Lake-Pulaski station and a comprehensive strategy of transit-oriented development that would anchor revitalization in the West Garfield Park neighborhood.

The pattern suggests that for some community developers the "new solution" found at the regional level might be better described as "new resources"—untapped opportunities for attracting investment (e.g., mixed-use housing and affordable housing projects, workforce develop-ment programs, and social service programs) and for leveraging pub-lic and private investment dollars back into inner-city and inner-ring suburban neighborhoods. This is particularly clear in the case of Bethel New Life: the region was the scale at which its members found *a* solution but not *the* solution, meaning that they did not embrace social movement regionalism in a way that deeply changed their organization's approach to its work. They saw a regional approach as *tactical:* that is, they recognized the region as an arena in which to secure resources and supporters and/or to expand the scope of services and development.

The Region as a New Frontier for Building Power

Other organizations, however, perceive the region as a *strategic* arena for policy intervention and for building power to influence decision-making. Labor efforts, like that of Working Partnerships (and LAANE in Los Angeles; see chapter 4), tend to think that large numbers of people will more easily recognize unequal power dynamics at the regional level and be willing to do something about it if labor is seen as a reliable ally and leadership development is broad and ongoing. Urban Habitat's advocacy and coalition-building strategies also extend from a regional analysis and leadership program—and its caring and careful feeding of the regionwide Social Equity Caucus represents its attempt find a new voice in regional policy debates.

Regional equity has been a way not only to build power but also to respond to power. In the Bay Area, social movement regionalist strategies emerged in response and in parallel to business regionalism led by organizations such as Joint Venture: Silicon Valley Network and the Bay Area Council. Working Partnerships discovered that taking a regional perspective was in sync with the nature of the new economy; this insight allowed them to pose a counterweight to business and created the space for new campaigns to promote equity, such as the Children's Health Initiative. In this view, regionalism represents a necessary arena where new values for economic growth and development can emerge from the needs and leadership of working people and their families. Theirs has been a long-term vision, replete with ideas for alternative structures, processes, and economic activity.

But again, there are tensions in such an explicitly power-focused approach. The comprehensive community initiatives funded by the Hewlett Foundation combined an operational model and a theory of social change that sought to address unequal power relationships and policy issues through community-building and leadership development. Yet as regional intermediaries, Mayfair and One East Palo Alto also needed to seek private- and public-sector funding and resources. Taking a power-based and community-organizing approach to policy and planning, however, sometimes bumps up against ongoing collaborations with traditional power brokers. Bethel New Life has also found itself playing a combination of "inside" and "outside" games—pressuring the powerful for policy change even as it strikes deals with those same elites to get city resources. This difficult balancing act suggests that those groups operating in the terrain of social movement regionalism will need either to sort out the conflicts or to streamline themselves into different and perhaps separate sorts of organizations.

Coming Together for Change

Do the groups we have portrayed here see themselves as part of a movement for regional equity? Yes and no. For the Gamaliel affiliates—MOSES in Detroit and the Interfaith Federation in northwestern Indiana—the answer is clearly yes. Gamaliel runs regular training programs on regional equity for affiliate leadership, bringing together people from across the country to share experiences and develop common leadership-development strategies. Within Detroit, MOSES clearly sees itself as part of a political movement that is trying to shift the political terrain through aggressive organizing and alliance-building. The central labor councils in Milwaukee and Silicon Valley see their regional power-building efforts as part of a broader effort to reinvigorate the labor movement and to become the voice of working families and disadvantaged residents—their is a social movement unionism with a clear regional equity agenda.

For community development organizations, with their mission and histories grounded in the business of bricks and mortar, the answer is mixed. In Chicago, Bethel New Life sees regional equity as important to understanding and advancing local development, but founder Mary Nelson (2006) stresses that regional equity is missing the "moral center" that is needed to inspire a movement. For Detroit LISC, the shift to regional equity is not a movement at all; it responds in part to a directive from the Ford Foundation. Still, it is having an important impact on local thinking by encouraging cross-border neighborhood revitalization, something that would not have arisen but for a regional equity frame.

It would seem hard to weave the tapestry of a national movement from so many threads. But before we draw too pessimistic a conclusion, it is useful to consider what may be the clearest example of where and how social movement regionalism has taken root. Los Angeles, we argue in the next chapter, is a place where the region has been identified as a source of problems, a lever for solutions, and a level for organizing. And it is a place where one of America's most antilabor, racially segregated, and sprawling metropolises has become one of its most hopeful beacons for the possibilities of new regional politics and policy.

CHAPTER FOUR

Coming Back Together in Los Angeles

In 1989, UCLA regional scholar Ed Soja published his influential *Postmodern Geographies: The Reassertion of Space in Critical Social Theory*. This breakthrough book emphasized the evolution of polycentric Los Angeles, and by doing so, it helped break through the traditional paradigm of the so-called Chicago school—the metropolitan configuration in which a central city surrounded by its suburbs was considered the archetype for all of urban America. And among the text's singular achievements was one of the boldest—perhaps most brazen—chapter titles in the urban studies literature: "It All Comes Together in Los Angeles."

It was a brave pronouncement, informed by a sense that Los Angeles represented the future of urban America. If L.A. was where it all came together, the years after the book's publication also brought a sense that L.A. was where it all fell apart. As the 1990s began, Los Angeles, already famous for its sprawling development patterns and the poverty conditions of its urban neighborhoods, saw its economy wracked by waves of plant closures and manufacturing job loss due to both defense spending cutbacks and a broader pattern of deindustrialization.

In 1992, the city and the region exploded into civil unrest. While the immediate trigger was the surprising verdict in the Rodney King police brutality trial, observers stressed that the pattern of property damage was caused more by poverty than by racial animus (Oliver et al. 1993; Pastor 1995). Further scrutiny, in turn, raised serious questions about local progressive leadership: if there was this much raw emotion and this much resentment over disparities, why was it channeled into a riot rather than a social movement?

The years after 1992 brought a dramatic rethinking and reworking of organizing, coalition-building, and progressive policy. With L.A.'s middle class still shrinking and the number of working poor on the rise, a wide array of new efforts began to emerge. When regional business leaders clamored for an expansion of the trade-serving logistics industry, primarily through expansion of the ports and retrofitting of rail lines in South L.A., a local coalition of faith-based organizations and community development groups called the Alameda Corridor Jobs Coalition rose up to demand local employment—and secured a local hiring program that soon became the largest one associated with any public works program in U.S. history.

When regional decision-makers in the transit authority continued their push for the expansion of light rail, the Bus Riders Union was founded to steer resources back to the buses that served the working poor—and secured through organizing and legal action a consent decree that directed the transit authority to do just that. When management for the regional air district created an emissions credit trading system that allowed local polluters to avoid reductions in already toxic neighborhoods, environmental justice advocates answered back with protests and a lawsuit—and eventually stopped one part of the trading program and secured the air district's adoption of environmental justice principles for future decision-making.[1] And when developers sought to expand the Staples Center, a regional arena that hosts the Los Angeles Lakers and a wide range of conventions, labor leaders and grassroots community groups raised the specter of protest—and secured a community benefits agreement that promised job training, affordable housing, and open space to local residents.

These new efforts had several common factors, including a laser-sharp focus on reducing the gap between rich and poor, a tendency to bring together multiracial coalitions, and a pragmatism in policy objectives. Each response was also accompanied by explicit attention to transforming power through building a mass base of constituents. Longtime labor and community organizers and activists entered the electoral arena and created a base of progressive leadership, particularly African American and Latino, at local and state levels which eventually led to the 2005 election of Antonio Villaraigosa, the first Latino mayor of Los Angeles since

---

[1] For one analysis, see Drury et al. 1999.

the 1870s. But these leaders also exhibited an important new willingness and marked ability to shift scale—to organize for policy change at the regional level (as with the metropolitan transit agency and the air district), and to leverage local improvements from regional investments (such as the Staples Center and the Alameda Corridor).

Los Angeles, in short, had taken an important progressive turn, and many of the effective policy strategies, such as targeting regional authorities and securing community benefits, have become a standard part of the toolkit for regional equity efforts. Most significantly, from our point of view, many of the actors were quite conscious of organizing and base-building within the context of a long-term social movement: they sought to privilege the transformation of power over specific projects and policies, to bring together new allies and resources, and to keep their eyes on the bigger prize of social justice.

To explore the ways in which regional equity goals, strategies, and organizing have fueled the progressive transformation of the city of Los Angeles and the surrounding metro area, we focus specifically on three emblematic groups. The Los Angeles Alliance for a New Economy (LAANE) is a multifaceted organization with strong ties to the labor unions and roots in the labor movement. Action for Grassroots Empowerment and Neighborhood Development Alternatives (AGENDA) is a community-based organizing institution in South Los Angeles, the traditional African American center of the region. And Strategic Actions for a Just Economy (SAJE) is a neighborhood-based organization in the Figueroa Corridor, a community that lies in the shadow of downtown Los Angeles.

Though the three organizations share the twin goals of economic and community justice, they arrived at the regional equity perspective in different ways. Taken together, however, their efforts have reframed community development and urban policy debates with an overt focus on the regional economy and regional decision-making. Utilizing core strategies of direct organizing, coalition-building, research, and policy advocacy, their efforts have resulted in significant reforms addressing poverty and income gaps across the region—and, in concert, they have revitalized a broad progressive political movement in Los Angeles.

As usual, some qualifications are in order. First, we acknowledge that many other groups contributed to L.A.'s progressive transformation or have been a key part of the new shift to equitable development. The Bus Riders Union and the Alameda Corridor Jobs Coalition, both mentioned above, pioneered regional targeting, organized broad interjurisdictional constituencies, and changed the political calculus for decision-makers in Southern California.[2] The community development field also saw a noticeable shift to a regional approach: the Community Development Technology Center (CD Tech), based at Los Angeles Trade Tech College, has trained a new generation of community developers who see their work entirely in a regional context. CD Tech has also helped to support networks of inner-city manufacturers and played a key role in the implementation of community benefits agreements. And, of course, no L.A. story would be complete without an acknowledgment of the broader role of labor, particularly of immigrant worker organizing (see Milkman and Wong 2001; Milkman 2006).[3] Still, since some narrowing is necessary, we think the three organizations reviewed here—LAANE, AGENDA, and SAJE—were among the most important in framing a new debate in L.A.

Second, we are aware that not too much should be made just yet of the L.A. "success story." When a June 2006 study by the Brookings Institution documented the decline of middle-income neighborhoods across the nation between 1970 and 2000, Los Angeles could sadly boast of having the sharpest decline of any of the 100 largest metropolitan areas in the country (Booza, Cutsinger, and Galster 2006). An earlier Brookings report listing the 100 poorest suburban places (ranked by the ratio of per capita income to regional per capita income) found that 10 percent hailed from the areas surrounding L.A. (Swanstrom et al. 2004). Increasing numbers of L.A. households are becoming the "working poor," many who live in urban core neighborhoods are already challenged by persistent and concentrated poverty (Pastor and Scoggins 2007). Housing prices in 2006 were so high that just 19 percent of the population could afford the median-priced home (Dreier and Steckler 2007). And as Ethington, Frey, and Myers (2001) note, since the 1960s, residential segregation amongst whites, blacks, Latinos, and Asians has been increasing in the region, bucking a general (albeit slow) national trend toward desegregation.

But with the dramatic change that has occurred in the balance of power, the word on the street is that help—or rather self-help—is on

[2] For more on the Bus Riders Union, see Brown 1998; Mann et al. 1996; Pastor 2001; Soja 2000; Grengs 2002. On ACJC, see Matsuoka 2005; Pastor 2001; Ranghelli 2002; Swanstrom and Banks 2007.

[3] For more on CD Tech, see Blackwell and McCullough 1999.

the way. With an economy that is relatively diverse and robust and a mayor who himself came from labor and progressive circles, there is a new backdrop for policy efforts. The landscape of social change is now populated with community benefits agreements, unionization drives in the low-wage service sector, and the institutionalization of community-based workforce development programs, all of which may finally yield significant improvements for distressed community residents.[4]

A New Economy, A New Agenda

The new economy came early to Los Angeles—but its public face was not the glitter of high-tech that is so often associated with, say, the Silicon Valley. Instead, by 1990 the Los Angeles economy had already been deindustrialized and reindustrialized—its manufacturing sector had both shrunk and been reconfigured with lower-wage labor and lower-skill production. The years that followed simply exacerbated the trend: according to the researchers at the California Budget Project (CBP), Los Angeles was "the center of the bust in the early 1990s and the periphery of the boom in the late 1990s" (CBP 2006, 3).

The CBP publication *Left Behind: California Workers and Their Families in a Changing Los Angeles* (2006) offers a succinct picture of the transformation. Between 1990 and 2005, manufacturing jobs fell 41.4 percent in Los Angeles County—a loss of 335,700 well-paying jobs accessible to relatively low-skill workers, many of them union positions.[5] Lower-wage industries and service jobs with few labor protections took the place of manufacturing; between 1990 and 2005, manufacturing's share of total employment declined by 7.8 percent, while the service sector increased its share by about the same percentage. Within manufacturing itself, the hourly wage of the typical worker in Los Angeles fell by 12.2 percent between 1989 and 2002, largely led by the decline in average hourly wage of nondurable goods employment (CBP 2006, 7).

The growth of low-wage work was accompanied by a rapid ethnic transition in the labor force. Between 1979 and 2005 both the Latino and Asian shares of the workforce doubled, while the non-Hispanic white

---

[4] For earlier accounts of these efforts, see Gottlieb et al. 2005; Nicholls 2003; and Pastor 2001.

[5] The CBP analysis is based on Employment Development Department Data, accessed February 13, 2006, from http://www.labormarketinfo.edd.ca.gov/.

share fell by half. Much of the growth for Latinos and Asians was due to immigration: between 1960 and 1990, the region's immigrant share of the population grew from 8 to 27 percent, an increase of 3.3 million foreign-born residents (Waldinger and Bozorgmehr 1996). Between 1990 and 2000, the number of foreign-born workers rose by nearly 230,000, an increase reflected across all sectors but most heavily concentrated in non-durable goods manufacturing, where immigrants made up 65.8 percent of the workforce (CBP 2006).

As the economy shifted toward lower-wage manufacturing and service industries, such as hospitality and tourism, labor realized the need to chart a new course. If unionized jobs in manufacturing were being lost, labor needed to organize immigrant workers in the rapidly growing service sectors—and it began to do so with a vengeance.

Starting in the late 1980s, for example, L.A. Local 1877 of the Service Employees International Union began organizing janitors and eventually called a citywide strike that mobilized support from other labor, community, and faith institutions, as well as regional, state, and national elected officials.[6] The strike was neither easy nor peaceful—but it birthed a new labor presence in the city and the region. On June 15, 1990, the primarily Latino and immigrant janitors and their supporters held a peaceful march and demonstration in front of a prominent Century City hotel where SEIU was seeking a contract. The protest ended with police attacking the marchers—and although some worried that the brutality would chill the atmosphere for immigrant organizing in the city, the Los Angeles Police Department's use of force actually created a backlash against the hotel owners as well as against the LAPD itself. With the wind of public opinion at their back, SEIU signed union contracts in nearly all the Century City buildings, the largest private-sector organizing success led by Latino immigrants since the United Farm Worker victories twenty years earlier (Waldinger et al. 1996).

Ten years later, the shift in the public mood was clear. In April 2000 the janitors and their union, SEIU Local 1877, struck again and marched again in Century City. This time the march began downtown, was led by elected city officials, and cheered by bystanders along the eight-mile route. The eventual results of the three-week walkout were, well, striking: workers won a 25 percent increase in their wages over a three-year

---

[6] See also Berman 1998; Waldinger et al. 1997; Savage 1998; Pastor et al. 2000; and Soja 2000.

period, more than any other janitorial contract in the previous twenty years. Other considerable gains included a $500 bonus, five sick days, and a commitment by employers to absorb increases in health insurance costs.[7]

All this activism and movement in the context of a shifting economy and a city long known for its antilabor history? Described in 1910 as a "wicked city" with "heavily guarded gates" (Milkman 2006, 36), L.A. was fiercely inhospitable to unions in the early 1900s; industrialists viewed its low wages and antiunion stance as a regional competitive advantage over high-wage, union-dense San Francisco.[8] In the 1930s and 1940s, union density finally began to grow, peaking at 37 percent in 1955; it then followed national trends and declined steadily. In recent years, however, unionization rates in the Los Angeles area have been on a gradual rise, even as national rates have been on the decline.[9] In Los Angeles, labor finally seems to have gained some momentum.

New Institutions for a New Economy

The rise of labor's voice stemmed from several factors. One was the shift to organize, rather than discount, immigrant workers. Another was the relative vacuum left by a business class that found itself weakened by the departure of large corporations and the growing role of small, and sometimes fragmented, businesses. Yet another was the growing sophistication about electoral politics on the part of the County Federation of Labor. But one outstanding expression of the "new" labor movement in Los Angeles was the formation and evolution of the Los Angeles Alliance for a New Economy.

LAANE was the outgrowth of an earlier institution: the Tourism Industry Development Corporation. TIDC was the brainchild of Maria Elena Durazo, leader of the largely immigrant Hotel Employees and

---

[7] Cleeland, 2005. SEIU has had other successes: in 2001, in partnership with Hotel Employees and Restaurant Employees (HERE) Local 814, 2,000 baggage handlers, security screeners, and food service workers at the Los Angeles Airport gained union membership as a part of the Respect LAX organizing project.

[8] This characterization, made in July 1910 in the San Francisco building trades journal *Organized Labor*, was quoted in Kazin 1987, 202, and also in Milkman 2006, 36.

[9] Whereas unionization in the U.S. and Los Angeles labor forces was tied at around 15 percent in 1996, L.A.'s rate in 2005, was 15.5 percent and the nation's was 12.5 percent. See http://www.irle.ucla.edu/research/pdfs/unionmembership-bw.pdf.

Restaurant Employees (HERE) Local 11, and Madeline Janis, former director of the Central American Refugee Center (CARECEN), an immigrant and refugee rights organization. Along with a set of community and university supporters, they created TIDC in 1993 as a research and policy organization designed to offer support for organizing campaigns in low-wage industries in Los Angeles.[10]

The name was seemingly odd for a social justice group: Tourism Industry Development Council does not immediately conjure in one's mind the face of the working poor struggling for their fair share of the pie. But this was exactly the point: TIDC hoped to make it clear that the health of the industry depended on the health of its workers. It sought to make ties with small businesses and ethnic neighborhoods that were often left off the tourist trail, and it hoped to capture a new spot in the debate by framing its efforts as an antidote for the ailments of a struggling regional industry.[11] Thus, one of its first actions was to take advantage of fact that Los Angeles was hosting the 1994 World Cup soccer games; TIDC provided detailed information on working conditions in the industry to reporters who arrived for the event, as well as maps to the lesser-known tourist destinations in East and South L.A. It was tourism promotion all right—but it was really intended to raise tourist and policymaker consciousness.

The initial efforts were slow in producing results, however, and TIDC soon decided that rather than targeting individual employers or even industries, it might be able to lift up the region's working conditions through improving the wages and benefits of firms doing business with the city. TIDC was rechristened as the Los Angeles Alliance for a New Economy in 1995—a skillful renaming and reframing designed to package the group as focused on the future, not griping about the past. LAANE then formed the Living Wage Coalition, bringing together members of

[10] The establishment of TIDC was supported by the research of the UCLA Community Scholars Program led by Gilda Haas, who later founded and now directs SAJE; interlocking directorates are apparently common in progressive as well as corporate circles. One of this book's authors (Pastor) was also on the founding board for the first few years of TIDC and was able to track the evolution of the LAANE vehicle from that vantage point. "Accidental Tourism" was the initial report by the UCLA Community Scholars Program; see http://www.spa.ucla.edu.

[11] It was also an explicit response to the criticism of a video produced HERE Local 11 called "City on the Edge," which attacked the hotel industry for forcing down wages. Accused of sabotaging the tourist sector, TIDC offered a new and more positive face for the same critique.

SEIU Local 1877 and HERE Local 11 with church and community leaders throughout the City who shared the mission of addressing ever widening income disparities in the region. Their first win—passage of the Workers Retention Act in 1996 by the L.A. City Council requiring contractors who worked with the city to retain employees who had done the work prior to subcontracting—saved the jobs of nearly 1,000 workers at the Los Angeles Airport (LAX).

A year later, in 1997, the LAANE-led coalition successfully pushed the Los Angeles City Council to adopt the Living Wage Ordinance. The landmark legislation covered not only all city workers but also those employed by companies with city contracts or city subsidies for their business, and it ensured a wage well above the $5.15 federal minimum: at least $7.25 an hour if benefits were provided and $8.50 an hour if there were no benefits.[12] It was passed despite strong opposition by the Republican mayor, Richard Riordan. The coalition relied on the elected leadership of City Councilmember Jackie Goldberg, a long-time progressive activist. She championed the issue and the ordinance, also applying the wage standards to a number of large-scale development projects in her district, which encompassed Hollywood and Silver Lake.

The development standards approach soon morphed into an equitable development strategy known as "community benefits agreements" (CBAs). LAANE's first major CBA victory occurred in the neighborhoods between the University of Southern California Campus and the Staples Center, where in 2001 the Figueroa Corridor Coalition for Economic Justice, in an effort to ensure "tangible benefits for people," negotiated a landmark agreement with the Los Angeles Arena Land Company.[13] The terms of the agreement: in exchange for $70 million in public subsidies, 70 percent of the new jobs would be unionized and/or pay a living wage;

---

[12] As of December 2006, the ordinance required firms to pay either $10.64 an hour, or $9.39 with health benefits, and to provide 12 paid days and 10 unpaid days off per year. According to a study by Fairris et al. (2005), the law raised wages for an estimated 10,000 workers, most from poor and low-income families, and employment reductions amounted to just 1 percent of all affected jobs, or an estimated 112 jobs. Following the successful citywide campaign, LAANE targeted the county and pushed the Board of Supervisors to adopt a living-wage policy there, which became effective on October 22, 1999. The county ordinance specifies that full-time contract employees must be paid $8.32 per hour with health benefits of $1.14 per hour or more, or $9.46 if health benefits are not provided. See http://lacounty.info/doing_business/living_wage.htm.

[13] On the Figueroa Corridor Coalition for Economic Justice, see http://saje.net/pro grams/fccej.php.

50 percent of the new jobs would be filled with local hires; a minimum of 20 percent of housing units would be affordable to low-income residents; a zero-interest revolving loan fund for affordable housing development would be created; and $1 million would be paid by the developer for parks and recreation facilities—among other environmental, parking, and community decision-making provisions.

Working with residents and community-based organizations, LAANE then helped carry the CBA banner into other areas, negotiating community benefits agreements with living-wage jobs, local hiring, a neighborhood improvement fund, a youth center for a project in the San Fernando Valley, and, later, a similar set of provisions in exchange for a $35 million public subsidy for the Santa Barbara Plaza retail and housing project in South L.A.

In 2003, LAANE and other accountable development activists turned their attention to one of the largest public assets in the region: Los Angeles International Airport (LAX), one of the world's busiest passenger and air cargo facilities. The target of an earlier living-wage campaign, LAX now became the focus of a campaign to secure community benefits from a proposed $11 billion modernization plan. LAANE established the LAX Coalition for Economic, Environmental, and Educational Justice, which involved labor unions, community organizations, environmentalists, and school officials in a package that secured $500 million for soundproofing houses and classrooms, developing job-training and local-hiring programs, and creating opportunities for local minority-owned firms to participate in the business growth.[14]

In 2004, this irresistible force for accountable development met a seemingly immovable object of corporate power: Wal-Mart. Even while in the throes of negotiating the airport agreement, LAANE worked in the inner-ring suburb of Inglewood to form the Coalition for a Better Inglewood. The coalition took on a ballot measure sponsored by retail giant Wal-Mart that would have allowed the chain to construct one of its Superstores the size of seventeen football fields without having to go through city oversight and environmental review. The measure was handily defeated, and although Wal-Mart still intends to build in Ingle-

---

[14] The Los Angeles World Airports (LAWA) oversees four airports in the region owned and operated by the City of Los Angeles: Ontario International (ONT), Van Nuys (VNY), and Palmdale Regional (PMD) in addition to LAX.

wood, it will now go through formal public planning and permitting processes. And what a process it will face: on July 11, 2006, the Inglewood City Council voted unanimously to approve an ordinance requiring the developers of proposed superstores to pay for an economic impact analysis that must be shared at a public hearing before the project can be approved. Inglewood is only the third jurisdiction in the United States to enact this kind of legislation.[15]

LAANE's history has not been a simple string of successes. In 2002, LAANE and Santa Monicans Allied for Responsible Tourism worked to put Measure JJ on the ballot—a living-wage ordinance that would have required larger downtown and coastal employers in Santa Monica (bordering Los Angeles on the coast) to pay employees $12.50 per hour, or $10.50 plus health benefits. Despite leading in the polls up to election day, Measure JJ was defeated.[16] This failure did not stop LAANE and its allies from working for a living-wage ordinance, and after several more years of struggle, in 2005 the Santa Monica City Council passed a living-wage ordinance covering workers employed by businesses that contract with the city.

In any case, it has been an impressive run for social justice proponents in the city and in the region, and LAANE's research, organizing, and coalition work has been a critical component in setting forth a new model for responsible development in Los Angeles (Broder 2004). What explains the successess? Aside from technical expertise—solid research, first-rate organizing, broad coalition-building—we think that the LAANE approach combines two distinct ideological strategies: reframing and rerooting.

By *reframing*, we mean the offering of a new analysis, rhetoric, and story—a strategy that is part and parcel of the new social movement theory. LAANE has focused not only on particular policies but also on changing the vision of government's role in addressing poverty and working conditions. It has not argued for enhancements in welfare spending; instead, through the living-wage and community benefits campaigns, it has suggested that those businesses receiving public contracts or public

[15] For more information on the Inglewood and Walmart campaign, see http://www.laane.org/projects/inglewood/index.html and http://www.laane.org/walmart/.

[16] A controversy over deceptive campaign practices erupted after it became known that day laborers had been hired to stand on street corners holding "No on JJ" signs. See http://www.laane.org/pressroom/stories/smart/sm030702smmirror.html.

subsidies should not strip resources from families. This sort of story sidesteps entirely the debates about market forces versus the role of the state; it starts from the presumption that they are related and that the real question about government intervention is whether it truly benefits a broad section of the public. And the activists and leaders are quite conscious about their approach: according to LAANE director Madeline Janis, "This frame and strategy have a primary goal of holding global corporations accountable to communities" (2005).

By *rerooting,* we mean understanding that globalization does not mean just a wave of footloose firms but rather the sort of regionalization of the world economy which we noted in chapter 1. Thus, LAANE has focused on reforming "sticky" industries in Los Angeles, with the implicit notion that the limited options for exit allow for better bargaining by workers. The fight for living wages reflects one part of that equation— jobs that are essentially created by the public sector are not leaving for Mexico or the Philippines. The strategy to secure CBAs reflects another part—jobs are also rooted in regional attractions such as the Staples Center or the airport, places that serve the local economy and are thus relatively immobile.[17]

Rerooting has also led to a new focus on what is termed the goods movement industry—the way in which commodities from the international economy stream through L.A.'s ports and then flow to the rest of the country. In 2006, LAANE initiated a coalition and campaign focused on the conditions facing the port's truck drivers, particularly owner-operators who are nominally independent but are, in actuality, highly dependent on large firms for contracts. The Coalition for Clean and Safe Ports involves typical labor allies, such as the Teamsters, but also new allies, including mainstream environmental organizations such as the Natural Resources Defense Council, the Coalition for Clean Air, and community-based environmental justice groups such as East Yard

---

[17] As part of this targeting, in 2006 LAANE launched "Campaign for a New Century," aimed at the tourism and hospitality industries—which clearly have nowhere else to go, since their very appeal is that they are in Los Angeles. These industries suffered from the post–September 11 economic and travel downturn, but now that they (and tourism in general) are reviving, labor is trying to organize workers at the hotels surrounding LAX. The campaign focuses on improving conditions for thousands of hotel workers, securing benefits for nearby working-class communities, and establishing new processes of economic development decision-making in the tourism industry (Flaming, Burns, and Haydamack 2006, 2).

Communities for Environmental Justice and the Coalition for a Safe Environment.[18]

This labor-environmental-community coalition was instrumental in securing the precedent-setting Clean Air Action Plan in 2006, which will require (among other air-quality improvements) the retrofitting of 16,000 trucks—to both reduce the community and environmental impacts from truck traffic and port activity and, at the same time, make it easier to unionize workers, since only the larger (and more easily organized) trucking companies can realistically afford the retrofits.[19]

While we think LAANE's reframing owes something to the regional equity framework—which does, after all, stress that market forces, properly directed, can help inner-city communities—we are even more convinced that rerooting owes a great debt to regional analysis. As LAANE has come to regional scale in its work, it has also grappled with the implications of this scale—and its focus on regional attractions, regional industries, and the concerns of inner-ring suburbs—even as it targets the central city of Los Angeles—suggests that the metropolitan area is an emerging level for policy and politics.

What's the AGENDA?

On May 10, 1999, more than 100 residents, workers, labor and community representatives, and church leaders packed Los Angeles City Hall to urge council members to approve a development agreement between a grassroots coalition called the Los Angeles Metro Alliance, the City of Los Angeles, and DreamWorks SKG, a major entertainment corporation owned by Steven Spielberg, Jeffrey Katzenberg, and David Geffen. For over two years, seventy organizations had gathered under the umbrella of the Los Angeles Metropolitan Alliance to pressure the city and the studio. Their goal: tie the development of a DreamWorks production and entertainment center to job opportunities in the burgeoning entertainment industry for low-income and working-poor communities

---

[18] For more information on the coalition, see www.cleanandsafeports.org.

[19] In March 2008, the Los Angeles Harbor Commission approved a Clean Trucks Plan which included a concession model requiring licensed motor carriers to hire employee drivers in order to enter into drayage contracts with the Port. Although the City of Long Beach joined with L.A. to adopt the Clean Air Action Plan as its joint policy framework, Long Beach later adopted a trucks plan that included retrofits but did not mandate employee provisions.

of color. After a rush of last-minute negotiations, the city council voted to adopt a developer agreement that met the Metro Alliance's demands for a private-sector-funded workforce development program. The deal promised to create 21,000 permanent jobs and careers in multimedia and entertainment through DreamWorks, in exchange for fulfilling the studio's request for public subsidies totaling somewhere between $70 and $90 million (Berbeo 1999).

Although the negotiations seemed to have reached a happy ending worthy of a Hollywood epic, DreamWorks eventually decided not to go through with the new studio project. Yet something had happened to the parties in the process of getting to know each other across the bargaining table—remarkably, the studio remained committed to the establishment of a job-training program and funding mechanism as outlined in the agreement. As a result, 5 million dollars from DreamWorks seeded the establishment of a regionwide employment training organization, Workplace Hollywood. As mandated by the development agreement, representatives from the Metro Alliance and other community-based organizations now sit on the decision-making body of Workplace Hollywood, helping distribute funds and overseeing development of job training curricula designed by private-sector entertainment firms, community colleges, and community-based training organizations.

The deal involved the most dynamic and rooted industry in Southern California and hard-nosed activists for social justice from some of the poorest communities in L.A. How in the world did the two come together? The answer really starts with what seemed like L.A.'s most dismal moment: the ashes of the 1992 civil unrest. For longtime community leader Anthony Thigpenn, the 1992 uprising was a wake-up call that made clear not just the gap between rich and poor, Anglo and minority, but also the chasm between activist organizations and the restless grassroots. In his view, neighborhood-based CDCs had focused on service provision but failed to engage and mobilize local constituencies. Community organizers had, in turn, focused on mobilization but tended to stress immediate and winnable interests rather than a long-term agenda. This nearsightedness left larger policy work in the hands of intermediary policy groups—akin to what we have called policy reform regionalists—which included representatives from many organizations but did not reach deeply into the affected communities. As a result, deep-seated community anger over economic and other conditions had few positive outlets and instead became the fuel for conflagrations.

A new approach was clearly needed. Thigpenn, born and raised in Los Angeles, was a veteran organizer who had been involved with the Black Panther Party, campaigns against police brutality, and precinct-level electoral organizing. He envisioned a base of grassroots community leaders who had sufficient power to change the rules of decision-making and development in South Los Angeles. In the settling dust of the uprising, Thigpenn founded Action for Grassroots Empowerment and Neighborhood Development Alternatives (AGENDA), which sought to combine strategies of consciousness-raising, community organizing, and direct action with sophisticated research, strong coalitions, and long-term alliances. Most important, the vision and analysis of AGENDA focused on transformations of power at the regional scale: "If you want to help South L.A., you can't talk about South L.A. apart from the region" (Thigpenn 2004).

To realize its regional vision, AGENDA took a multipronged approach. First, it built its membership and mass base in South Central L.A. with a combination of educational and grassroots organizing strategies. Second, it sought to build bridges between the region's lower-income communities through the Metro Alliance, a group that included other AGENDA-related organizing efforts in West Los Angeles and Silver Lake–Hollywood–Echo Park, additional community-based groups in South L.A., faith-based organizations and unions, and the other organizations we profile here, LAANE and SAJE. Third, it sought to develop a sophisticated in-house research arm that could help identify likely regional campaigns, an effort that was eventually formalized in 1998 as the Community Institute for Policy, Heuristics, Education and Research (CIPHER).[20]

Among AGENDA's priorities was the development of a long-range strategy to obtain well-paying, secure union jobs for its members and other low-income residents of the region. In AGENDA's view, this required targeting industries and sectors that exhibited (1) a history of steady regional growth; (2) a range of jobs that started at entry level but offered career potential; (3) a baseline wage that met living-wage standards; and (4) a high level of, or potential for, union density.

---

[20] AGENDA's umbrella organization, Strategic Concepts in Organizing and Policy Education (SCOPE), has restructured, integrating the research work of CIPHER into a comprehensive Training and Policy Education (TPE) Department whose mission is to build "a more powerful social justice movement through the strategic development and management of SCOPE's research/analysis and training/technical assistance programs": www.scopela.org.

The entertainment and multimedia industry clearly met the bill. It was a growing sector in the Los Angeles regional economy; it included a range of employment opportunities; and it was heavily unionized. It was also vulnerable to political leverage because of the fact that DreamWorks was seeking to create a new state-of-the art multimedia studio and entertainment complex on the largest remaining piece of open land in Los Angeles, an area two miles west of LAX, and was hoping to receive up to $90 million in city subsidies.

A regionally rooted sector and a large public subsidy—it was the perfect combination for educating communities about regional equity. With the campaign slogan "Public Money for Public Good," the Metro Alliance officially kicked off a campaign in fall 1997 to secure a job-training and placement program from DreamWorks. The alliance moved swiftly to enlist the support of then-Councilmember Mark Ridley-Thomas, who represented a large portion of South Los Angeles, as well as Councilmember Jackie Goldberg, who had played a leadership role in the Living Wage Ordinance secured just a year earlier. Less than two years later, the deal was signed.

The developer agreement codified by the city council elevated Metro Alliance from a passive community beneficiary to a development partner along with the city and the studio developer. The terms of the agreement also required private-sector funding for a workforce development program situated in the community college system. And because the agreement and the council decision were the results of a long and visible public campaign, the victory created a visible policy precedent that tied public subsidies to the provision of public benefit in all future development in the City of Los Angeles. In this regard, it was an especially elegant complement to the reframing around accountable development that had been the focus of LAANE and others.[21]

The Metro Alliance soon turned its regionalist focus to the growing health care field in order "to meet the training and employment needs

---

[21] Alliance members were also involved in a two-year campaign as federal welfare reform arrived to ensure that workforce investment monies be used for programs providing the necessary training and social support services for welfare recipients to make the transition to the workforce. Organizing and political pressure generated by the Metro Alliance resulted in a model program that has changed the way the city develops programs and administers Workforce Investment Act (WIA) funds: no longer simply "work first" approaches, the programs now provide training, placement, and social service supports, and ensure living wages and benefits (Ito 2007).

of the unemployed and underemployed but also address the growing demand for health care workers" (Ito 2007). Its efforts eventually led to the Healthcare Career Ladder Training Program (HCCLTP), a collaborative effort of the city's Community Development Department, its One-Stop Career Centers (or WorkSource Centers), organized labor, and AGENDA's Metro Alliance. By 2006–2007, Workforce Investment Act funds, along with employer matching funds, guaranteed $1.69 million for the Health Care Careers program. The result: between 2002 and late 2006, a total of 782 people enrolled in training or were directly placed in health care jobs, with an 82 percent completion rate of training and an average post-training placement wage of $14.92 hour. Moreover, as CIPHER's director Jennifer Ito notes:

> The Health Care Careers program has really influenced the overall WIB (Workforce Investment Board) strategy. In addition to keeping a focus on the training and support services as critical to workforce development, the WIB has replicated the HCC model and applied it to other industries such as logistics and goods movement, construction, private security officers, child care, and hospitality. (Ito 2007)

In 2005 a new organizational umbrella for AGENDA was formed, Strategic Concepts in Organizing and Policy Education (SCOPE). Integrating AGENDA as well as the Metropolitan Alliance, CIPHER, and a training arm called the Environmental and Economic Justice Project (EEJP),[22] SCOPE's mission is "to develop multi-dimensional approaches that reduce and eliminate structural barriers to social and economic opportunities for poor and economically disadvantaged communities and communities of color."[23] SCOPE now leads a statewide coalition—the California Alliance—that comprises organizing groups throughout the state such as ACORN, Working Partnerships, and Urban Habitat. Together, they aim to develop a long-term plan for systemic reform of California's state policies and the formulation of ballot initiatives to organize around and spur electoral action.

[22] EEJP and CIPHER have now been organized into a new department, Training and Policy Education (TPE).

[23] See SCOPE's full mission statement on its website: http://www.scopela.org/index.html.

The Metro Alliance has initiated the Progressive Electoral Project (PEP), which currently functions in seven regions—Los Angeles, Oakland, San Francisco, San Jose, San Diego, Fresno, and San Bernardino—to build the electoral organizing capacity of fifteen leading community groups within each region. In the midterm November 2006 election, more than thirty-seven organizations participated in regional get-out-the-vote efforts, mobilizing more than 600 neighborhood precinct leaders and volunteers and contacting over 80,000 voters in low-income, working-class communities throughout the state (SCOPE 2006).

From South Central L.A. to the region to the state and, increasingly, to the nation as well, SCOPE continues to build its relationships, capacity, and influence. In 2005, SCOPE began discussions with the national Apollo Alliance, an effort led by such groups as the Sierra Club and the United Steelworkers to create jobs and secure energy independence by promoting investments in the domestic clean-energy sector. More than thirty national, state, and local unions as well as more than thirty environmental and community organizations are members of the national Apollo effort. SCOPE is now represented on the national advisory board and has taken the lead in convening a local chapter of the Apollo Alliance in the Los Angeles metropolitan region. Sabrina Smith, SCOPE's organizing director, notes that Apollo constitutes a new proactive strategy for economic development: "We've proven our ability to secure community benefits from the regional economy through policy wins; we're now testing our ability to develop alternative economic directions to provide permanent solutions to poverty and the problems our communities face" (2006).[24]

Furthering its national agenda, SCOPE has begun to work with a set of community-based organizations that have experimented with ways to link organizing with new strategies for electoral politics. The Pushback Network involves grassroots organizing groups from California, New Mexico, New York, Kentucky, Mississippi, and Alabama which emphasize long-term planning and execution over tactical and reactive campaigns;

---

[24] Smith further, notes "The regional face of the Apollo Alliance–L.A. differs from the earlier Metro Alliance in several ways. The most important is that the Metro Alliance represented a loose configuration of the power base that AGENDA had hoped to build regionally—it was broad but not deep; it included many different communities but it was episodic and driven by particular campaigns. In contrast, Apollo Alliance–L.A. represents a smaller number of member institutions and individuals who contribute specific political and technical resources to the Alliance goals. It was a deliberate and focused effort to build long-term strategic partnerships with some of our key allies" (2006).

developing state electoral alliances and partnerships from the bottom up; targeting communities of color, poor people, and marginalized communities to expand the electorate; and integrating community organizing with electoral work.

It has been an impressive trajectory that reflects scaling geographically, analytically, and politically. The geography is straightforward: when AGENDA/SCOPE decided to lift its eyes from the neighborhood to the region, it saw a hopeful path toward building power also at the state and national levels. Analytically, SCOPE began with a model of securing a fair share of local employment and increasing training opportunities from growing regional employment sectors—and it is now pushing investment toward whole new forms of economic development. And politically, SCOPE has moved from protest and resistance to crafting alternatives, taking power locally, and building statewide and national influence.

A Right to the City

It's one thing to hitch one's wagon to a thriving regional industry (say, entertainment) or to an important regional asset (say, the airport). It's another to try to prevent the bulldozer of progress from burying your community in its wake. That has been the difficult balancing act attempted by the Figueroa Corridor Coalition for Economic Justice.

Like many efforts in Los Angeles, the FCCEJ grew out of an earlier labor history, particularly involving struggles in the late 1990s at the University of Southern California (USC)—a major institution in the Figueroa Corridor—to organize service workers (janitors, housekeepers, dining workers) who believed that their jobs were threatened by the university's decision to subcontract certain activities. With the worker organizing led by SEIU Locals 399 and 1877 and HERE Local 11 (the unions responsible for launching other campaigns in the growing regional tourist industry), a number of additional organizations—among them, SAJE, the Student Coalition against Labor Exploitation (SCALE), LAANE, and AGENDA—came forward to form the Committee for a Responsible USC.

The thread linking the labor and community groups was the belief that conditions at work, and in the adjoining neighborhoods, were threatened by the university's corporate behavior and strategic plans to expand. On the one hand, service workers were vulnerable to the cost efficiencies of contracting out; on the other, residents who lived in the surrounding neighborhoods were vulnerable to displacement as USC sought to expand campus facilities (Leavitt 2005). The coalition thus organized repeated acts of direct action and civil disobedience to challenge the university's employment practices, and the campaign quickly acquired a high profile: USC is one of the largest private-sector employers in the city, and the uneasy relationship between the university, its employees, and the neighborhoods mirrored the social and economic inequities of the city and region (Wilton and Cranford 2002).

In 1998 the members of the coalition turned their attention to another major regional project proposed for the Figueroa Corridor: the expansion of the Staples Sports and Entertainment Center. Well known as the home of the Lakers and the Clippers, the arena also hosts large-scale conventions, a notable one being the Democratic National Convention in 2000. The proposed expansion included plans for two hotels (a 1,200-room convention facility and a smaller 600-room hotel); over 1.1 million square feet carved out for retail, entertainment, office, and residential uses, including medical offices and a sports medicine center; a health/sports club; an open-air plaza; and, acknowledging the primacy of the automobile in Southern California transit, over 5,000 new parking spaces.[25] Recognizing the scale of the project, neighborhood organizers and activists along the Figueroa Corridor anticipated that a broader coalition was needed in order to save their community (Leavitt 2005).

The Committee for a Responsible USC thus changed its name to the Figueroa Corridor Coalition for Economic Justice (FCCEJ) and ultimately created a coalition including thirty community organizations and five unions representing the immigrant Latino and the African American families who lived in the core downtown neighborhoods. The coalition was staffed by SAJE, a group founded by organizer, educator, and economic development specialist Gilda Haas in 1996. The evolution of SAJE, seen through the lens of this struggle, helps to reveal the circumstances under which community development and social movement regionalism can come together.

SAJE was founded "on the premise that many of Los Angeles' social problems have economic roots" (Haas 1999). Unlike LAANE and AGENDA, SAJE has focused less on engaging the regional economy than on the right of residents to live in safe and healthy communities despite

---

[25] See Leavitt 2005 for a detailed case study of the Figueroa Corridor Coalition's campaign to leverage community benefits from the proposed Staples Center expansion.

the pressure of gentrification. Its initial campaigns focused on the lack of affordable banking options for low-income people, particularly welfare recipients; and on neighborhood housing problems, including landlord abuse, lead paint, and code violations. One of the group's signature documents is called "We Shall Not Be Moved"—and this is meant literally as well as politically (Haas 2004). SAJE has focused on criminalizing slumlords, securing tenants' rights, and preserving people's ability to stay in their neighborhoods even in the face of development and redevelopment.

To focus on preventing displacement, SAJE could hardly have picked a more apt case than the Figueroa Corridor, which is the doorstep to the Staples Center and links the downtown core to the growing USC complex. Here, the wealthiest landowners and the most economically vulnerable communities coexist—as Haas (2005) has noted, it is where "the richest and poorest dance on the same floor." As of 2000, nearly all the residents were people of color—74 percent Latino (primarily immigrant), 12 percent African American, and 8 percent Asian. More than eight in ten households were renters, and the median income was less than half that of the region (Community Scholars Program 2005). But the demographics seem slated to change: during the day, even as the area's 200,000 residents fan out to work in low-wage garment, service, or informal economy jobs, the sounds of new condo construction, destined to appeal to the hip urban gentry, rings across the corridor's landscape.

The whispers of land speculators may be harder to hear, but they are driving the new retail and residential construction—and an implicit part of their strategy is a marginalization of current residents. Their preferred method for sweeping through the area is simple: increase the rents. And those residents have only to look in the other direction to see that the heavy hand of eminent domain stands at the ready as well, because 87 percent of the census tracts in the neighborhoods are within city redevelopment areas. While this designation could potentially suggest opportunities for the neighborhood, it also allows for the possibility of taking land and using the neighborhoods to siphon property taxes and issue bonds (Community Scholars Program 2005). Although the threat of displacement has been particularly acute in the Figueroa Corridor, it is a pressure felt by many low-income communities in the city. Modeling a new development approach in the Corridor was therefore of broad regional interest, and SAJE and its partners found a new leverage point when the Staples Center expansion was proposed.

Some local residents had reason to be wary of the expansion: they had already been displaced when the Staples Center was originally built in 1998–99, after having acquired more than $12 million from the Community Redevelopment Agency for land acquisition and site preparation. Those residents had received vouchers to help them relocate, but this assistance had time limits, and the limits were coming up just as the expansion was proposed. Other residents thought the Staples expansion was likely to displace even more households, and they wondered about their own security.

Why would developers who had so often had their way in Los Angeles be worried? Part of the reason was the shifting political economy of Los Angeles: the living wage had just been passed over the objections of a business-friendly Republican mayor, the city council was increasingly dominated by labor-friendly liberals, and the scent of the DreamWorks deal was still fresh. For the Staples expansion to go forward, the council needed to approve a rezoning of the area, and doing so with community support rather than resistance was much more likely to result in success. Negotiations ensued, with Madeline Janis from LAANE and Gilda Haas from SAJE leading the community-labor side. The ultimate result was a precedent-setting community benefits agreement in May 2001, the highlights of which (reviewed in the preceding discussion of LAANE) included job guarantees, housing help, parks, and additional parking spaces for neighborhood residents.

In the years since the agreement was struck, zero-interest loans to promote affordable housing have been made to help launch projects by two Figueroa Corridor nonprofit developers: Esperanza Community Housing Corporation and 1010 Development Corporation (Environmental Defense 2006). A study and public participation process was completed to identify potential park sites and park development.[26] The Figueroa Community Jobs Program, a partnership between SAJE and the L.A. Trade Tech College, has been created to train community residents for jobs created in the area, particularly through the CBA; by March 2006, thirty people had already obtained living-wage union jobs through the program.[27]

---

[26] In 2002, Mia Lehrer and Associates, Landscape Architects, produced the study that examined existing facilities, identified the needs and priorities of the community, and developed a series of options for open space and recreation.

[27] Information taken from the SAJE website: www.saje.org. See also Environmental Defense 2006.

Balancing the organizing and the implementation has been a challenge. SAJE is a group firmly rooted in a social movement frame, but it is also now responsible for the sorts of details (such as job-training design) that often turn community developers inward and away from the broader picture. An equally difficult juggling act exists between SAJE and its partners, at least at the ideological level. SAJE has broad goals of social justice, but it is essentially place-based in its analysis and its actions. Its key priorities are neighborhood preservation and tenants' rights, and whereas SAJE and other advocates see the region as a critical factor in the lack of affordable housing in poor and working-poor communities, they have concentrated their efforts on key local policies such as inclusionary zoning and a housing trust fund.[28] SAJE's approach is all about helping people stay in place—*not* about insuring mobility and movement across the region.

This philosophy risks a potential conflict with other progressive allies. In San Diego, for example, the labor institution parallel to LAANE—the Center for Policy Initiatives—split with a longtime ally, a place-based environmental justice group, over the particulars of a CBA that put more emphasis on obtaining quality jobs than on preventing displacement. In Los Angeles too these tensions exist, but the groups have thus far managed to negotiate differences in emphases and perspectives, partly thanks to their long history of working together. And collectively, the groups have realized that they are onto something big: the community benefits agreement and the coalition that won it have begun to establish the outlines of a new model of urban development.

Like LAANE and AGENDA, SAJE has had ambitions to scale up, engaging with similar organizations across the country who share SAJE's mission of protecting and revitalizing low-income urban neighborhoods. Discussions with the Miami Workers Center and the Tenants and Workers Support Committee in Virginia have given rise to a growing

---

[28] SAJE worked on the trust fund with a coalition of housing trust advocates under the umbrella of a coalition called Housing LA. The coalition is supported largely by leadership from the Southern California Association of Nonprofit Housing (SCANPH). The trust fund is supposed to be $100 million and would be used to catalyze the production of affordable housing. While no permanent source of monies for the fund has been established, in July 2005 the city council approved a $1 billion affordable-housing bond measure for the midterm November 2006 ballot. Voters supported the measure by nearly a 2 to 1 margin, but it failed by a few percentage points to reach the necessary two-thirds threshold required under California law to approve new bond measures.

network of place-based regionalists fighting for neighborhood revitalization and neighborhood sustainability in the face of gentrification. In January 2007, SAJE and these other groups—plus Just Cause of Oakland; City Life/Vida Urbana of Jamaica Plain, Massachusetts; Committee against Anti-Asian Violence; and FIERCE of New York City—launched a new Right to the City Alliance, developing a common frame and approach to unify their diverse struggles for housing, social wages, public space, and culture.[29]

SAJE is an example of community development regionalism with a social movement twist. Unlike Chicago's Bethel New Life—an organization that also seeks to create safe, secure, and stable neighborhoods with regional levers but views its social movement work as apart from that—SAJE intertwines its local focus, regional analysis, and social movement ambitions in a tumultuous but ultimately successful mix. It is a neighborhood-based approach that nonetheless has an explicit social change agenda—and it has been an important part of the revolution in Los Angeles politics.

Why Regions?

Each of the organizations profiled above is important in its own right, but perhaps the most interesting aspect of the Los Angeles experience is the way in which they have intersected and have woven their organizing threads into an overall movement for regional equity and social change. It is impossible to tell the story of SAJE's evolution without recounting its collaboration with LAANE on community benefits agreements; it is difficult to understand how AGENDA's struggle for an accountable workforce strategy could have succeeded without the pressures that LAANE and SAJE put forward regarding accountable redevelopment; and it is clear that LAANE could not have moved so far beyond its original labor roots without the community base that other organizations such as AGENDA and SAJE brought to the table.[30]

---

[29] See www.righttothecity.org.

[30] Even the Villaraigosa victory of 2005 involves a complex tale: when L.A.'s Central Labor Council could not agree to support Villaraigosa against a labor-friendly incumbent—with the decision defended on the grounds that labor should always reward incumbents who deliver—it was the executive director of AGENDA who slipped out of his position to run the field campaign, a task that would normally have fallen to forces more closely associated

These interactions are not just the stuff of casual coalitions. In June 2005, right after the Villaraigosa victory that seemed to symbolize the triumph of a progressive alliance, the three authors of this volume convened a discussion panel consisting of Haas, Janis, and Thigpenn. In attendance were some of what might be termed leading lights in the regional equity movement: Angela Glover Blackwell (founder of PolicyLink), Bruce Katz, john powell, David Rusk, and others. With ease and familiarity, the three L.A. leaders laid out their visions and their conflicts, their histories and their futures. They have circled around each other—and circled with each other—for nearly twenty years, and this solidarity is evident not only in their friendships and honest conversation but also in the broader movement-building in which they have participated.

For all these groups, "going regional" was an intentional perspective spawned by what would become powerful new approaches for organizing, coalition-building, and urban policy focused on neighborhood revitalization, reduction of poverty, and the creation of economic opportunity for all. Old and new coalitions—including the Bus Riders Union, the Alameda Corridor Jobs Coalition, the environmental justice advocates in Communities for a Better Environment, and many others—have intentionally sought to link labor with social and environmental justice in a strategic recast from local-level politics to regional organizing. But what brought about the regional shift?

Reading the Region

If regionalism was in the business air in the Silicon Valley of the early 1990s, it was permeating community and labor circles in Los Angeles as well. Much of the shift can be dated to the 1992 unrest in Los Angeles and the way it forced experienced grassroots and activist leadership to consider alternative strategies for addressing the conditions of low-income neighborhoods in the city.

One prominent regionalist approach, beyond the three groups we've profiled, was led by the Labor/Community Strategy Center and its founder, veteran activist Eric Mann. Mann initiated discussions over the period of a year to develop a shared analysis and new—and explicitly

---

with LAANE—which signifies the importance of connecting with and mobilizing the African American vote to win races in Los Angeles.

regional—responses to the events of April and May 1992.[31] As the Labor/ Community Strategy Center's literature explains:

> If the discussion of jobs in South L.A. is focused simply on "new" jobs located within local geographic boundaries, then existing employers and new employers in San Fernando Valley, Orange County, or even downtown L.A. would not be tapped.... The fight for jobs in South L.A. must be part of a fight for higher-wage jobs for working people and people of color in the entire region—otherwise we will have neighborhood versus neighborhood competition for scarce resources rather than demands on the entire system to provide more jobs in total. (Mann et al. 1993, 24)

The analysis couldn't have been clearer: the center decided that it needed to move up quickly to the region. As it began this shift toward a broader view, Mann explains, "we stumbled onto mass transit" and soon went on to form the Bus Riders Union (BRU) in 1994 (Mann 1999). Its two-year civil rights campaign against transit discrimination successfully pushed the County's Metropolitan Transit Authority to redirect funds from rail-oriented projects to bus transit projects that directly targeted the mobility of the transit-dependent working poor. This was a regional equity effort that preceded and inspired many other transit justice efforts around the country—and partly as a result, L.A. now has one of the cleanest bus systems in the nation (with 80 percent of the buses using compressed natural gas), and other improvements to the system have taken place, such as new routes for heavily traveled areas (Dreier and Steckler 2007).

Another regionalism effort was one in which one of us was intimately involved: Pastor was one of the cofounders of the New Majority Task Force in the late 1980s, a leadership group focused on redevelopment in the distressed neighborhoods of Los Angeles, and in late 1992 and early 1993 the New Majority met regularly with the Multicultural Collaborative (an organization founded after the civil unrest to promote interethnic communication) and the Coalition of Neighborhood Developers (an alliance formed in 1990 of over fifty organizations, anchored by a group of ten community development corporations based in Central, South, and East Los Angeles). Together, they sponsored a 1995 document called

---

[31] The written documentation of the year-long process is captured in Maan et al. (1993).

Economic Strategies for Multi-ethnic Communities in Los Angeles (Grigsby and Wolff 1995), which argued that community developers should get involved in regional conversations and whose evaluation of several regional economic initiatives was based on whether they were likely to promote revitalization in minority enclaves.

Regionalism was also in the mix for environmental justice groups. This was not an entirely new phenomenon: in the late 1980s, jurisdictional and community lines were crossed when a largely African American group, Concerned Citizens of South Central Los Angeles, came together with a Mexican American organization, Mothers of East Los Angeles, and successfully fought back the siting of a region-serving garbage incinerator in Southeast Los Angeles. Yet it reached a new apex in the mid-1990s when Communities for a Better Environment (CBE) sued the regional air-quality district about a "car scrapping" program associated with an emissions credit trading program called RECLAIM. The CBE claim was that the program allowed oil companies simply to buy older, highly polluting cars and take them off the road rather than reduce pollution coming from their own tankers. Such pollution trades may have had some effect on relieving regional pollution, but they also created toxic "hot spots" where the tanker-related pollution went unabated.

Organizing around the issue showed residents both how regional decisions could have a tremendous impact on local communities and how linking together across the areas of hot spots was necessary to realize their own regional voice. Under legal pressure, oil companies were ordered to reduce tanker pollution despite having purchased scrapping credit: And under political pressure, the South Coast Air Quality Management District (AQMD) adopted environmental principles in December 2001. CBE, based in Huntington Park, is now working with Coalition for a Safe Environment in Wilmington, East Yard Communities for Environmental Justice (in the City of Commerce), and Comité Pro Uno, an immigrant rights organization in Maywood, all in a regional effort to improve air quality in the southeast areas of Los Angeles County.[32]

This regionalist effort is not surprising: Huntington Park, Commerce, and Maywood are all inner-ring suburbs of Southeast L.A. (see figure 4.1). Once the manufacturing belt of the region, Southeast L.A. was

---

[32] The EJ Cumulative Impact Collaborative also includes the Community Coalition for Change in unincorporated Athens Park. On the adoption of EJ principles by the South Coast AQMD, see Clifford 1997.

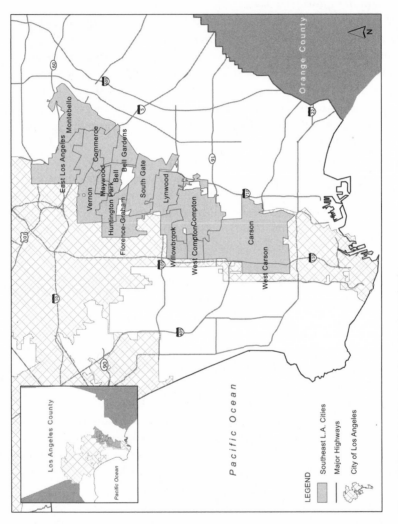

Figure 4.1. Southeast Los Angeles inner-ring suburbs

Note: The map comprises the cities of Montebello, Vernon, Commerce, Maywood, Bell, Huntington Park, Bell Gardens, South Gate, Lynwood, Compton, and Carson, and the unincorporated West Carson, West Compton, Willowbrook, Florence—Graham, and East Los Angeles.

hard hit by deindustrialization and went through a sharp demographic shift from mostly white working-class residents to largely immigrant and working-poor; it also suffered a sharp cut in federal funding for antipoverty programs (Goldsmith and Blakely 1992, 156). In older urban core communities, CDCs and other community-based development organizations struggled to pick up the slack by turning to philanthropic funds. But having missed the wave of federal programs in the 1960s, back when they were thriving suburbs, the inner-ring communities felt the impact of cuts without having the institutional backstop of CDCs to assist them with increasingly difficult social and economic challenges.[33]

Interestingly, it is not the usual regional equity issue of economic dislocation and the usual recipe of regional tax-sharing that has brought many of these municipalities together.[34] Rather, residents have been moved to make regional connections—that is, to build bridges to other communities in the region—while confronting questions of environmental injustice and abuses of immigrant rights. As with children's health in Mayfair, the route to regionalism is not as straight as some would think; there needs to be a visceral link that makes working at the regional scale both clear and compelling.

Coming to Regionalism

What about the three main groups we have profiled? What common threads can be found in their "coming to regionalism" moment—and in the strategies they have since used to scale up?

First, each of the organizations recognized the fact that business was highly fragmented in Los Angeles. Corporations had largely abandoned L.A. as a headquarters city by the mid-1990s (Holloway and Wheeler 1991), and despite having a Republican businessman serve as mayor from 1993 to 2001, business seemed disorganized and dispirited. Even as regional business collaboratives took root in other areas of California,

---

[33] Research by Joassart-Marcelli and Wolch (2003) found, for example, that the Southeast cities in Los Angeles County lack the infrastructure of nonprofit organizations, particularly those addressing the needs of low-income and working-poor populations.

[34] One of the regional collaboratives, the Gateway Cities Partnership, representing businesses and civic leaders in Southeast Los Angeles, works closely with the Gateway Cities Council of Governments on regional issues of workforce development and education and has recently established a Community Development Corporation to provide housing services and facilitate industrial and housing development in the Southeast cities.

including the Bay Area, San Diego, and the San Joaquin Valley, no such phenomenon happened in L.A. There were some smaller business pockets, including one in the so-called Gateway Cities near the ports and one in the San Fernando Valley, but none were centered in the City of Los Angeles—leaving a hole in the center of business regionalism.[35] Where Bay Area activists had responded to business regionalism by trying to squeeze their way into the discussion, Los Angeles activists responded to a business leadership vacuum by trying to create a new dialogue altogether.

Second, each of the three organizations was driven by the need to confront dramatic demographic changes in their constituencies—and "going regional" in their analysis and organizing was partly about going multicultural. The regional discussion of the economy helped LAANE make the connection between older white workers and the growing immigrant workforce. The regional emphasis on crossing racial, class, and geographic boundaries—and using organizing to knit together inner-city and inner-ring-suburban communities—also offered a path to unifying the inner city itself. AGENDA/SCOPE's place-based focus in South L.A. for example, required developing and implementing strategies to forge black-brown coalitions and long-term alliances in neighborhoods that were once traditionally African American but are now experiencing an increasing number of immigrants, primarily Latinos. Pursuing regional strategies in a broader vision of shared prosperity rather than fighting over a narrow turf pointed to one way out of this spatial and racial dilemma.

Third, although each of the groups had a regional frame, they also focused their initial efforts on policy within the City of Los Angeles. That focus reflected an understanding of the primacy of the city in economic development and related policymaking in the region, particularly the city's ability (and willingness) to provide incentives to economic developers. The city includes more than 38 percent of Los Angeles County's ten million people and represents the historic center of urbanization as well as industrialization for the region (Fogelson 1967; Scott and Soja 1996).[36] So why target regional scale when your analysis is informed by

---

[35] See Jonas and Pincetl (2006) on the Gateway Cities Partnership; they argue that the effort functions as a regional chamber of commerce rather than an inclusive collaborative.

[36] Population figures based on U.S. Census 2005.

an urban understanding of the economy and power dynamics? In the words of Anthony Thigpenn of AGENDA/SCOPE:

> We have a regional analysis for our work and know that the conditions in South Los Angeles are the very same as those in other cities such as Huntington Park or South Gate. The political reality is that the City of Los Angeles represents the arena where regional agendas are negotiated. So, our focus on the City of L.A. and the County represents a strategic decision to target a single public decision-making body, the city council, and a known set of decision-makers, leaders, rules, and policies that we can influence that will ultimately have positive benefit to a very large number of people. (2004)

In going regional, the three groups have followed the social movement path, focusing on power rather than just policy or projects. Part of this strategy has been an explicit commitment to engage in the electoral arena. The votes they helped mobilize fueled the 2005 election win of Mayor Antonio Villaraigosa, but before that, victories had been scored with the election of Karen Bass—the founder and longtime executive director of the Community Coalition in South Los Angeles—to the California State Assembly in 2004,[37] and the election of Martin Ludlow, a former organizer and political director for the Los Angeles County Federation of Labor, to the L.A. City Council.[38] Political appointments to various boards and commissions have also reflected the power of the movement—LAANE's executive director Madeline Janis was appointed to the board of the Los Angeles Community Redevelopment Agency

[37] Notably, Bass was appointed majority whip in her first year in the assembly. In her second term, beginning January 2006, she was selected majority floor leader by the Speaker of the Assembly, making her the first African American and first woman to hold that leadership position for the state of California. In May 2008, she became Speaker of the Assembly, the first African American woman in the country to serve in this important legislative position.

[38] With the sudden passing of Miguel Contreras in early 2005, Ludlow assumed the leadership of the powerful County Federation of Labor Though he resigned in 2006 in the midst of campaign election mishandlings, the transition from a dynamic Latino to an equally progressive African American in labor's key leadership role signaled the depth of the progressive movement, the increasing presence of people of color in the movement, and a conscious focus on maintaining an African American and Latino coalition around labor issues.

(CRA) by Mayor James Hahn and reappointed by Mayor Villaraigosa.[39] Our point: the three groups have focused on moving politics along, not shying away from an arena usually eschewed by community development groups worried about losing funding or other opportunities.

They have also chosen to stick together over the long haul. There are, of course, underlying structural tensions between them: AGENDA/ SCOPE relies most heavily on its direct organizing strategy with a broad geographic scope; LAANE on its labor and coalition-building focus and strategic partnerships for policy change; and SAJE on a place- and resident-based approach that seems to reflect a traditional community organizing effort to "let the people decide." But they have also recognized both the need to craft short-term coalitions to win specific policy battles such as living-wage campaigns *and* the imperative of having each other as long-term allies. The three groups—and others in Los Angeles—recognize that no single organization has the capacity or strength to win fundamental social change on its own and that all can be part of a social ecology of change. And maintaining a regional analysis has helped, in that it enables organizations to transcend ideological differences by focusing attention on how to build broad appeal (Kleidman 2004).

In any case, the L.A. story is clear: a new sort of community-oriented regionalism has come of age—and it has been driven by a series of actors committed to building a broader social movement for justice. Could this have happened without the dramatic shocks of the early 1990s, especially the social scarring of the civil unrest? We do not claim to know the answer—and we are not among those who believe that things getting worse is merely a prelude to their getting better (plenty of urban problems, after all, just seem to keep heading downhill). What we do know is that the unrest mattered, mostly because it spurred movement activists, both in the groups we profile and in others, to be open to trying something new.

[39] The mayor also appointed Jerilyn López Mendoza, from Environmental Defense and a chief architect of the LAX and Staples CBA, to cochair the powerful Harbor Commission responsible for overseeing the operations of the Port of Los Angeles, the busiest cargo facility in the nation; combined with the adjacent Port of Long Beach, it represents the fifth largest port in the world according to the United Nations Conference on Trade and Development (UNCTAD 2007, 8, table 46. See http://www.unctad.org/en/docs/rmt2007_ en.pdf (accessed January 13, 2008; see also http://www.aaenvironment.com/LongBeach Port.htm).

That something new turned out to be regionalism, or at least a shift in the scale of organizing that pointed in that direction. Though the jury is still out on whether this new paradigm will eradicate L.A.'s poverty, it has already moved regional politics in a dramatically different direction. The 2005 election of Antonio Villaraigosa as L.A.'s mayor was heralded as a major victory for Latinos—but just as important is that he campaigned on what was essentially a regional equity platform. Borrowing from concepts developed while serving as a Fellow at USC's Center for Sustainable Cities, he promised to help the city "grow smarter, grow greener, grow together, and grow more civic-minded."[40] Many of his first moves as mayor, such as resolving a labor dispute to protect the regional tourist industry and taking a leadership position in the regional transportation agency, signaled his understanding and commitment to a regional equity agenda.[41]

Can We Do This at Home?

Can all this be replicated elsewhere? We suspect so and would point to several critical elements in the experience, such as the central role of labor, the development of internal research capacity to identify issues, and the constant attention to organizing as the base for any forward movement. We would stress, however that the L.A. experience also owes much to the larger coordinating organizations such as LAANE, AGENDA, and SAJE, which provided continuity to the movement; created mechanisms for allies to engage in peer exchange and learn best practices through their "regional stories"; and independently cultivated and maintained relationships with various actors in the academy, the public sector, and elsewhere.

[40] As a part-time Fellow between his time in the state legislature and a new position on the city council, Villaraigosa co-facilitated a workshop on the future of metropolitan Los Angeles, which produced the volume *After Sprawl: Action Plans for Metropolitan Los Angeles* (see Fulton et al. 2003; a related and more academic work that emerged from a parallel process at the Center is Wolch, Pastor, and Dreier 2004).

[41] On the other hand, an ambitious effort to restructure and increase L.A.'s authority over the regional Los Angeles Unified School district faltered in the mayor's first year. His administration has now shifted strategy and is working on a more limited effort called the Partnership for Los Angeles Schools, intended to take over management of several low-performing high schools and their feeder schools, mustering philanthropic and other resources, and giving local school councils more control with the aim of improving performance. See Blume and Helfand 2007.

All these elements fall under the rubric of what Bert Klandermans (1989) and Alberto Melucci (et al. 1988; Melucci 1996) refer to as "organizational infrastructure." That such infrastructure is critical may not be recognized by romantic notions of social movements—don't they just arise from the frustrations of the masses and the stirring of populist sentiments? Social movement theory is, of course, more systematic in identifying the need to attract resources, recognize opportunity, and develop frames—and organizations with substance, skill, and scale are necessary. Nicholls (2003, 882) notes that in Los Angeles, organizational and institutional forms "allow decentralized and fragmented movements to mobilize the necessary human, intellectual, and financial resources needed to produce significant political change."

Within Los Angeles, LAANE, AGENDA/SCOPE, and SAJE serve as what Nicholls calls "coordinating mechanisms" to build trust, learning, and relationships. These "relational platforms enable the formulating frames for collective action, testing hypotheses, succeeding and building upon what is known, or failing, and the insertion of that knowledge into existing cognitive circuits" (Nicholls 2003, 883). In this way, organizational infrastructure facilitates not only mobilization of resources but also the relational frameworks that produce new linkages and strengthen already existing ones.

Funders, academics, and others are enthusiastic about smaller organizations—surely, if their budgets, staff rosters, and offices are small, then they must be truly grassroots. But moving policy and politics requires the capacity to develop relationships and mobilize resources, so size and scale matter, particularly when the target is the region. And doing this level of work requires "anchor organizations" that can spawn and support grassroots social movement activity.

Labeling these anchor organizations as "social movement intermediaries," the New World Foundation notes:

> The distinctive common characteristic of the new intermediaries is that they consciously integrate the intermediary roles of policy development and regional networking, with the infrastructure tasks of grassroots organizing, leadership development, and community empowerment....As the old division between intermediary and base-building roles is transcended, the old tension between national and local organizations seems less inevitable....Through collaborative peer-based intermediaries, community-based work can grow to the state and regional scale. (2000, 6, 14, 16).

Moving regional efforts, in short, requires regional scale. And this will be even more important if the social movement regionalists are to be able to achieve some degree of national influence (Chapters 5 and 6).

Excavating the Future (of Progressive Politics) in Los Angeles

We recognize that much of what has happened in Los Angeles will stay in Los Angeles.[42] The region has been the context for and the cause of several uncommon circumstances: the "shock" of a civil unrest, which prompted new thinking; the fragmentation of a business class which meant that the regional agenda was left open to other social actors; and a rare set of long-term relationships which allowed ideological differences to be hammered out in private while unity over public policy goals could be maintained in public.

Still, the view from Los Angeles reveals the mechanics of a long-term social movement approach resulting in important policy outcomes that advance regional equity: living wages, community benefit agreements, transit justice, and important shifts in workforce development. Perhaps more important, social movement regionalists in Los Angeles have not just steered regional equity policies but also catalyzed a broader progressive movement, one with a growing sophistication about both policy levers and the need to connect mass base-building with electoral arenas.

Even as the L.A. story offers hope for social movement regionalism, it also suggests challenges and risks. Although the local economy has avoided the full-scale slippage of Silicon Valley in the early 2000s, wage prospects in L.A. have not fully turned around—and regional equity activists may eventually need to turn their attention to getting growth going as well as getting it redistributed. Many of the inner-ring suburbs, such as Ventura, Orange, and Riverside—the outlying counties that complete the metro region—remain disconnected from the progressive turn. Differences in the strategies of the major groups in Los Angeles could hold the seeds of division, particularly in light of new economic opportunities and problems.

---

[42] Our section title is an obvious bow to the brilliant volume *City of Quartz: Excavating the Future of Los Angeles* (Davis 1990), focused on the historic dystopia of L.A. and the shifting roles of its power elite. Although his work, ranging from the travails of corporate-driven development to the repressive character of L.A. policing, presaged the events of 1992, it did not fully account for (and who could have anticipated?) the creative organizing that emerged thereafter.

Foremost among these challenges is the future of international trade and goods movements. Activity at the Ports of Los Angeles and Long Beach rose from approximately 5 million containers in 1995 to nearly 13 million in 2004, with trade volume expected at least to triple over the next thirty years; the costs to improve port and rail infrastructure to handle this increased load will run into the billions of dollars, creating job opportunities both in the trade industry and in the construction phase (LAEDC 2002, 2005). At the same time, many are worried that resulting increases in traffic will worsen the current environmental burdens faced by nearby minority communities. Efforts are afoot to resolve the tensions, combining economic and environmental justice in a new set of coalitions that aim to clean up current trucks and port activities, but trade-offs may be difficult to avoid. Keeping the new equity regionalists together—those who are concerned about attaching to Southern California's most vibrant sector and those who are concerned about protecting its most environmentally vulnerable residents—will be a delicate balancing act.

Careful navigation will also be necessary in managing relationships with political figures. The futures of LAANE, AGENDA/SCOPE, SAJE, and social movement regionalism, for example, are now dependent, at least in part, on the power and direction of the progressive elected officialdom. Mayor Villaraigosa has proved to be a reasonable ally, helping to put pressures on the ports for a more environmentally sensitive strategy and on developers for new community benefits agreements particularly in the improving downtown—yet any official can overstep and find his power eroded. The mayor, for example, flexed his political muscle early in his first term in an effort to restructure the Los Angeles Unified School District, and he stumbled when the Los Angeles School Board flexed its own political muscle and filed a successful lawsuit challenging the mayor and the city's role in the schools. Despite these and other setbacks, Villaraigosa's regional vision and bold steps create a terrain of possibilities for regional equity in the Los Angeles metropolitan area.

Meanwhile, as mentioned earlier, the L.A. groups have started to go national, working to seed and support other movements' efforts in other regions. Some may worry that attempting such a national movement is premature. But we should note that we were there as both academics and activists when the L.A. "experiment" in regional organizing began, and we recall that when we presented some of our initial studies suggesting that the region might be a useful "hook" (alas, we hadn't yet learned the word "frame") for analysis and problem-solving, some community developers protested; even more antipoverty organizers decried the shift from the neighborhood; and nearly everyone, including academic colleagues, worried about capacity.

A few activists did not protest. Instead, they pondered—partly because it was their own curiosity about regional possibilities that had led us to the research in the first place: was there indeed something in this stew of regionalist ideas that could offer a way out for L.A. in the dark and seemingly hopeless days that followed the civil unrest? Whether the experience of Los Angeles can shine some light on the future of regional equity work in the country is certainly up for debate; what is more certain is that the shift to a regional approach in Los Angeles has been a remarkable journey with more punch and more staying power that any of us anticipated.

CHAPTER FIVE

Making Regional Equity Work

From Los Angeles to Detroit, from Milwaukee to Chicago, community developers, organizers, and movement builders have come together to forge new regional understandings, new regional coalitions, and new regional policy experiments. But as impressive as any single case might be, some questions remain: Can these diverse and often specific organizing efforts overcome the challenges of localism and parochialism? Can they share a common vision? And can they connect strongly enough to have a major impact on equity and economic opportunity across the country?

We believe they can—yet this is by no means an inevitable future. Regional equity organizing could remain fragmented in dispersed local initiatives, devolving into a loose linkage of disparate struggles around different policy issues. It could fail to catch the public imagination, slipping into a series of technical challenges to unintelligible planning processes. It could be shipwrecked before it truly takes off, crashing on the same shoals of racism and economic disparity that created our unequal metropolitan landscapes in the first place.

To avoid the bleaker outcomes, we need to understand the challenges local organizers face, how they choose to address them, and whether they can actually scale up. We need, in short, to consider what is necessary to build a movement *within* a region and what is necessary to build a movement *across* various regions.

The answers require an honest assessment of the tensions and tightropes that confront many of the organizations we have profiled. Working Partnerships, for example, has had to determine how best to relate to the dominant and sometimes domineering business regionalism that exists in the Silicon Valley. LISC and MOSES in Detroit have had to determine how to cross the chasm of organizational difference, with one focused on community development and the other on community organizing. The Interfaith Federation and others have worried about whether to acknowledge evident divisions along race lines or focus on common issues that might unite. And the Los Angeles groups have faced what might seem a welcome but can also be a disconcerting challenge: what happens when you (or at least the mayoral candidate you support) wins?

To examine these tensions, unpack the possible outcomes, and scrutinize our cases (and a few others we lift up below) in more detail, we begin by examining both where regional equity organizing is emerging and how location affects the nature of issues chosen and strategies taken. We next ask whether regional organizers themselves see the region as a *tactical* means to a traditional end or a *strategic* and entirely new way of doing business. Along the way, we identify the tensions that emerge as groups seek to position themselves vis-à-vis other regional efforts, deal with differences among partners, and make a real and lasting link to people's lives. We then focus on policy and politics: the limits set by having so few regional policy levers, and the challenges that emerge when assembling unlikely allies.

The analysis of difficulties might lead some to pessimism, but we remain hopeful and consider in the next chapter how our optimism at a regional scale might be carried on up to a national level. We happily profile new attempts to share best practices, form new intermetro networks, and build on existing national infrastructure. We also cast our regionalist net widely, arguing that some of America's best organizing groups already combine region and equity—without necessarily viewing themselves as regional equity proponents—and we invite them to join the party. But that is jumping ahead of ourselves; let's start with the basic issues and challenges that are occurring region by region.

Are We Regional Yet?

Where are we seeing regional equity movements emerge? What are the conditions that facilitate their existence? How do those conditions structure the choice of issues and organizing strategies? Among the numerous factors at play, we focus here on three: the structure of local government, the strength of the local economy, and the demographic composition of the region.

Fragmentation and Cohesion

In the United States, governmental fragmentation seems to be the rule rather than the exception. The 2002 Census of Governments showed 3,034 county governments, 19,429 municipal governments, 16,504 township governments, 13,506 school districts, and 35,052 special districts (everything from air quality management and transportation districts to parking authorities and cemetery districts).[1]

Yet the size and structure of these local governments varies significantly throughout the country. Pennsylvania has a population of slightly over 12 million people and over 2,500 city and township governments; California has a population of over 35 million but only 475 city governments. The City of Los Angeles has a population of nearly 3.7 million and a single city government; the Pittsburgh metro area has a population of only 2.3 million but a total of 418 municipalities, nearly as many as the entire state of California.

How do these differing governmental structures and dynamics influence social movement regionalism? One perhaps obvious answer is that in regions with multiple local governments, it is harder to develop political or policy strategies that build from city to city within the region because of the greater number of policy targets. Thus, we might expect that regions with more fragmented local government structures are more likely to pay attention to county- and state-level policy levers, rather than pursuing policy initiatives on a city-by-city basis.

In Detroit, for instance, MOSES organizers spent a significant amount of time engaging with state government around policy issues such as "Fix-it First." The fragmented structure of the governments in the region made it essential to persuade the governor and state representatives to put pressure on reluctant local authorities. Similarly, the MOSES campaign to develop a land bank in Wayne County to promote rapid development of abandoned land was successful only after enabling legislation had been passed at a state level. Political infighting stalled efforts to establish a land bank within the city of Detroit; when Wayne County finally approved the land bank in June 2006, by a narrow 8 to 6 vote, the six county commissioners who largely represent Detroit all voted against it, reflecting the challenges of building a regional approach in this highly conflicted and fragmented region (Lee 2006).

[1] For more on these data, see the census website, http://www.census.gov/govs/www/gid2002.html.

Likewise, in Milwaukee, the fragmented nature of local government makes it difficult to develop truly regional bases of power. The various organizations in the Milwaukee area have primarily focused on building power within the City and County of Milwaukee rather than across the broader metropolitan region. According to John Goldstein, former secretary-general of the Milwaukee CLC:

> Our base of organizing has been in Milwaukee. This is not to say we wouldn't think about the metro region and do something suburban to the degree that it helped build the sorts of capacities we want to build, but our strategic focus is looking at places with a high concentration of minorities and where we have a huge potential for changing the politics of that community. From that base, we influence the politics of the state. Our focus is a little less on the Orfield vision of city-suburban spatial relationships, and more on trying to build the power at the urban core. (2006)

In Silicon Valley, by contrast, a region of 1.7 million people has only one county government and fifteen city governments.[2] Thus, organizers can immediately frame organizing efforts that focus on Santa Clara County policies in truly regional terms—it has been easier for Working Partnerships and the South Bay Central Labor Council, for example, to generate political allies and influence in the cities that neighbor San Jose.

Los Angeles, our prototypical region for social movement regionalism, provides a somewhat mixed picture in this regard. On the one hand, most analysts speak of the highly fragmented structure of local government in Southern California. Los Angeles County alone has eighty-eight cities, many of whose boundaries were originally drawn to maintain racial segregation and economic separation. And, for our purposes, the truly relevant region is the greater six-county area comprising Los Angeles County, Ventura County, Orange County, San Bernardino County, Riverside County, and Imperial County, far to the southeast.[3] Indeed,

---

[2] These figures are U.S. Census figures for Santa Clara County, the core of Silicon Valley. The definition of Silicon Valley used by Joint Venture: Silicon Valley is somewhat larger, including a total of twenty nine cities in portions of four counties, with a total population of nearly 2.5 million. See, for example, JV:SVN 2006.

[3] These counties make up the Southern California Association of Governments (SCAG), which is the largest council of governments in the United States and functions as the region's Metropolitan Planning Organization.

the various parts of the region are intertwined: rapid development and sprawl, particularly in the eastern "Inland Empire" of San Bernardino and Riverside Counties, is integrally linked with growth dynamics in Los Angeles County.[4] But driving from one end of this region to the other would take nearly five hours, assuming that there is no traffic—and there is always traffic, and plenty of it. Given this immense scale, it is extremely difficult to develop effective coalitions across the entire region.

Still, there is one rather "giant box" in Southern California—the City of Los Angeles—and although activists have not necessarily been successful in building coalitions that reach across the full *geography* of the region, they have been successful in building broad-based coalitions that reach across a range of regional equity *issues*. The City of Los Angeles is politically, economically, and culturally dominant in the county, and the county is centrally important in shaping development dynamics for the entire region. Consequently, movements at the city scale have a more profound impact in the Los Angeles region than in regions where the central city or county constitutes a smaller percentage of the regional population.[5]

David Rusk (1999) has argued that less fragmentation means more fiscal and social equity in a region—in his view, "little box" metros (regions with a large number of small and less powerful jurisdictions) have less ability to grow, lower overall fiscal health, and shoddier services. The San Jose and Los Angeles examples also suggest that a less fragmented local government structure—or one with a larger and more prominent central city—may create a more workable environment for regional equity organizing.

The State of the Market

The adage of the real estate business is that only three things matter: "location, location, and location." In the social movement regionalism

---

[4] Organizers in San Bernardino and Riverside, who note that the term "Inland Empire" derives from the region's historical legacy of the Ku Klux Klan, refer to it instead as "the Inland Valley."

[5] This fact does not necessarily translate into municipal cooperation. As Jonas and Pincetl (2006) point out, there is significant resistance to regionalism by local governments in California, partly because of unsuccessful earlier attempts to establish regional governance structures and partly because state policies (Proposition 13) that limit property tax collections have led to a constant pursuit of sales tax dollars by localities—and thus solidified home-rule stance by local governments and rigid resistance to regional planning and governance initiatives.

field, we like to say: "context, context, and context"—and though some of that has to do with political fragmentation, a very important part of the contextual background is the state of the economy.

One major set of economic differences—at least in the regional issues addressed and the cross-constituency coalitions possible—lies between what are called "strong-market" and "weak-market" cities. Weak-market cities, typically the older manufacturing centers of the Midwest and Northeast, have faced long-term economic decline over recent decades, with little job growth. Often, they have also undergone major population dislocation from the urban core, infrastructure deterioration, high levels of racial segregation, and radical patterns of decentralization. Here the challenges are primarily to revitalize the core cities and older suburbs, reclaim vacant and abandoned properties, and promote affordable housing options in opportunity-rich neighborhoods.

Strong-market cities, such as the rapidly growing regions of the Southwest and Florida, face a different set of challenges: escalating housing prices and growing immigrant populations in low-wage service-sector jobs that serve the expanding population. Here, the difficulties involve expanding affordable housing, raising wage and employment standards, and ensuring adequate community benefits from ongoing development initiatives in the region. One crucial challenge is to capture benefits from growth and simultaneously avoid the displacement of residents who have held on for years in distressed neighborhoods—but now, as the economy heats up, find themselves with few "rights to the city."

How do these different market conditions and equity issues shape social movement regionalism? In some ways, we might expect strong-market regions to be the more receptive hosts for regional equity organizing: the fiscal viability of their local governments is typically healthier, which makes local officials at least potentially amenable to regional equity demands. Businesses that are growing and profiting from expanding revenue are also more likely to be willing to make concessions such as agreeing to community benefit agreements. With increased economic resources in both the public and the private sphere, it would appear that strong-market regions would be the more fertile ground for social movement regionalists.

One confirmation of our hypothesis comes in a recent paper (Pastor, Lester, and Scoggins 2007) in which the authors geo-coded the addresses of the attendees at the two Regional Equity Summits hosted by PolicyLink and used a logistic regression to determine the probability that a given metro region would have Summit attendees. Though an imperfect measure of regional equity interest, the procedure revealed that higher levels of inequality, residential segregation, and immigrant presence all predict attendance—but so does rapid growth in per capita income.[6] This result suggests that the strains of rapid growth may cause a response on the part of equity proponents—and that this may be a more powerful driver of interest in the regional level than the strains of metro decline.

This is not to say that there are not opportunities in weak market areas. In these locations, it may be easier to tie the distress of the poor to problems of regional economic competitiveness and hence forge alliances with sympathetic business regionalists. This is part of the story of Milwaukee: wide-spread deindustrialization galvanized employers throughout the region to support the Wisconsin Regional Training Partnerships, since despite competing against each other, they all recognized the reality of global competition and the need to respond collectively to promote modernization and workforce training.

Still, we suspect that there may be more opportunities for successful regional organizing in strong markets than in weak ones. We are not saying that strong markets necessarily promote social movement building; we are saying that a growing economy facilitates economic opportunities. These prospects create a context in which regional business collaboratives are more open to the concerns of regional equity proponents and in which funding is more readily available to organizers. Of course, the test of a national movement is whether it truly has national reach— that is, does its frame, its language, and its strategies apply in multiple locations? Regional equity surely draws out the contradictions of a place like Detroit, where the stark dividing line between Detroit and its suburbs has fueled the work of MOSES. Regional equity may ripen best in certain places, but its seeds can be planted and thrive in many locales.

The Race of the Regions

The racial composition of metropolitan areas shapes the ways community and labor groups organize. In some places, a history of racial tension

---

[6] We included regional dummies in the regression to account for the concentration of slow-growing regions in the Northeast and Midwest. Interestingly, we discovered that higher levels of business interest in regionalism, as proxied by attendance at meetings of the Alliance for Regional Stewardship, prompted equity interest—but not the other way around.

presents a barrier to finding common ground; in other places, racial distinctions seem to be blurring, creating new opportunities. In all places, race is a fundamental element of the organizing landscape—and, in our view, needs to be a clear part of the conversation.

New Jersey, for example, seems to be a regionalists' dream: it has housing affordability requirements to ensure that every municipality takes on its fair share, and it has a 1998 court ruling, commonly know as the "Abbott decision," which mandates that the state use its own resources to equalize per-student spending in the schools (Bollens 2003; Corcoran and Scovronick 1998). But in southern New Jersey, organizers associated with the Gamaliel Foundation have been tackling a doughnut without the hole: they have a presence in the suburbs that adjoin Camden but little presence in the city itself. Partly this is so because another congregation-based organizing federation has a historic and ongoing presence in the city—but it is also because city residents resent the usual regional equity message that Camden's problems are spreading to other jurisdictions in the region. The message is meant to signify city-suburb commonality and solidarity, but it is heard as Camden being "the problem." Race relations in the city, which is 53 percent black and 39 percent Latino (Camden Reports 2006), matter deeply in explaining the mutual fears and hostilities, as they do in Detroit, Atlanta, and so many other places.

At the same time, the classic picture of white suburbs and black inner city, often used to characterize city-suburb differences, is often no longer accurate. Suburbanization rates for ethnic minorities still lag behind those of whites, but they have risen dramatically since 1980 (see figure 5.1).[7] But even if "a rose is a rose is a rose," not all suburbs are the same: as

[7] The data were constructed using the 1999 definitions of metropolitan statistical areas (MSAs) and their central cities. To construct the 1980, 1990, and 2000 figures, we utilized tract-level data from the U.S. Census for 2000, and 1980 and 1990 data as reshaped into 2000 tracts by Geolytics (see www.geolytics.com); we then tagged each tract by its presence in one of the MSAs or one of the central cities, and figured the suburban demographics as that part of the MSA not in the central cities. For the 2006 figures, we utilized the American Community Survey (U.S. Census 2006), reconstructing to the older MSA shapes through the country definitions and also selecting out city populations based on place-level data. Because doing so did not pick up all the central cities in the top 103 MSAs (those with a population over 500,000 in 2000), we restricted our consideration to 94 MSAs in that year. We then reran the 1980, 1990, and 2000 data for just those 94, estimated the difference between that figure and full coverage, and adjusted the 2006 demographics accordingly.

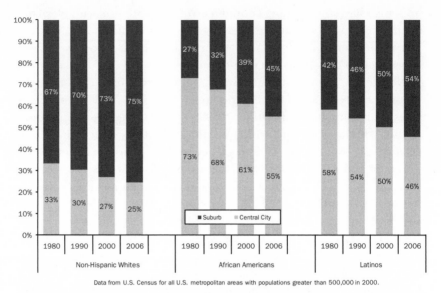

Data from U.S. Census for all U.S. metropolitan areas with populations greater than 500,000 in 2000.

Figure 5.1. City and suburbanization rates for major ethnic groups in America's largest metros, 1980–2006.
Source: U.S. Census 1980, 1990, 2000, and 2006 (American Community Survey).

Myron Orfield (2002) has shown, many minorities and new immigrants are settling in older suburbs that are experiencing the central city–like challenges of aging infrastructure, deteriorating schools and commercial corridors, and inadequate housing stock (see Orfield 2002). Even within broad racial groups, there are significant differences in experience. Think about the contrast between the African American workers in northern manufacturing centers who face problems of deindustrialization and the African American farmers in the South who face displacement because of either sprawling suburbs (e.g., Atlanta) or declining agricultural markets (e.g., Alabama).

The nuances of race can even lead to different regional equity strategies in different parts of the same region. Consider the difference between Mayfair and East Palo Alto, both in the Silicon Valley (and both profiled in chapter 3). As a predominantly Latino neighborhood, Mayfair has been a stopping point for new immigrants in the region—who then move on to other locales. Thus, throughout the region there are social networks that link Mayfair residents with other Latino communities and with Latino political and business leaders. For organizers in this neighborhood, developing a regional equity frame was a stretch, but it was also consistent with the patterns of outmigration.

East Palo Alto, by contrast, was a community created from an unincorporated area by black residents who felt politically and socially neglected and abused by the region, and thought that a separate jurisdiction would provide some defense and some autonomy. The city is now predominantly Latino, but a regional approach, particularly consideration of the benefits of a regional attraction such as IKEA, was a tough sale: older African American residents were historically wary of the larger region and its designs, and mostly wanted to slow traffic-inducing development.

If race influences organizations' strategies and successes in such a complicated way within a region or even a neighborhood, how can we develop generalizations about the dynamic between race and the possibilities of social movement regionalism? Although it has limits, William Frey's breakdown (2001) of the 102 largest metropolitan areas of the country into five different categories, as follows, is useful (metros in each group are listed in order of population).[8]

- Melting Pot Metros (35 of 102 metro areas): metropolitan areas in which no single racial group forms a majority, and there are significant Asian, Latino, and African American populations. They include cities such as Los Angeles, Miami, New York, and Chicago. People of color make up more than a quarter of the suburban population.

Los Angeles-Long Beach, CA PMSA	Houston, TX PMSA
New York, NY PMSA	Dallas, TX PMSA
Chicago, IL PMSA	Riverside-San Bernardino, CA PMSA
Washington, DC-MD-VA-WV PMSA	Phoenix-Mesa, AZ MSA

[8] Frey (2001, 16) adds: "Melting Pot Metros denote those where non-Hispanic whites [constitute] no more than 69 percent of the 2000 population and where the combined populations of Hispanics, non-Hispanic Asians, Hawaiians and Other Pacific Islanders, Native Americans and Native Alaskans, other race and two or more races, exceed 18 percent of the population. Largely White-Black Metros denote remaining areas, in their respective regions, where blacks [make up] at least 16 percent of the population; and Largely White Metros denote the residual areas in each region. 'South and West' pertains to metros located in the South and West census regions. 'North' pertains to metros located in the Northeast and Midwest census regions."

Orange County, CA PMSA

San Diego, CA MSA

Oakland, CA PMSA

Miami, FL PMSA

Newark, NJ PMSA

San Francisco, CA PMSA

Fort Worth-Arlington, TX PMSA

San Jose, CA PMSA

Orlando, FL MSA

Sacramento, CA PMSA

Fort Lauderdale, FL PMSA

San Antonio, TX MSA

Las Vegas, NV-AZ MSA

Bergen-Passaic, NJ PMSA

Austin-San Marcos, TX MSA

Middlesex-Somerset-Hunterdon, NJ PMSA

Fresno, CA MSA

Honolulu, HI MSA

Tucson, AZ MSA

Ventura, CA PMSA

Albuquerque, NM MSA

El Paso, TX MSA

Bakersfield, CA MSA

Jersey City, NJ PMSA

McAllen-Edinburg-Mission, TX MSA

Stockton-Lodi, CA MSA

Vallejo-Fairfield-Napa, CA PMSA

- Largely White/Black South Metros (19 of 102): metropolitan regions in the South where there is a large African American and white population but small concentrations of other racial groups. They include cities such as Atlanta, Raleigh, Nashville, and New Orleans.

Atlanta, GA MSA

Baltimore, MD PMSA

Norfolk-Virginia Beach-Newport News, VA-NC MSA

Charlotte-Gastonia-Rock Hill, NC-SC MSA

New Orleans, LA MSA

Greensboro-Winston-Salem-High Point, NC MSA

Nashville, TN MSA

Raleigh-Durham-Chapel Hill, NC MSA

Memphis, TN-AR-MS MSA

Jacksonville, FL MSA

Little Rock-North Little Rock, AR MSA

Charleston-North Charleston, SC MSA

Mobile, AL MSA

Columbia, SC MSA

Richmond-Petersburg, VA MSA

Greenville-Spartanburg-Anderson, SC MSA

Birmingham, AL MSA

Baton Rouge, L.A. MSA

Wilmington-Newark, DE-MD PMSA

- Largely White/Black North Metros (6 of 102): regions in the North where again there are large African American and white populations, but small concentrations of other racial groups. They include the cities of Detroit, Cleveland, Milwaukee, and Philadelphia. The white percentage in the central cities ranged in 2000 from a high of 49.4 percent in Milwaukee to a low of 10.6 percent in Gary, Indiana (both profiled in chapter 3).

Philadelphia, PA-NJ PMSA

Detroit, MI PMSA

St. Louis, MO-IL MSA

Cleveland-Lorain-Elyria, OH PMSA

Milwaukee-Waukesha, WI PMSA

Gary, IN PMSA

- Largely White North Metros (29 of 102): cities such as Pittsburgh and Minneapolis–St. Paul in which the white population forms a significant majority within the metropolitan area, albeit with important concentrations of black and other racial groups in particular neighborhoods. One of the most celebrated examples of tax-sharing regionalism, Minneapolis–St. Paul, is among the whitest of these areas.

Boston, MA-NH NECMA	Dayton-Springfield, OH MSA
Minneapolis-St. Paul, MN-WI MSA	Albany-Schenectady-Troy, NY MSA
Nassau-Suffolk, NY PMSA	Syracuse, NY MSA
Pittsburgh, PA MSA	Omaha, NE-IA MSA
Kansas City, MO-KS MSA	Akron, OH PMSA
Bridgeport, CT NECMA	Allentown-Bethlehem-Easton, PA MSA
Cincinnati, OH-KY-IN PMSA	Harrisburg-Lebanon-Carlisle, PA MSA
Indianapolis, IN MSA	Scranton—Wilkes-Barre—Hazleton, PA MSA
Columbus, OH MSA	Toledo, OH MSA
Buffalo-Niagara Falls, NY MSA	Springfield, MA NECMA
Hartford, CT NECMA;	Youngstown-Warren, OH MSA
Monmouth-Ocean, NJ PMSA	Ann Arbor, MI PMSA
Rochester, NY MSA	Wichita, KS MSA
Grand Rapids-Muskegon-Holland, MI MSA	Fort Wayne, IN MSA
Providence-Fall River-Warwick, RI-MA NECMA	

- Largely White South and West Metros (13 of 102): regions such as Denver, Seattle, Tampa, and Portland, Oregon, which are also largely white but have lower levels of racial segregation and a more diverse economic base than their counterparts in the North. They also tend to be more racially homogeneous, partly because many, having come of metropolitan age more recently, have less rigid ethnic lines.

Seattle-Bellevue-Everett, WA PMSA	Louisville, KY-IN MSA
Tampa-St. Petersburg-Clearwater, FL MSA	Tulsa, OK MSA
Denver, CO PMSA	Tacoma, WA PMSA
Portland-Vancouver, OR-WA PMSA	Knoxville, TN MSA
Salt Lake City-Ogden, UT MSA	Sarasota-Bradenton, FL MSA
West Palm Beach-Boca Raton, FL MSA	Colorado Springs, CO MSA
Oklahoma City, OK MSA	

Where do our case studies fit in? Los Angeles and the San Jose/Bay Area are melting pot metros, as is Chicago; Gary, Indiana, is clearly a largely black-white region, as are Detroit and Milwaukee. None of our core case studies are of largely white regions. This is partly a reflection of our case selection—we did not, for example, examine Boston, although there has been some interesting regional equity work there—but may also indicate that regional equity initiatives in largely white regions are likely to be less social movement–oriented than initiatives in regions with larger communities of color.

The racial composition of a metro can also influence the institutional base of organizing. Metropolitan regions that have a large concentration of African Americans, for example, tend to be those where the community development movement of the 1960s took root. In the newer melting pot regions of the Southwest and West, community development corporations (CDCs) are less common (see Matsuoka 2005).[9] Thus, regional equity movements in the largely black-white metropolitan regions are most likely to emerge out of a community development tradition, with an emphasis on housing and physical redevelopment of rundown neighborhoods. In Detroit, for example, LISC's program for city-suburb development initiatives represents a move from traditional community development work in inner-city neighborhoods toward a regional equity focus, and yet LISC still retains much of its community development culture. And although Bethel New Life is situated in melting pot Chicago, CDCs there did have strong roots and histories, and the pull of a community development orientation is strong.

Regions with large populations of Latinos, primarily the melting pot metros, may have an advantage in social movement building. Immigrants who have been exposed to (or have actively taken part in) social mobilizations and movements in Mexico and Central America (Delgado 1993) may be more likely to identify with social movement strategies in the United States.[10] Pastor (2007b) has also argued that Latinos might be

[9] As noted in chapter 4, Joassart-Marcelli and Wolch (2003) explore this distinction in the context of Los Angeles, showing how the Southeast cities lack a CDC tradition and other social services.

[10] A rich literature examines the role of race in organizing and coalitions, including the tensions and obstacles in forming coalitions between African American and nonwhite immigrants, some suggesting that cross-race efforts, particularly between immigrant and native-born communities, are few and far between (Rogers 2004) and others offering a more hopeful view of the commonalities (Pastor and Marcelli 2004). In our view, the regional equity frame can facilitate coalition formation on the basis of shared regional issues as well as regional power and thus help with these coalitional tensions (see Pastor 2007a).

especially open to Smart Growth and regional equity arguments—partly because of their urban living patterns and partly because their tendency to be working poor rather than jobless poor means that they can more easily benefit from improved transit links and affordable housing closer to suburban jobs.[11]

In largely white metros, the level of nonwhite population within the central city itself seems to be significant. While all of the largely white metros have a maximum of 30 percent nonwhite population in the total metropolitan area (by definition), at least two (Rochester and Hartford) have a majority nonwhite population in the central city, and at least another six (Denver, Bridgeport, Cincinnati, Harrisburg, Buffalo, and Youngstown) have more than 40 percent nonwhite population in the central city. A large concentration of communities of color in central cities may provide a stronger constituency for social movement regionalism. For example, Hartford has the highest percentage (66.5) of nonwhite population of any metro region in this category. It is also home to the Greater Hartford Interfaith Coalition on Equity and Justice—a local affiliate of the Gamaliel Foundation—which includes forty-four faith communities representing eight municipalities in the Greater Hartford region.[12] This coalition has launched campaigns to reform state tax structures in order to increase support for public education and reduce the reliance of public schools on local property taxes.

Denver has the highest percentage (48.1) nonwhite population of any largely white metro in the West and South. It is also home to one of the more social movement–oriented central labor councils in the country. The story of the Denver Area Labor Federation (DALF) and its nonprofit affiliate, the Front Range Economic Strategy Center (FRESC), closely resembles that of Working Partnerships and the South Bay Labor Council. DALF founded FRESC in 2002 to help promote labor-community alliances and link organizing with research and policy action, with an explicit goal to "set in motion a broad social movement to expand economic opportunity and to strengthen local communities."[13] In collaboration with a range of community organizations, including a local ACORN chapter, the labor movement in Denver helped pass a living-wage

---

[11] See also Suro and Singer (2002) on the dispersal of Latino populations to new metropolitan destinations.

[12] See http://www.ghicej.org/ (accessed August 17, 2006).

[13] See http://www.fresc.org/ (accessed August 17, 2006).

ordinance, challenged a subsidy for a new convention center, and created the Campaign for Responsible Development to promote community benefits agreements for major development projects in the area (Luce and Nelson 2004).

Metros with smaller percentages of nonwhite populations in their central cities have also seen regional initiatives emerge, but these have been primarily proposed by business interests, or have been more focused on policy than on social movement–building. Indianapolis, for example (31.6 percent nonwhite population in the central city), has consolidated many of its public services, including planning, building regulation, and parks, with surrounding Marion County, but such consolidation has been sponsored by political elites, rather than grassroots groups. Likewise, Pittsburgh (33.1 percent nonwhite population in the central city) has a long history of regionalism, but it has been propelled primarily by business and political leadership through the Allegheny Conference on Community Development and its affiliated organizations.[14]

Most of the largely white metros with the smallest percentages of nonwhite population in their central cities, such as Scranton–Wilkes Barre (8.0 percent), Omaha (22.4 percent), Knoxville (20.2 percent), and Fort Wayne (26.9 percent), have not been prominent in national regionalism movements. One exception is Portland, Oregon, where the central city has a nonwhite population of 23.1 percent. Portland is known for its urban growth boundary (UGB), established as the result of a 1973 state land-use law. To advocates of Portland's approach, the UGB has produced less sprawl, greater-inner city reinvestment, and lower levels of regional disparity than many other places. Yet many of Portland's regional accomplishments have been concentrated on broad land use and environmental issues rather than on regional inclusion and equity.[15] And though there is certainly broad support for regional planning in Portland, it is hard to conclude that the activities there are self-consciously seeking to contribute to a new social movement.

On one level, it makes intuitive sense that metropolitan areas with large majorities of white neighborhoods would be less likely to have

[14] See www.alleghenyconference.org.

[15] Indeed, some have argued that the urban growth boundaries may have resulted in negative equity effects by raising housing costs. See the special 2002 issue "Does Portland's Urban Growth Boundary Raise House Prices?" *Housing Policy Debate* 13 (1).

social movement regionalism. Social movements require a constituency or mass base of people with quite a lot at stake, and people of color have, in general, been hurt the most by patterns of regional inequality. On another level, some of the black-white areas that have been the most damaged by regional disparities are also the least active hubs of regional organizing; racial polarization gets in the way of bridge-building, and it requires the special, concerted efforts of groups like the Interfaith Federation in Gary to overcome regional divides. This pattern suggests that much of the action for social movement regionalism may be in the more fluid melting pot metros—places where the political and ethnic lines are in flux and new regional futures can be crafted.[16]

Tensions and Tightropes

Structure of government, strength of the economy, racial composition—these are all factors that we have argued are important in shaping the potential for social movement regionalism to emerge in different metros throughout the country. But a consideration of such structural factors must also be linked with an understanding of the political and social dynamics in different regions. It is important to examine how regional equity organizers are relating to the other political forces that exist in their regions, both allies and opposition. What lessons can be learned from the ways social movement organizers are balancing the various tensions and walking the tightropes of these interactions?

Consider, for a moment, the Justice for Janitors (J for J) campaign. Since its founding in the mid-1980s in Denver by the Service Employees International Union, this movement has succeeded in organizing more than 200,000 property service workers (both janitors and security guards) in more than twenty-nine cities around the country. Many elements of the Justice for Janitors campaigns are similar to regional equity strategies: they depend, for example, on building broad-based public

---

[16] This squares with the findings of the New World Foundation (2005), which defines new majority structures as civic alliances that connect and integrate multiple constituencies, are proactive and escalate their demands, and combine strategic planning with leadership development. New World identifies twenty-two metropolitan areas in which it has provided funding for such alliances; of these, twelve regions (or 54 percent) are classified as melting pot regions, whereas only 34 percent of the 102 largest metros in the country are classified as melting pots. They provide funding in six largely white metro regions, accounting for only 27 percent of their total compared to 41 percent of metros that are predominantly white in Frey's categorization.

support for their cause and, through that process, mobilizing assistance from a range of regional constituencies, including religious, political, and community leadership.

J for J campaigns emphasize the inherent inequality between the well-paid professionals who use office buildings during the day and the low-paid, frequently immigrant, workers who clean them at night. Furthermore, by addressing the linkages between janitors and security guards, property service firms (cleaning and security companies), building owners, and companies that lease building space, the J for J movement directly addresses the regionally embedded nature of many economic transactions, especially in the service sector.

But J for J does not explicitly utilize a regional equity framework in its organizing efforts. Its approach highlights an industry and an occupation, and its organizers pursue their goal of building union membership region by region.[17] Their regional *organizing* efforts involve issues of regional inequality, but the solutions they offer—creating or improving contractual relationships between workers and employers—do not necessarily involve regional *decision-making processes*. The regional equity movement, by contrast, has come to be identified with changing the "rules of the game" at a metropolitan scale, specifically in regard to policy and planning processes. The region is not just an *instrumental* or *tactical* level on which to operate; rather, it is considered fundamental and *strategic* to an analysis of the problem, the framing of solutions, and the building of power.

Such regional fundamentalism is not uniform. For some organizations, adopting regional equity strategies or frameworks is tactical, not strategic, and designed to strengthen particular campaigns or projects. The main goal of Bethel New Life, for example, is the development of Garfield Park as a "community of choice," and Bethel might use "regional equity" as a way to attract support for transit-oriented development or to enhance a neighborhood attraction like the Garfield Park Conservatory. But the group does not necessarily buy into a strategic goal of building a regional power base.

For other organizations such as the Gamaliel Foundation groups or Working Partnerships, the region is fundamental or strategic: they define social and economic opportunities and problems at the regional

---

[17] The SEIU has recently engaged, for example, in global efforts to organize Group 4 Securicor, the largest global provider of security guards. See http://www.focusong4s.org/.

level; they think that influencing regional processes, such as transportation systems, land-use decisions, housing markets, and so on, is key. Still others, such as SCOPE, do not consider regional processes as the only or even main cause of social problems but believe it is the regional scale at which broad national patterns of disparity in wealth and poverty are directly *experienced*. In this view, operating at these spatial dimensions helps to expose origins of social problems in a powerful way, and organizing on that scale is valuable in building political consciousness and social movements.

With so much in the mix—some organizations don't see themselves as part of a regional equity movement; others see different roles within it—it is unsurprising that there are tensions and tightropes involved in doing regional equity organizing. We explore four issues: (1) how best to relate to the other regional efforts, particularly business regionalism, that are out there; (2) how to deal with differences between groups focused on regional equity; (3) how to address race and racial inequality in building visions and organizations; and (4) how to link the lived experiences of people in their homes, neighborhoods, and workplaces with the broader economic, political, and social processes operating in the region.

Playing Well with Others

Regionalism is not "hot" just among equity advocates; the ideas are buzzing in business, urban planning, and public administration circles as well. Within the business and economic development community, for instance, there is a strong emphasis on regional cluster promotion. Numerous efforts have been made to create regional public-private organizations that can address economic needs, transportation infrastructure, and quality of life. Similarly, within the environmental and urban-planning communities, Smart Growth and New Urbanism have emerged as efforts to promote more energy-efficient and environmentally sustainable urban development. In the public administration and political realms, there are efforts to promote greater coordination among municipalities within a region; in the most far-reaching cases, these have led to the structural consolidation of different municipal structures.

How does the existence or absence of such different kinds of regionalism affect the opportunities for social movement regionalism? In some ways, the Smart Growth movement is a good, if sometimes uneasy, fit with social movement regionalism. Anything that will steer development back to central cities is likely to help regional equity—although it can also lead to gentrification in the absence of proper safeguards.

The task here is to broaden the vision of Smart Growth and New Urbanism. These movements tend to imagine urban revitalization as a flowering of cappuccino bars and art houses; as a 2006 report by the Center for Transit Oriented Development argues, the transit developments favored by new urbanists are actually very diverse in terms of both income and class. Thus, paying attention to the constituencies that also support regional equity would seem to be a natural fit.[18]

In our view, however, the most important relationship is with business regionalism, partly because this is where the most powerful potential opposition lies but also because business interests can help pave the way for regional approaches, thus shifting the opportunity structure in regions. In essence, there are cases where its presence helps, cases where it hinders, and cases where it offers a combination of the two.

Take the example of Silicon Valley. When the Joint Venture: Silicon Valley Network was launched in 1993, the Central Labor Council and Working Partnerships were invited to be part of its board of directors. Ultimately, John Neece from the building trades agreed to serve on the board and played an active role in Joint Venture's activities. But many leaders of the labor movement, including the head of the labor council, Amy Dean, worried that issues of equity and opportunity for disadvantaged sectors of the Valley's population would be buried under Joint Venture's primary focus on economic competitiveness.

Nonetheless, as a strong and growing organization in the region, JV:SVN helped contribute to social movement organizing in at least three ways. First, Joint Venture positively reinforced the sense of Silicon Valley as an interconnected region with a common destiny. Its focus on relatively large-scale and long-term initiatives, such as improving education in the Valley, promoting investment in new industries, and permanently streamlining permitting processes, grew out of the notion that business would and should "stick" to the region—and that to do so, it might need to consider issues of human capital and social connectivity.

Second, Joint Venture, largely unintentionally, served to isolate a local business opposition to labor-sponsored policy; it focused on the needs of high-technology industries and large multinational corporations—while

---

[18] See Pastor 2007b; Dreier and Steckler 2007; and Center for Transit-Oriented Development 2006.

the San Jose Chamber of Commerce, more the province of local real estate and small business, became increasingly perceived as a creature of less forward-looking enterprises. When Working Partnerships campaigned for a living-wage ordinance in the City of San Jose, for example, the Chamber of Commerce opposed it vehemently. Joint Venture, however, was largely silent on the issue: although its business leaders were generally opposed to a living wage in principle, the policy was unlikely to affect them (as they were generally not contracting with the city and tended to pay higher wages). Moreover, Mayor Susan Hammer was a strong supporter of the policy, and a key participant in Joint Venture. As a result, the recalcitrant and less-connected Chamber of Commerce had diminished political clout with the San Jose City Council, and the Living Wage Ordinance passed.

Third, Joint Venture served as a useful foil. Having a clear opponent typically makes the organization of strong community sentiment easier, and while Joint Venture was never actually a target for such campaigns—specific campaigns were organized around city and county government policy, or broad issue areas such as the Children's Health Initiative or affordable housing—in community meetings and door-to-door organizing efforts, organizers could point to Joint Venture as the "other" regional voice in the Valley, and surely, they argued, Joint Venture should not be the only voice. This approach generated a sense of urgency around a counterpoint of community-based regional organizing and policy efforts.

Sometimes, the existence of business or policy-led regionalism hinders the development of social movement regionalism. In Pittsburgh, for example, regional discussions have been dominated by the business-led Allegheny Conference on Community Development, whose focus over twenty years has primarily been on downtown revitalization and promotion of industries linked with the region's large educational and medical institutions. The conference leaders combined their strong, organized connections to media outlets, regional politicians, and local funders with a paternal openness to CDC-oriented neighborhood groups. This cluster of power has marginalized more oppositional groups, making it difficult for them to gain traction in the public arena.[19]

In comparison, the absence of effective business regionalism created an opening in Los Angeles. The relative weakness of business was most

---

[19] On the Pittsburgh story, see Lubove 1996; Hamilton 2004; and Ferman 1996.

evident when the 1992 uprising exploded into the region's (and nation's) consciousness and led to the creation of Rebuild L.A.—which did little to mobilize corporate investment for the areas affected by the unrest. By the time it shut its doors five years later, it had shifted to a strategy of supporting small business development, reflecting the ongoing business fragmentation. With the field wide open, community organizers developed their own regional vision for lasting and far-reaching structural changes. In this context, it is little wonder that progressive candidate Antonio Villaraigosa actually found strong business as well as labor and community support in his 2005 campaign for mayor. Business had essentially ceded ground and realized that a social justice commitment would be the price they would have to pay to get any political figure who could support large-scale regional economic investment and real estate development.

But absence does not always make the social movement heart grow fonder. In the highly fragmented Detroit area, MOSES has struggled to create a regional transportation authority and a single countywide land bank. With few others pulling their weight, making the region come together is a challenge.

All our profiled groups must make decisions every day whether to dance with business interests or box with business representatives; as hard a choice as that may seem, it is neither the least nor the last of the difficulties they face—for they also face each other.

When Regional Equity Worlds Collide

Community world views may generally differ from business world views, but they are neither singular nor homogeneous. Organizations may have a tight or a loose association to regional equity principles, or they may tend to focus more on projects, policies, or power. Bringing these varied perspectives under the same tent can often be a challenge.

This dynamic was particularly evident between Detroit LISC and MOSES. LISC is a classic example of a community development approach to regionalism. Before 2002, Detroit LISC focused almost exclusively on traditional approaches to community development, assisting neighborhood revitalization primarily through helping community development corporations in their efforts to build affordable housing and revitalize commercial strips. Even though LISC participates in the Metro Detroit Regional Investment Initiative (and though currently it does emphasize projects that bridge the boundaries between Detroit and its suburbs), its focus is still primarily on project development.

This project-oriented approach contrasts sharply with MOSES's approach to regional equity. MOSES's very origins are in some ways *reactions against* project-oriented community development. MOSES emerged from three previously existing neighborhood community development organizations that had been working separately to address quality-of-life issues through traditional community development processes but had been frustrated by their limited progress at a neighborhood scale. MOSES was created specifically to address the broader processes that were undermining neighborhood revitalization initiatives, and the focus was clearly on power-building and democratic accountability.

According to the MOSES organizers, Detroit LISC was a latecomer to regional equity, embracing regional strategies only in 2003 and yet garnering large amounts of attention and millions of dollars for work that essentially only modified traditional community development approaches; LISC paid little attention to policy, advocacy, or power-building. Meanwhile, MOSES, which had been pursuing regional strategies since its founding in 1997, continued to struggle for every penny. MOSES staff felt that policy work and advocacy-oriented organizing efforts should be a higher priority for funding than the project-oriented work Detroit LISC pursued.

For their part, Detroit LISC staff acknowledged both its late start in implementing regional strategies and the fact that it had been prompted by external inspiration, both from National LISC and from the Ford Foundation. Yet they also argued that the nature of development work requires large amounts of money, which led them to align themselves closely with banks and corporate economic development organizations. At times, they suggest, many people have viewed MOSES as being oppositional and obstructionist.

MOSES and Detroit LISC were able, however, to overcome many of these organizational and tactical differences. It may have helped that both groups were led by African American women working in environments historically dominated by men (church structures and financial/corporate institutions, respectively); given this sense of shared experience, the two met regularly to talk. From this friendship came mutual understanding, and they were soon able to help their organizations find common ground, most importantly around efforts to develop a land bank in Detroit. Yet the tensions between their organizational approaches reflect some of the real difficulties of uniting project, policy, and power-building regional equity strategies.

Even in cases where there is significant overlap in visions of regional equity, real tensions can surface. We saw this in the case of Milwaukee's Campaign for a Sustainable Milwaukee (CSM), founded by the Central Labor Council. When sufficient financial resources became available for workforce training, CSM joined forces with the Wisconsin Regional Training Partnership (WRTP) under the umbrella of the Milwaukee Jobs Initiative (MJI). MJI was a separate organization but subcontracted its training work to CSM—and CSM worked closely with the WRTP because of the latter's expertise in training and its ability to place training recipients in high-paying union jobs.

CSM thought that it would be able to leverage its training work to gain support for its organizing efforts, but it had difficultly doing so. According to John Goldstein, the last executive director of CSM, the organizing and service components of CSM operated separately in practice, and people who received services were rarely substantially involved in the organizing efforts. With mission drift becoming mission split (as described in chapter 3), CSM eventually collapsed.

The tensions between equity agendas and between organizing and implementation do not necessarily result in groups' abandoning their regional collaborative work; Detroit LISC and MOSES continue to see their futures as intertwined, and they find ways to collaborate whenever possible. Many CSM members remain active in the Good Jobs and Livable Neighborhoods Coalition and see the more programmatic work of the WRTP as an essential part of retaining and building a strong political base in the region. In many ways, then, it is the regional economic and political processes that provide these groups a way of navigating the tensions of different ideological perspectives and varying organizational activities.

Race, Regions, and Destiny

Perhaps the single most important issue simmering in the regional equity world is the role of race: more specifically, the extent to which regional processes are important in understanding racial inequality. Conversely, to what extent is an explicit focus on racial inequality needed to understand regional processes? In this context, regional equity strategies find contradictions. On the one hand, racial inequity and segregation have been key factors in creating the unequal metropolitan landscape of America—many early leaders in the regional equity movement, be they white, black, Latino, Asian, or other, cut their organizing teeth on some variant of the civil rights movement. On the other hand, the effort to find common ground across city and suburb, rich and poor, white and minority has sometimes led to politics where issues of race are set aside or diffused to build regional coalitions or work on specific issues (such as transportation, housing, or Smart Growth).

Consider the Detroit–Grosse Pointe Park Collaborative, a city-suburb neighborhood revitalization effort on Detroit's eastern border. The contrast between black and white could hardly be more stark: Gross Pointe Park was developed as an exclusive suburb, housing wealthy executives and managers from Detroit's auto firms; in 2000 the city's population was 93 percent white and 60 percent college-educated, with a median household income over $80,000. In the adjacent Detroit community, the population was nearly 90 percent African American, only 9 percent college-educated, and the median household income was $25,020.[20] Despite these evident disparities, both white and black leaders chose *not* to focus on these differences but, instead, to organize around building a cross-border (city-suburb) neighborhood business association and fostering communication through sports leagues and other recreational activities for children—that is, to attempt to bring blacks and whites together without talking about racial differences.

Compare this strategy with that used by the Wisconsin Regional Training Partnership to organize workers within the construction industry in Milwaukee. Here, the historic racial inequalities had also been quite stark: well-paying unionized construction jobs were largely reserved for white men, and people of color were largely excluded from the building trades and relegated to lower-paid laborer positions (Waldinger and Bailey 1991; Butler 2006). Yet in the late 1990s, union leaders recognized the intersection of two major trends. First, the level of unionization in the construction trades was declining across the board; second, increasing numbers of Latino immigrants and African Americans were being employed in construction.

Deciding to capitalize on this observation, union leaders sought out new ways of rebuilding union strength by leveraging labor agreements on projects involving direct public expenditures or subsidies and

---

[20] As measured by the U.S. Census (2000) in zip code 48215.

by concurrently reaching out to minority constituencies. To succeed, they had to demonstrate credible commitment to expanding diversity in both the rank and file and the leadership of construction unions. They established trust by investing significant amounts of time and resources in BIG STEP, a pre-apprenticeship program for inner-city African American residents, designed to provide pathways into the better-paying apprenticeship programs in the building trades. In essence, attention to race and historical patterns of racial discrimination became central to their regional organizing strategies.

The question of how much to emphasize race and racial differences in American politics is not unique to the regional equity movement—indeed, it runs through nearly every aspect of policymaking and coalition-building in this country. Yet it is a particularly sharp tension in this arena precisely because the urban form—struggling central cities and isolated suburbs—is in many ways the physical manifestation of highly racialized processes of segregation. Race, in short, is an inescapable part of America's regional histories and racism a part of its social institutions. If regional equity is to become, in Rev. Cheryl Rivera's words, the "civil rights movement of the twenty-first century" (2003), it is hard to see how it can triumph without bringing race and racism into the light.

Talking about race is difficult—both for whites who may be uncomfortable with the implication that they benefit from unfair privileges, and for people of color who are tired of being seen only through the prism of race. In large part, the conversation about race revolves around political power—who has it, who doesn't, and what it will take to get it (Thompson 2002). In some sense, regional equity tries to sidestep the issue. It celebrates Richard Hatcher of Gary, Indiana, for becoming the first African American mayor of a large U.S. city, but it also stresses that he inherited a restructuring economy that had deprived Gary of its resources and left it with a shrinking public-sector capacity to address the increasing social and economic needs of its people. Regional equity proponents thus argue for a focus on the regional economic common ground—but it seems clear that we cannot build up the economic capacity of the inner city without addressing the visibility and viability of inner-city political leadership as well (Thompson 2005).

This effort to embrace regional common ground and to address historical political discrimination simultaneously leads to contradictions in the support bases for regionalism. It is easy to think, for example, that since so much of the regional equity agenda could benefit disadvantaged areas, there is a natural constituency for regional equity in communities of color. Yet many of these same communities have long been suspicious of regionalism, particularly in places where minority political power stems from geographic concentration; higher levels of regional governance are seen as potentially diluting hard-won political voice. In Louisville, Kentucky, for example, the African American community was largely opposed to a city-county merger for exactly that reason. In Cleveland, Ohio, African American leaders perceived regionalism as being primarily driven by white suburban communities (Savitch and Vogel 2004). Interests must be viewed through a historic, and often discriminatory, context; building new alliances without directly addressing the racial dimensions of politics and power would be difficult and inadvisable.

With all this talk of race, we are especially struck by lessons from the election of Antonio Villaraigosa, the first Latino mayor in L.A. in more than 130 years. His victory, we have suggested, was partly due to regional equity proponents who had worked to win landmark community benefits agreements, build a new metropolitan labor movement, and change the politics of the city and the region. Villaraigosa had proved himself to be an effective advocate for racial justice in his previous public stances; he invested campaign time and resources to bring together African American and Latino constituencies; and he was seen as someone who understood the racial realities of the city's politics. But despite his commitment to racial equality, he downplayed race in his campaign, instead lifting up common aspirations for education, public safety, and economic betterment and stressing a universal narrative of hope and promise for Los Angeles. In short, Villaraigosa's run for mayor embodied the tension of the regional equity movement—the need to have credibility on issues of race while crafting a vision and policy package that can create broad agreement and a sense of common destiny.

Keeping It Real

Speaking to the immediate needs of people struggling on a day-to-day level while providing a compelling understanding of the regional processes that are involved in creating those experiences is yet another delicate balancing act. The link between everyday experiences and larger processes of social change is one of the central dimensions that characterize all social movements. How this link is achieved and its quality are critical to shaping the nature of any social movement—the targets of action, the kind of organizing, and the constituency that is mobilized.

Consider, for example, the historical differences between the U.S. civil rights movement and the Black Power movement. Both movements grew during roughly the same period (with obviously strong interconnections), and both were built upon the daily lived experience of discrimination and structural racism faced by African Americans in the United States. But each offered a differing vision of social life, social change, and social action. The emphasis of the civil rights movement was on ending discrimination, primarily based on race, but also on gender and disability. Although in practice the civil rights movement directly confronted power relations in society, its vision was built around a human rights framework and a discourse of equality of opportunity. This vision created a broad appeal and an opportunity for building (sometimes unlikely) alliances with a range of constituencies and institutions—though this approach was also criticized as being "accommodationist" and ineffective in gaining sufficient benefits for African Americans.

The Black Power movement, in contrast, emphasized self-determination among African Americans and direct challenges to white hegemony. This more radical approach limited the size of the constituency that it mobilized, but it also made invaluable contributions not only to confronting discrimination in American society but to understanding and addressing deeper ways in which race structures culture, identity, and unequal socioeconomic relations. Without debating the relative contributions of the two distinct but interrelated movements, our point is simply that linking the day-to-day experience of discrimination with a more expansive vision of social change was critical in both movements, and that the nature of *how* that linkage was made was quite different for each movement (Lawson 2003; Joseph 2006, 2007).

Making connections between people's day-to-day lives and a vision of regional equity can be extremely challenging, especially when an organizing target has indirect impact on people's daily lives (Groarke 2004). Few people see regional processes as directly affecting the quality of their jobs, the affordability of their homes, the accessibility of health care, or the quality of their lives. Similarly, people's sense of identity is rarely rooted in a region. More frequently, people's sense of their own race, nationality, gender, occupation, family role, spiritual life, or even neighborhood is stronger than their sense of metropolitan identity.

For most people, the region they live in is a geographic abstraction with little relevance to their daily lives, or it is just the background terrain for the things that really matter in their lives. Yet the need to clarify the relationships is clear. As Fisher notes:

> Neighborhood organizing movements develop in an historical context that includes but transcends local community borders.... [S]ocial developments are part of a total economic and political system—a political economy—in which all strands of life, from the national to local level, intertwine with each other. The challenge for the regional equity movement is to make visible and tangible the link between regional processes and people's material aspirations and well-being. (1994, 159)

How are the organizations involved in the nascent regional equity movement making these associations between day-to-day experiences and economic structures as well as a larger social vision? Sometimes the link is not explicitly to "regional equity" as a vision or goal but rather to specific issues of opportunity or inequality that happen to have regional dimensions. Bethel New Life founder Mary Nelson (2006) questions whether regional equity is a compelling concept for mobilizing communities—in her words, "What's the moral imperative of regionalism?" Nevertheless, she and Bethel New Life organized specific campaigns based on regional opportunities and used this as a basis for building support. Furthermore, their efforts to revitalize the Garfield Park Conservatory depended on a vision of the conservatory as a regional resource whose state of disrepair was important to the entire region. While regional equity was not seen as the ultimate vision driving the organization, the vision that Bethel presented—the possibility of reversing socioeconomic decline in a single neighborhood by looking outward—was a regional equity vision that in the end united diverse constituencies.

For even those organizations that have explicitly focused on regional equity, bringing together people's daily experiences and regional equity goals has been a long, slow, and careful process. Affiliates of the Gamaliel Foundation, for instance, have developed a sophisticated and detailed organizing process for making these connections. At the core of their process are "one-on-ones"—direct individual meetings between Gamaliel organizers and individual members of the various congregations. These meetings are designed to make personal connections with residents of the region, discover their key day-to-day concerns, highlight the problems they are experiencing, clarify what they see as important priorities, and identify people with strong leadership capabilities to drive campaigns for collective action.[21]

This process of building on individual meetings and then expanding from this one-on-one base to collective actions is a process customary to all of the faith-based organizing networks that have grown from the Alinsky tradition, including the Industrial Areas Foundation (IAF) and the PICO National Network (formerly Pacific Institute for Community Organizations). What distinguishes the Gamaliel affiliates is their strategic emphasis on the importance of regional processes in shaping patterns of inequality and poverty. During their one-on-ones they concentrate as much on building a regional consciousness as on building social capital, leadership capabilities, and even inspiration. As Gamaliel's cofounder, Mary Gonzalez, puts it:

> We find that whoever [whatever] we're talking about, there is so much isolation in communities. We're looking at, in terms of values discussions, moving towards collective communities. We're looking at how do we operate in every community. Decisions are being made out of fear, and we need to move to hope, not fear. We need to push abundance, rather than scarcity. So we start discussions around where in the region is there abundance.[22]

Working Partnerships in San Jose takes another tack to approaching day-to-day experience and transforming it into regional equity understanding. At the core of WPUSA's approach is the Labor Community Leadership Institute (profiled in chapter 3). The curriculum enables the participants to step back from their day-to-day operations and broaden their world view, and this unhurried learning process helps build the deeper collaborations that do not occur in tactical short-term coalitions. As WPUSA founder Amy Dean says, "You don't build relationships in the middle of a fight; you have to create deliberate space to understand each

---

[21] This is an example of what Themba (1999, 3) calls the best sort of policy initiatives, one that "engage[s] the community that shares the problem and ensures that it is part of the solution. These initiatives match the desired policy with the capacity of the community to advocate for change, while seeking to expand the base of support for such advocacy efforts in the future."

[22] Quoted from a meeting of the Conversation on Regional Equity (CORE) held in Detroit on October 4, 2004.

other's interests" (CORE 2006, 39). Understanding differing interests—having conversations that forgo the lowest common denominator in favor of frank discussions to reach the highest common ground—makes it easier to develop policy proposals and campaigns that can provide win-win opportunities for multiple constituencies.

For Gilda Haas, whose Figueroa Corridor Coalition has achieved regional equity policy and organizing successes, keeping it real requires popular education. She notes:

> Popular education is education for a genuine democracy. It provides tools for collectivizing knowledge and experience around shared problems, for analyzing power and structural dynamics, and for democratically devising solutions and actions to attain those solutions. It is important, however, not to confuse popular education's tools with popular education's purpose to produce social change for a more democratic and equitable society. With this end in mind, popular education must always include an action component, for it is only through collective action that social change can occur. And it is only through collective reflection and analysis of those actions that we continue to learn and to build our movement. (2002, 94).

Regionalism cannot be imposed as an external solution—and when presented as an abstract concept, it frequently carries little sense of immediacy in people's lives. Thus, it does not serve as a mobilizing force. Nor are academic discussions of regional policies, such as the urban growth boundary in Portland, necessarily compelling; such conversations tend to launch conferences, not social movements. By contrast, in those efforts that are contributing to building a social movement, regionalism is not perceived as an external concept or abstract notion. Instead, using popular education based on sophisticated research and analysis, regional equity organizers can demonstrate how regional strategies can bring community and individual aspirations to life.

Building an Agenda, Creating the Will

Even if regional consciousness is forged, groups face challenges in identifying targets and building organizations. How, after all, do you change the rules of the game on a regional scale when there are few obvious formal targets for clear regional solutions? What does it take to put together and maintain unlikely alliances?

Where's the Game?

David Rusk (1999) has argued that community developers spend too much time on the "inside game" of neighborhood revitalization and too little time on the "outside game" of regional planning and tax rules that have stripped resources from distressed communities. It is a compelling vision and a powerful admonition—but what do you do when there is no playing field on which to engage?

In Detroit, MOSES identified transportation as a major issue and took on investment in regional transportation infrastructure and coordination as a strategic goal. Yet Detroit had no regional authority responsible for transportation planning—there was, in fact, no formal regional government structure for groups seeking regional options to identified problems. MOSES therefore sought to create DARTA, the Detroit Area Regional Transportation Authority (discussed in chapter 3). Unfortunately, the preexisting transportation authorities (one for the City of Detroit and the separate authority called SMART, which runs the suburban transit system) and the local authorities in the area were reluctant to cede powers of taxation or regulation to a new transportation authority. They refused to merge existing structures into a new one.

This refusal created problems for MOSES not only in transportation policies but in transportation politics. In the initial efforts, residents of the region could see the importance of organizing for regional transportation solutions. But when the proposed solution was frustrated, so were the residents—and MOSES experienced growing levels of disillusion within its constituency. As sentiment grew that regional solutions were not the most productive ones, MOSES began working closely with other Gamaliel affiliates throughout Michigan to pursue state-level solutions to the problems they were experiencing in Detroit. Regional equity still remains an important mobilizing framework for MOSES, but it is now pursuing practical solutions on a different scale. To play the game, it seems, you must first find—or create—the right field.

In Los Angeles, where responsible and powerful regional entities reign, there are still gaps in the reach of regional governance. For example, LAANE's Coalition for Clean and Safe Ports is pushing for independent truck drivers to become employees of the concessionaire trucking firms that contract with the Ports of L.A. and Long Beach. The strategy of establishing a single, fiscally responsible employer to come to the bargaining table follows on the heels of a successful labor strategy won earlier. In 1995, SEIU Local 434B (now known as SEIU Local 6434, the United Long-Term Care Workers' Union) successfully lobbied to have the state's In-Home Supportive Services (IHSS) become employer of record for the 74,000 home care workers in the state. The victory not only ensured the union a bargaining entity but also represented the biggest organizing victory for the U.S. labor movement since workers at Ford's River Rouge plant joined the United Auto Workers in 1941 (see Stone 2000).

There is a lack of structural levers also when it comes to addressing the unequal tax bases of different municipalities. Although regional tax base sharing has been suggested by Orfield (1997) and others, such plans have been implemented in only a few locales: for example, the Minneapolis–St. Paul metro and, on a more limited basis, regions such as Pittsburgh–Allegheny County. The problem is that in the absence of an existing regional authority, regional tax base sharing would require agreement from all municipalities involved, a highly unlikely achievement in most regions. For example, a limited version of such tax base sharing in the Sacramento region of California, complete with extra incentives for Smart Growth–style projects, ran into a buzz saw of opposition from the League of California Cities, Sacramento suburban advocates, and other key political actors, and eventually it was stopped cold by the state senate.[23]

In the absence of regional policy levers, regional equity organizers must either build incrementally, city by city, within the regional context or leapfrog the region entirely and search for policy solutions at the state level.[24] In places where the scale of the county is large enough to allow significant regional solutions, county governments can be effective vehicles for regional social movement organizing. In San Jose, for example, Working Partnerships' very first policy initiative was focused on providing accountability for property tax rebates through the Santa

---

[23] The effort was part of a bill passed by the California Assembly in 2002. It proposed a relatively modest strategy: run a pilot experiment in the rapidly growing Sacramento region that would take the growth in sales taxes generated by new retail development and split it across the region, with one-third going to the local jurisdiction, one-third for regional sharing on a per capita basis, and one-third specifically to reward Smart Growth development (see PolicyLink 2002a).

[24] See Wood 2007 on the efforts of PICO groups in California to work at the state level.

Clara County government. Similarly, their groundbreaking policy to promote children's universal access to health insurance successfully targeted the county. The coalition's success in achieving a unanimous vote by the county's board of supervisors to invest their proceeds from the national tobacco settlement in the Children's Health Initiative was critical to persuading the City of San Jose and local foundations to invest in that initiative as well.

Innovative targets have included other major regional government bodies. In the busy hub of Los Angeles, the airport is a major regional asset administered by Los Angeles World Airports, a self-supporting branch of the City of Los Angeles government, which also administers three other airports in the region: Ontario, Van Nuys, and Palmdale. When LAANE successfully signed a community benefits agreement with LAX, not only did it have regional implications because of the prominence of the airport as a regional asset, but it also established immediate implications for other airport renovations and expansions in the region. Similarly, in Chicago, when Bethel New Life wanted to maintain and improve the rail line through its neighborhood, the pivotal target was not an overall regional government (which doesn't exist) but rather the Chicago Transit Authority, which administers the transportation system for the City of Chicago and forty surrounding suburbs—the second largest public transit system in the country.

These cases illustrate the potential of regional approaches, even in the absence of regional special district authorities, or an overall regional government. Indeed, although it would seem ideal to have regional governments that would facilitate regional equity policies, in practice, advocating for regional policy coordination will be more effective than advocating for structural change in regional government in the form of a new body. Moreover, consolidations or mergers of local governments into a single regional body tend to be treated with some suspicion by regional equity constituents, partly because they do not want to dilute neighborhood-based political power. In a 2004 presentation to regionalist advocates, john powell argued that even though mergers might promote efficiency in the delivery of services and perhaps improve fiscal health, they are unlikely to have a significant impact on regional inequality unless they directly address the most important processes perpetuating inequality—primarily the forces shaping land use, fiscal disparities, housing, and education (powell 2004).

Rounding up the Unusual Suspects

Strengths and weaknesses are usually a package deal. While regional equity is a "broad tent"—capable of encompassing a wide range of approaches and organizations—connecting across diverse constituencies, balancing a wide range of perspectives and experiences, and linking with other "regionalisms" can be a difficult balancing act. Alliance building that focuses on long-term relationships to endow a sense of common purpose is often a lengthy process of give and take that can be challenging to negotiate.

LINKING CITIES AND SUBURBS

One major tension in regional equity efforts occurs between suburbs and cities. Whereas the traditional picture is one of affluent and homogeneous suburbs seeking to separate from their neighboring central city, the migration of ethnic minorities and the rising concentrations of poverty have transformed the face of many older, inner-ring suburbs—which would seem to make it easier for inner-ring residents to recognize the common interests they have with residents of the central city. This argument is also pursued by Weir, Wolman, and Swanstrom (2005) in their examination of central city–suburban government coalitions that influence state policy and legislation.

Whether the actors are state structures or civil society organizations, building cross-jurisdictional coalitions and alliances is a long, painstaking process that raises numerous issues. Metropolitan Detroit provides an example. Here, the Detroit LISC initiative focused explicitly on forging cooperation between the city and its immediately adjacent suburbs in three strategically chosen development corridors. The focus of these initiatives was on both physical development, particularly the revitalization of commercial strips, and social development through various partnerships and social programs. Crossing political jurisdictions, however, has been a serious hindrance. In the case of the Van Dyke–8 Mile Gateway, for example, despite consistent government support from the suburb of Warren, support from the City of Detroit has been uneven and unreliable. For Warren, as a small suburb bordering the city, the revitalization of the neighborhood is clearly a high priority. For Detroit city planning officials, however, the 8 Mile Gateway is simply one neighborhood among many, and officials seem more focused on downtown revitalization and the Riverwalk development. Policymakers whose priorities differ and whose interests are nested in many relationships complicate collaboration across jurisdictional boundaries (V-8 Collaborative 2006).

Milwaukee also illustrates the difficulties of building truly regional alliances around programmatic efforts. The Wisconsin Regional Training Partnership and the Milwaukee Jobs Initiative had a vision of regionwide training, industrial upgrading, and job placement. In practice, however, most of their activities have focused on Milwaukee County. The significance of even this scale of activity should not be minimized; their efforts to improve job access for inner-city residents within the county labor market have made significant improvements possible. Yet they have had little success in addressing the patterns of urban sprawl in the region beyond Milwaukee County. In essence, the suburbs are still going it alone.

One of the newest spatial frontiers involves ties between rural communities and city dwellers. In 2000 the Community Farm Alliance (2003)[25]—a grassroots organization whose mission is "to organize and encourage cooperation among farmers, rural, and urban citizens, through leadership development and grassroots democratic processes"— successfully persuaded the state of Kentucky to devote some of its $3.4 billion tobacco settlement money to help family farmers transition out of growing tobacco and into growing food for new local markets. The CFA spearheaded the design and implementation of an integrated, diverse, and long-term strategy for a local food system that has included new direct marketing opportunities, such as urban farmers' markets, as well as loans to farmers for building small-scale food-processing plants, diversifying crops, and experimenting with innovative production techniques. In western Louisville, low-income residents frequently lacked access to health and nutritious foods, since commercial grocery stores were dramatically underrepresented. CFA therefore worked with local residents in the Portland neighborhood to develop a local farmers' market, providing healthy, and affordable, locally produced food in an accessible location— which has subsequently become an important gathering point for building neighborhood cohesion.

This project and others like it have linked rural and urban constituencies, bridged historic racial divides, and promoted rural economic diversification and urban neighborhood revitalization (Funders' Network 2005, 107–10). A number of similar programs, bringing together farms and urban schools in order to create new markets and improve nutrition,

[25] For more information, go to http://communityfarmalliance.org/.

have popped up across the country.[26] Crossing the city-suburb and urban-rural lines is not easy, we admit, but some organizations are showing how the usual divides of space and place can be overcome.

REACHING ACROSS RACE

In America's racialized metros, regional equity organizing necessarily involves linking multiple racial and ethnic communities. The case studies reveal both the challenges faced and successes achieved in building multiracial alliances and the careful work and deep understanding that must go into forming these ties. Sufficient time is needed to foster a quality of relationship that can move beyond the historical divisions and lack of understanding.

Highly segregated Detroit provides a particularly compelling example of the challenge. With few opportunities for whites and blacks to interact in their neighborhoods, building cross-racial organizations requires conscious effort. Patrick Gahegan, a white pastor in a predominantly African American congregation in the City of Detroit and one of the leading pastors within MOSES, described the dynamic to Chris Benner:

> Initially, I didn't get involved with MOSES.... In this divided region [when I was first exposed to the organization], MOSES was seen as a white organization and couldn't cut it in the black community.... [A]t the time [1998] the organizers were all white. Gamaliel itself was perceived as all white. That is still the perception in most of the black churches.... In the suburbs, MOSES is seen as a black organization. It is all relative. Detroiters aren't used to walking in a room and seeing half white and half black. That is out of the context of what goes on here. African Americans see all the white people and say this is a white organization. White folks see all the African Americans and say this is a black organization.... [T]he leadership of MOSES...have helped address this, but the truth is that Detroit has become so polarized. It is who we are. It is built into the DNA of us as a people. (Gahegan 2006)

[26] See the National Farm to School website (http://www.farmtoschool.org/), which is hosted and staffed by the Urban and Environmental Policy Institutes Center for Food Justice at Occidental College (www.uepi.oxy.edu). The UEPI website also points to a growing movement of farm to institution programs that draw rural and suburban food resources to important institutions such as hospitals and prisons.

To overcome these historic racial divisions, MOSES built an organization with congregations throughout the Detroit metro region, congregations sometimes predominantly African American and sometimes predominantly white. For MOSES, focusing on metropolitan equity has become a means of overcoming racial divides, and relentless organizing has started to forge a sense of shared destiny between white and black residents of the region.

The barriers against building cross-racial majoritarian movements are different in the multiracial regions of California. In both Los Angeles and the Bay Area, whites no longer represent a majority of the population and have not for years. With rapid growth in the Latino population and large numbers of Asian residents, both regions truly reflect a demographic tapestry of race and ethnicities.[27] Although white/nonwhite tensions are still important, there are also important stresses across the range of races and ethnicities. African American neighborhoods in South L.A. and East Palo Alto (Silicon Valley), for instance, have experienced a rapid influx of Latino immigrants, resulting in rising tensions that have sometimes exploded into violence. Korean communities in Los Angeles and Vietnamese communities in San Jose face particular challenges associated with being smaller enclaves in a wider urban context (Martinez and Valenzuela 2006).[28]

In the context of these majority-minority regions, community and labor organizations developed experience in building trust across racial lines. They did so not out of pure altruism or goodwill: political coalitions that cut across racial lines were the only way to achieve any victories in the context of changing neighborhoods and a changing region. But multiracial coalitions must be fundamentally rooted in shared goals such as achieving genuine political equality and building the capacity of communities of color to participate fully as leaders in political coalitions and

[27] In Los Angeles County, for example, 47 percent of the population was of Hispanic or Latino origin in 2004; white non-Hispanics represented 29 percent, Asians and Pacific Islanders 13 percent, and African Americans 9 percent. In Santa Clara County (San Jose area), the white non-Hispanic population represented 40 percent of the population, Asians and Pacific Islanders 30 percent, Latinos 25 percent, and African Americans 2 percent (U.S. Census, 2004).

[28] Part of the cross-racial communication comes from the lower levels of residential segregation in these regions. In Los Angeles, for example, while whites became more residentially isolated from people of color over the 1990s, the residential proximity of African Americans and Latinos was on the upswing, and so too was the need to forge new lines of communication.

in policymaking (Thompson 2002). Building such powerful cross-racial alliances is clearly not easy, even in these regions, and it has required a time-intensive process of developing trust.

FORGING LABOR-COMMUNITY ALLIANCES

Alliances between communities and labor throughout the United States have generally been more the exception than the rule[29]—partly because the separation between residential space and work space contributes in turn to the lack of connection between labor politics and community politics. Community issues are indirectly joined to broader employment structures, and rarely do workplace issues directly address areas of traditional concern for community organizations such as housing, transportation, and neighborhood commercial viability (Katznelson 1981). In many contexts, the labor-community divide is reinforced by a racial divide, particularly in the building trades, where people of color have often been excluded from the better-paying union jobs. Collaboration has traditionally been limited to labor's calling on community organizations for temporary support in particular organizing campaigns, or community organizations' requests for labor's endorsement of particular initiatives.

In our profiles, we find that the labor-community relationships reflected similarities as well as variances in structure, strategy, and ultimately outcome. As a starting point, however, all efforts mirror the rise of social movement regionalism, where unions ally themselves with community and social movement organizations (Nissen 2004; Frege, Heery, and Turner 2003; Rathke 2004; Turner 2005). In San Jose, Los Angeles, and Milwaukee, the three cases we examined where labor played a significant role, there were essentially three methods through which labor-community ties were established: political (electoral) processes, programmatic and policy work, and longer-term leadership development and training. And in each region, central labor councils were critical.

In Los Angeles and in San Jose, much of the impetus for labor-community alliances came from the political process, and specifically in response to state-level initiatives. Starting in 1994, a series of statewide ballot propositions affected the constituencies of both labor and community organizations. All these initiatives were put on the ballot by conservative advocates, and the campaigns to defeat them provided

[29] Though there are important exceptions: see Brecher and Costello 1990.

platforms for labor and community groups to work together and, some-times, to succeed.[30]

The propositions on the 1998 ballot (226 and 227) were particularly significant in that they directly attacked both unions and immigrants, giving labor and community groups something specific to rally around. There is nothing like a shared battle to forge relationships and bring together unlikely allies, a form of "common-cause coalitions."[31] Fighting alongside community allies allowed labor unions to demonstrate their interest in arenas beyond workplace issues, such as community benefits agreements and regional health insurance campaigns. Through these electoral struggles and other moments of resistance, community groups have come to understand the potential strength coming from unions and the value of maintaining ongoing union ties. Over time, the coalition's relationships would intensify, morphing into an "integrative coalition" (Frege, Heery, and Turner 2003).

In Milwaukee, politics also played a role in bringing together labor and community organizations. As in California, the living-wage initiative of the mid-1990s, and later efforts to promote community benefits agreements proved to be important ways of making valuable personal connections and nurturing a sense of commonality between labor and community groups. Beyond the policy campaigns, programmatic initiatives were also critical to generating labor-community ties. In particular, the job training and placement programs run by the Milwaukee Jobs Initiative and the Wisconsin Regional Training Partnership were

---

[30] Proposition 187, passed in 1994 but later overturned in a federal court, made it illegal for undocumented residents to access social service programs. Proposition 184, passed in 1994, was one of the first "three strikes, you're out" laws in the nation and had a disproportionate impact on people of color. Proposition 209, passed in 1996, eliminated affirmative action programs in California's public institutions. Proposition 226, defeated in 1998, would have restricted unions' abilities to raise political monies from its members. Proposition 227, passed in 1998, eliminated all spending for bilingual programs in the state of California. Proposition 38, defeated in 2000, would have provided vouchers for private schools.

[31] See Frege, Heery, and Turner 2003. These authors utilize a typology that categorizes labor-community coalitions in three types: (1) vanguard coalitions, where community groups play a subordinate role to the union; (2) common-cause coalitions, characterized by complementary union and community interests and cooperative, joint action; and (3) integrative coalitions, where unions "offer unconditional support to their non-labor partners" and adopt the objectives of those partners as their own. Interestingly, as Nissen (2004) notes, Heckscher and Palmer (1993, 72) assert that unions are capable of forming only "vanguard" coalitions, not "common-cause" ones (72). Nissen critiques this argument, as do we.

important vehicles of collaboration: they placed disadvantaged inner-city residents into well-paying and often unionized jobs, benefiting both labor and community.

In San Jose and in Los Angeles, leadership development and training programs have been important for building strong labor-community ties: in San Jose, the Working Partnerships Leadership Institute (discussed previously); in Los Angeles, the Community Scholars Program at UCLA.[32] Jointly sponsored by the Department of Urban Planning and the Center for Labor Research and Education, that program brings labor and community leaders together for a two-quarter training program focused on specific community development issues in the region; topics have ranged from popular education to banking in communities, to the impact of Walmart. The very first program in 1991–92 focused on the Los Angeles tourism industry and played a critical role in the founding of the Tourism Industry Development Corporation, the predecessor to LAANE. Similar to the Working Partnerships Leadership Institute, the Community Scholars Program gathers labor and community leaders in a shared environment to study and develop solutions to regional problems, and it has broken down barriers between labor and community groups.

Of course, relations between labor and community in even these "success stories" have their difficulties. Stresses continue to exist, rooted in a range of issues such as different organizational structures, unequal power, diverse constituencies, and sometimes conflicting goals. Community groups, in particular, remain wary of labor's power. Though unions may seem toothless compared to business, they are an overwhelming force for many smaller community groups. Yet in all three areas, labor and community have moved beyond cooperation only around specific campaigns or fashioning coalitions whose sole aim is to achieve discrete outcomes. Through ongoing, long-term communication and collaboration, labor and community groups have networked to form a dense "civic infrastructure" with a mutual understanding of regional programs and a sense of interdependency (Dean and Reynolds 2008).

BRINGING BUSINESS IN

Perhaps one of the most surprising aspects of regional equity organizing efforts is the potential to forge alliances between business and regional equity advocates. Business is frequently viewed by both labor and

---

[32] See http:// www.spa.ucla.edu/ dept.cfm?d=up&s=academic&f=scholars.cfm.

community organizers as being, at best, indifferent to issues of inequality in the region and, at worst, outright hostile. Whereas businesses emphasize competitiveness and profits, social justice advocates tend to emphasize equitable distribution of benefits for workers, communities, and the surrounding environment. And even though some business leaders have adopted the banner of "inclusive development," particularly those associated with the Alliance for Regional Stewardship, community-based organizations are usually wary that business's words and deeds will not go together.

There are, however, places where regional equity proponents have found reasons to collaborate closely with business. Part of the reason is that regional equity organizers tend to take market realities into account more than do activists in other social movements. They know that business can make money and do good in underserved communities, and they understand that companies need to remain economically viable while also paying higher wages. The WRTP, for example, helped solve a "collective action" problem within regional manufacturing industries: the reluctance of firms to invest in training because of the fear that other firms would "poach" highly trained employees. By organizing a coordinated increase in training, the WRTP helped firms remain viable in the face of growing global competition—and by combining training with union representation and job placement for inner-city unemployed workers, the WRTP coupled regional competitiveness with regional equity.

Organizers are also finding that business leaders can be indispensable allies for promoting particular regional equity strategies, especially those related to housing and infrastructure. The Atlanta Neighborhood Development Partnership (ANDP), along with other groups like the Enterprise Foundation and LISC, have actively sought to engage businesses, including lenders and developers, in their Mixed Income Communities Initiative (MICI) network—and garnered a striking level of support. The Social Equity Caucus, which grew out of the Bay Area Alliance for Sustainable Communities, has collaborated with business on the Community Capital Investment Initiative and the Bay Area Family of Funds, intended to promote Smart Growth development.

Learning to work together can provide unexpected results. In Los Angeles, even after DreamWorks decided not to build a new studio, it still stuck with the Workplace Hollywood effort that it had generated in earlier negotiations with SCOPE and Metro Alliance. In San Jose, the ties that Working Partnerships and the South Bay Central Labor Council built with regional business leaders over issues such as affordable housing and transportation ensured a level of trust, illustrated when SEIU Local 1877, representing janitors in the region, hit a roadblock in contract negotiations with building owners, and several business leaders expressed support for the janitors' demands. Approached by the Central Labor Council, key executives from Hewlett-Packard, Genentech, and Cisco all made public statements supporting the janitors. The most striking was that of Eric Benhamou, chairman and CEO of 3Com at the time, who wrote in an editorial in the *San Jose Mercury News* that

> [Silicon Valley is underpaying] an (intolerably) high percentage of the population.... It is a matter of dealing with the guilty feeling one experiences at the thought that yesterday's business lunch leftovers were magically cleaned up at night by someone who lives in a storage shed.... As leaders of the high-tech industry, we are being put to the test.... While some may ignore a serious problem in the making for a while longer, I trust many will join me and San Jose Mayor Ron Gonzales and see in the janitors' case an opportunity to make our ideas known about which kind of a Silicon Valley we stand for. (Benhamou 2000)

We are not Pollyannas in our view of the business-community link: class interests have not disappeared; many businesses remain opposed to any interference with markets; and the "win-win" dreams of some regionalists are often just that—dreams. Still, there are numerous possibilities for securing a "double bottom line" of reasonable profits and improved community outcomes—and the repeated interactions implicit in these transactions can lead to transformations where business participates in creating an equitable region, even as social justice proponents learn more about the market (Pastor 2006).

Dialogues and Transformations

The discussion of business alliances returns us to a central rule of the famous organizer Saul Alinsky: there are "no permanent enemies." Many organizers within the regional equity movement have embraced what we term transformative pragmatism—an approach to regional equity that focuses on achieving real victories while being flexible on some principles. This pragmatism comes from the fundamental rule of social movement building that movements need successes and victories in order to take off, sustain, and grow. But even in the case of accepting compromise for the goal of achieving some progress, regional equity organizers are seeking out victories that can lead to big changes in the rules of the game at a regional scale.

We have no naïveté about the challenges they face. Maintaining credibility on race while crafting a vision and policy package that can create consensus, drawing the connection between regional issues while highlighting neighborhood distresses, balancing the need to agitate for justice with the desire to attract private capital, dealing with fragmentation by jurisdiction, geography, and politics—these are just some of the difficulties regional equity activists juggle. We get tired just listing them; organizers seem tireless in tackling them.

Nor are we sanguine about the resistance ahead. For-profit real estate developers, wealthy suburban residents, and certain other business interests certainly do benefit from regional inequality and fragmentation, and social movement regionalists are not shy about addressing that conflict. At the same time, by dealing with the conflict, naming it, and confronting it, they are able to move beyond the polarized roles that are usually the stuff of political kabuki theater. By not demonizing opponents but, instead, recognizing differences and engaging in efforts to resolve them, activists are demonstrating that conflict in one arena does not necessarily preclude cooperation in others. These strategies are an attempt to achieve "transformation"—a shift in the body politic toward mutual conversation and engagement and toward strategies that lift up all sectors and all places.

Social movement regionalism, in short, is going beyond building coalitions to build movement infrastructure capable of lasting over the long haul. At their best, coalitions build relationships and power between unlikely allies, but they are generally short-term and episodic, revolving around specific issues and tactical goals. They are important in pursuing well-defined goals, particularly in a constrained period of time. But building regional equity as a transformative politics requires paying attention to creating long-term alliances, institutions, and networks that are concerned with cultivating cross-constituency relationships, creating strategic partnerships between different sectors of a region, and developing institutions that can help key leaders develop common understandings of the regional economy and structures of power and influence.

There is definitely something happening here. Working across race, place, and issue silos, and negotiating power relations are all steps forward. Yet, reaching across local political barriers is not always enough. Margaret Weir, Jane Rongerude, and Christopher Ansell (2007; see also Weir and Rongerude 2007) argue that achieving regional policy outcomes will be limited if coalitions do not have the vertical reach to power and policy levers as well.

> Horizontal collaboration by itself can do little more than promote new ideas and hope for the best. Horizontal collaboration in regions may help build consensus and alliances that can work in more powerful state and federal venues to promote regional capacity.... Whether such efforts are successful depends not only on the horizontal consensus building process but, more critically, on the power relationships—alliances, coalitions, enemies—that prevail in these alternative venues." (Weir, Rongerude, and Ansell 2007, 35)

The challenge of progressive regionalism thus involves building multilevel power, not simply engaging in regional processes. It involves reaching up to regional policy, as Weir contends—but it also involves employing a set of strategies to connect not just actors within a region but also actors across America's metropolitan regions. It is to this issue of scaling up to a national movement that we now turn.

CHAPTER SIX

Moving on Up

In early 2007, two of us were asked to attend an invitation-only conference in Los Angeles. The mention of select invitations may raise the image of the World Economic Forum in Davos, Switzerland—but instead of hobnobbing with the heights of the business community, we were rubbing elbows with some stars of the community-organizing world.

From New York, Washington, Boston, and Miami, as well as from Katrina-ravaged New Orleans and the host city of L.A., grassroots activists who were worried about gentrification came together to talk about common concerns and strategies. One might have expected a rehash of policies and tactics, including, for example, coalition-building strategies to pass tenant eviction protections. The talk, however, was all about whether or not they should collectively agree on a new "frame" revolving around "the right to the city"—a theory first promulgated by French intellectual Henri Lefebvre—and how they might use such a frame to build a national movement.[1]

Talk about putting theory to practice—or, perhaps more accurately, about theorists needing to catch up to practice! Indeed, our central point in this book is that a new social movement in America—one that could blend equity and growth, link city and suburb, and provide a new narrative that permits communication across the chasms of race and

---

[1] Lefebvre 1996 (English translations); see also the review in Purcell 2003. Watching this process of theorizing and reframing reminded us of community-based efforts to come up with a collective grounded theory (Glaser and Strauss 1967).

place—is actually in the making. For it to gain traction at the levels of policy and politics, it will need to overcome the local challenges and obstacles and then figure out how to move up to a national strategy and language.

Such an upward move is already under way. The Gamaliel Foundation groups, as a case in point, have incorporated regional analysis into their national training and into their regional organizations; from San Diego to Atlanta, from Trenton to Detroit, all claim regional equity as a driving goal. In 2005 the various labor-community groups that have pushed for community benefits agreements in numerous metropolitan areas formed the new Partnership for Working Families National Network that stretches from New Haven to Denver and from Seattle to Washington, D.C. It's formation had an explicit and focused movement strategy: "Drawing on the extensive organizing, research and policy experience of our founding members, the Partnership is building a nationwide movement to transform the economic development process."[2] And for the antigentrification forces to come together as they did at the Los Angeles conference was a groundbreaking moment. This set of groups concentrated on defending particular places but believed that such a defense would require plugging into and combining the fluid constituencies of organizers from many different regions in America.

Having already focused on the challenges facing regional equity movements *within* regions, here we stress the promise and possibilities of these movements *across* regions. We begin by considering the gap between local and national organizing. We argue that regional equity groups are beginning to build a middle ground, relating people's everyday concerns to a larger, regional set of political dynamics; more and more, these same groups are also forming national networks and federations. We profile their efforts to increase the scale of organizing and also consider their relationships to other emerging and existing networks, pointing to the parallels and potential conflicts. We then address the resource issues so

---

[2] The quotation is from www.californiapartnership.org, accessed on November 30, 2006. The Partnership for Working Families, whose website has since migrated to www.commu nitybenefits.org, initially hired veteran labor leader John Goldstein, the force behind the successful Campaign for a Sustainable Milwaukee, as well as Julian Gross, the civil rights attorney who represented LAANE and other community-based organizations in their successful CBA campaigns. The executive director is Leslie Moody, former president of the Denver Area Labor Federation.

prominent in social movement theory—and talk about how policy inter-mediaries and funders could help.

We conclude by arguing that the regional equity movement can make a profound contribution to a revitalized national progressive movement, partly because it underscores a deeply felt democratic discourse about the trends and forces that are affecting our lives. We acknowledge that this view is necessarily speculative; although we are excited to be re-searching a movement in progress, we must confess that the analytical work would be both clearer and easier if the groups had already arrived at an established benchmark. But this is, it seems, exactly the point: the movement is at a critical juncture, and we hope our work will contribute to both its construction and any future scholarship on the topic.[3]

Making the Middle

Prominent Harvard University scholar Theda Skocpol is well known for her 2000 book *The Missing Middle: Working Families and the Future of Ameri-can Social Policy.* In it, she posits that working families are all too often neglected in debates on American social policy. This "missing middle," she argues, falls victim to generational neglect, sandwiched between debates on Social Security and welfare reform for the elderly, on the one hand, and discussions of school reform and public assistance to poor children, on the other. Working families are also overlooked socioeco-nomically, as liberals attempt to defend social programs for the poor and the underprivileged, while conservatives champion tax cuts and eco-nomic policies that benefit the privileged. Placing the needs of working men and women of modest means at the center of social policy debates, she contends, is critical to the progressive revitalization of American society.

But Skocpol's "missing middle" is not limited to the demographic groups she sees as neglected in American policies; she uses the term also to refer to a missing organizational structure in American politics—the

---

[3] Our conclusions and generalizations are built by synthesizing what we have seen and experienced across the country within an analytic frame anchored by social movement theory. For more on this method of developing grounded theory, see Snow and Trom's 2002 chapter on case studies and social movement research; Glaser and Strauss's 1967 volume on qualitative research; and George and Bennett's 2005 book on case studies and theory-building.

relative absence of institutional bridges between local movements and national politics. Emerging out of her research on the history of American civic engagement and voluntarism is her argument that the solution to civic health does not require that people be active in a dense array of local political, recreational, and cultural associations—a view popularly espoused since Alexis de Tocqueville's well-known account of early 19th-century America. Instead, she documents the importance of federated relationships between local and national organizations, arguing that the true source of civic health lies in "the nature of connections between powerful supralocal institutions and local or particular endeavors" (Skocpol, Ganz, and Munson 2000; 542).

Skocpol asserts provocatively that the challenge of American politics today is not so much that people are inactive in social life—a thesis elaborated at some length by her Harvard colleague Robert Putnam in his *Bowling Alone* thesis (2000). Indeed, she contends that between the mid-1960s and the early 1980s, grassroots groups organizing on a countless range of issues at a local level have proliferated, and professional groups, trade associations, and think tanks with a strong presence in Washington, D.C., have all increased their numbers. What has declined since the 1950s, she argues, is the "missing middle" of effective links from national politics to local groups, which has made it harder for "Americans to band together to get things done—either through or in relationship to government" (Skocpol 1997, 18).

For regional equity efforts to influence national politics and policy, organizers will need not only to overcome the challenges and obstacles incurred at a local and regional level but also to determine strategy, language, and infrastructure that can connect them to one another as well as to other movements for progressive social change. If they are able to build this missing middle, linking the multiple regional equity initiatives around the country and integrating them with other local-national federated networks, they may help to fashion a fresh, progressive American future.

Connecting the Strands

National networks—of faith-based organizations, labor organizations, community groups, and policy advocacy organizations—have begun to emerge in exciting new ways. Some, such as the interfaith Gamaliel Network, are explicitly committed to utilizing a regional analysis, regional policy proposals, and regional power-building strategies to achieve an equity end. Other networks—such as Jobs with Justice or ACORN—are organizing to promote equity primarily on a regional scale *but* do not necessarily see their mission as regional equity per se (at least in terms of the notion of changing the rules of the game at a metropolitan level).

We would argue that it is important to consider both types of initiatives in analyzing the potential for putting together a national regional equity movement. The first kind of network might be understood as using the region as a *strategic* level for understanding and affecting economic, social, and political processes. The second kind treats regions as *tactical,* as one among many possible scales for building power and helping organizations achieve success in their strategic efforts. Even those initiatives that fall in the more tactical camp, however, share important values and visions with those networks that are strategically focused. Thus, tactical-scale organizers are important potential allies for strategic-level organizers in building a national movement.

But our argument about the importance of such allies goes further. Remember from our discussion of social movements in chapter 2 that we see the regional equity movement as emerging along three dimensions: the region as a source of social *problems,* the region as an inclusive place for developing *solutions,* and the region as a scale for building social *power.* We think that this movement grows in part out of the material conditions of our urban areas themselves and in part out of the political vision of those leading the movement—and their strategic networks reflect a commitment to looking at regions in terms of problems, solutions, *and* power.

Those national networks that have a tactical take on regionalism can be thought of as responding to the same material conditions of urban areas that have prompted a specific regionalist approach: they focus on regional power-building when they encounter processes or solutions that operate on that scale, but they do not always have a strategic commitment to focusing on building regional power. But, if we are correct in identifying the potential power of a regional equity vision for building a national social movement, then we might also expect the regional focus to become more central to their strategic efforts over time. Thus, we need to study the ways both types of networks have engaged with regional processes and try to assess the capacity of one or both to become a national effort eventually.

Strategic Regional Equity

Among the mix of cases we examine are a number of national initiatives that have explicitly focused on trying to build and organize a national regional equity social movement. The Gamaliel Foundation, a prime example, has adopted metropolitan equity as a central organizing lens and works to promote this perspective throughout its network of sixty affiliates in twenty one states. The Partnership for Working Families, a network spanning eighteen affiliates in ten states, has developed a new model for urban growth and social justice that analyzes regional sources of inequality and utilizes community benefits agreements. Certain central labor councils around the country, organized through AFL-CIO channels and more informal national partnerships, are building regional power around a progressive regional equity agenda. Other less prominent efforts are also making the regional equity connection. The Right to the City Alliance brings together from around the country groups that are fighting gentrification by equating their power-building efforts with regional equity goals and a human rights frame. Each network has its own set of processes, as well as distinct challenges, in moving their regional work up to the national level.

The Gamaliel Foundation, as previously noted, is an organizing network working across the United States (and in five provinces in South Africa). Unlike other Alinksy-inspired organizing networks, which tend to allow local issues and populist sentiment to drive the focus of local organizing, Gamaliel has been willing to articulate particular ideologies and provide direction on issues and strategies from the national office. Since 1996, it has adopted a regional approach to community organizing, building metro-wide organizations and increasingly focusing on issues of regional equity (Kleidman 2004).

Gamaliel's commitment to regional-equity organizing first emerged when its Minneapolis affiliate ISAIAH began to work with Myron Orfield in the early 1990s. Persuaded by Orfield's analysis of the problems embedded in metro dynamics, ISAIAH engaged in a successful regional campaign to clean up brownfield sites that were deterring economic growth in the central city. ISAIAH organizers then arranged for Orfield to address the senior staff of the Gamaliel network in 1995, and the network soon thereafter adopted regional equity organizing as a core focus. Gamaliel then established formal strategic partnerships with Orfield and two other leading regional equity policy experts, David Rusk and john powell. These strategic partners work with both local and national leadership to develop and strengthen regional organizing strategies; they assist with strategic analysis of development trends in the regions, speak at public outreach and education events, and serve as technical advisers in organizer training sessions.

Robert Kleidman (2004) maintains that the Gamaliel network's commitment to a regional organizing approach has helped local affiliates navigate the tensions between populist and ideological approaches to organizing. As Kleidman puts it:

> Populism's general sentiments and immediate appeal help in recruiting and retaining participants and in maintaining a moderate, respectable image. Populism, however, provides only a vague vision, analysis, and strategy. Political ideologies provide a clearer vision, more complex and consistent analysis, and longer-term strategy, but they often lack broad and immediate appeal. (2004, 410)

Kleidman argues further that regionalism is enabling Gamaliel's local groups to articulate a more consistent progressive vision, with a clearer analysis of processes shaping inequality and poverty on a regional scale. He stresses that Gamaliel retains a strong focus on "relational organizing," which involves one-on-one meetings and leadership development that stresses an individual's personal understanding of local problems. He also notes that many local affiliates have struggled with understanding regional equity, and regional solutions have been difficult to achieve in many places. Still, the network has embraced the regional equity framework and language while maintaining an organizational commitment to building both local power and a national network.

National networks of labor unions have also been a significant supporter of regional equity organizing initiatives around the country. A strong nationwide commitment to regional organizing first developed in 1996 with the AFL-CIO's Union Cities Agenda. Following the election of John Sweeney and the "New Voices" slate to the leadership of the AFL-CIO in 1995, a number of strong leaders of central labor councils around the country, including Amy Dean from San Jose and Miguel Contreras from Los Angeles, pushed to have the role of central labor councils represented more strongly within the federation.

The Union Cities initiative, which grew out of a meeting of 150 labor councils in 1996 and was adopted by the AFL-CIO Executive Council in 1997, was explicitly designed to promote regional power through re-vitalized central labor councils. By 2001, more than 163 of some 600 councils had been designated by the AFL-CIO as having met the re-quirements of promoting union cities. Much of the activity was modeled on the activities of the central labor councils in San Jose, Los Angeles, and other places where CLCs had engaged in regional issues that affected all working families, not just union members (Kriesky 2001; Ness and Eimer 2001).

Ironically, just as the number of CLCs embracing the Union Cities Agenda increased, other dynamics took central stage within the AFL-CIO. With the creation of the New Unity Partnership in 2003, debates re-volved around proposals for union restructuring and resource allocation for organizing—debates that ultimately led to a split within the AFL-CIO and to the departure of seven large unions to start the Change to Win Coalition. In this context, regional organizing and the role of central labor councils declined in significance within the federation, some labor leaders arguing that, though valuable, these regional power-building ini-tiatives did little to build union membership and thus were a distraction from the core of organizing.

Central labor councils around the country, however, have continued to share experiences and support one another's work. This networking takes place through AFL-CIO structures but also through other national networks. One example of a labor-linked national organization that focuses on regional equity organizing is the Partnership for Working Families.[4] This organization was founded in 2002 by four labor-linked organizations in California that had prominently promoted community benefits agreements and other strategies for producing more account-able and beneficial economic development strategies.[5] It had grown to include eighteen organizations in ten states by the end of 2007.

The Working Families organizations aim to influence land use and eco-nomic development decisions in their regions, moving decision-makers away from narrow concerns with tax revenue and toward more complex community needs such as decent health care, affordable housing, and living-wage jobs. Their primary tool is community benefits agreements,

---

[4] See http://www.communitybenefits.org/.

[5] The four organizations were Working Partnerships USA in San Jose, Center for Policy Initiatives in San Diego, Los Angeles Alliance for a New Economy, and the East Bay Alliance for a Sustainable Economy.

but the ultimate goal is a wider development of the movement and increasing community benefits in all land-use and economic development decision-making processes. The organization is a forum for member organizations to share best practices and provides a space to coordinate strategies and build a stronger national movement around community accountability in economic development projects.

The similarly titled group Building Partnerships USA (BPUSA) was founded in 2005 by Amy Dean with the objective of creating a decentralized organization that could help support central labor councils around the country. Its practical goal was to create "a peer-to-peer technical assistance and leadership development network: an alliance to help activists in other cities create successful coalitions of their own."[6] Its focus has been on building Civic Leadership Network Institutes, modeled on the Labor Community Leadership Institute in San Jose, which can help labor organizers build regional coalitions with common frameworks for progressive social change within the region. In its initial year, the BPUSA network helped seed, promote, and support the development of five labor and community coalitions that work to build regional power in Denver, Atlanta, Boston, Milwaukee, and New Haven and Hartford, Connecticut.[7]

Another initiative is the Transportation Equity Network (TEN), originally founded under the aegis of the Center for Community Change, a longtime national community development intermediary. Once focused primarily on capacity-building for community development corporations, CCC now recognizes the potent role of organizing in social change and as a result has realigned its national strategy to support local and state community development efforts by organizing around equity. TEN includes regional equity champions such as the Alameda Corridor Coalition and the Bus Riders Union (Los Angeles), MOSES (Detroit), the Northwest Interfaith Federation (northwestern Indiana), the Metropolitan Congregations United (Missouri), and the West Harlem Environmental Action (New York). Though the Gamaliel affiliates help anchor TEN, the network provides important and specific national infrastructure for other equity advocates as well—it has scored important national successes, including the insertion of language in a 1995 federal transportation bill that encourages local hiring and secures employment

---

[6] See http://www.building-partnerships.org/home.html.
[7] For background on BPUSA, see http://www.building-partnerships.org/.

for low-income communities (Swanstrom et al. 2007; Swanstrom and Barrett 2007).

The Right to the City Alliance, the national coalition launched in January 2007 by base-building organizations from across the nation's largest metro areas, has developed a set of goals that have regional equity at their core. These goals include (1) strengthening local capacity of local grassroots campaigns through technical support, policy development, and campaign research; (2) supporting community reclamation in New Orleans and the Gulf Coast, an "essential battleground for an urban movement to develop in the U.S."; (3) facilitating regional and cross-regional collaboration through organizational dialogues and exchanges; and (4) advancing a national platform to influence national policies that affect local conditions.[8] The alliance is made up of twenty-four organizations in eight metro regions: Los Angeles, New York, Washington, D.C., Boston, Oakland, Providence, Miami, and New Orleans. At the U.S. Social Forum held in Atlanta in 2007, the "right to the city" mantra to fight displacement and gentrification resonated loudly among national and global groups. The Gulf Coast organizers shared the story of their fight against gentrification and displacement for "the right to remain," and those from Miami spoke about their struggle for "the right to return" to public housing from which they had been displaced (National Organizers Alliance 2008).[9]

Tactical Regional Equity

In addition to the national networks focused strategically on building region-based movements for equity, a number of national organizations focus on regional equity in a tactical way. One example is Jobs with Justice (JwJ), which was founded in 1987 with the mission of improving

---

[8] See http://www.righttothecity.org/.

[9] For the regional equity movement, the challenge of gentrification is crucial. As Gihan Perera from the Miami Workers Center notes, "The major progressive centers throughout the country are formed around cities; that's where they are now. But through this widespread gentrification, not only race and class demographics are being shifted but also political demographics. We've been calling it redistricting by development, where longtime progressive voting bases are basically being wiped off the map" (Tides Foundation 2007, 28). At the same time, regional equity proponents often favor mixed-income housing and deconcentration of the poor (a tension discussed below). Squaring these two strands will be a major task in coming years; here we are merely stressing the need to develop a national network in this policy and organizing arena, among others.

workers' standard of living, fighting for job security, and protecting the right to organize. Since that time it has grown to include labor, religion, student, and community organizations in forty cities across twenty-five states. Their focus is on workplace justice issues, including contract campaigns and the rights of immigrant workers, but local coalitions have also organized around affordable housing, living-wage ordinances, economic development policies, and public services.

Jobs with Justice was founded as a more progressive, social movement–oriented labor effort at a time when most mainstream labor unions were dominated by a service approach rather than an organizing approach. Arguably, after John Sweeney and the New Voices slate of leadership was elected to head the AFL-CIO in 1995, with a new focus on organizing and a more social movement emphasis, there was less need for Jobs with Justice. Many local organizers, however, continued to see the desirability of building local JwJ chapters: they were an effective way of sustaining community-labor coalitions in places without strong social movement–oriented unions.

Local JwJ chapters are autonomous, with their own structures and fund-raising efforts. The national office, which in 2006 had a staff of eight to ten, helps set national campaign priorities (along with members of the national board) and provides organizing advice, informational resources, and analysis to support local efforts. In many regions, JwJ coalitions are exciting examples of multiracial organizing in which the region becomes an important arena for identifying allies and mustering political strength—but they generally concentrate more on workplace rights and standard-of-living issues than on the usual buffet of regional equity issues (Early and Cohen 1994, 1997).

Another prominent national network that has pursued equity, often at a regional level, is the Industrial Areas Foundation. Originally founded by Saul Alinsky in Chicago in 1940, by 2007 the network comprised fifty-six local organizations in twenty-one states. Building on the Alinsky tradition, IAF affiliates are focused more on power, leadership development, and organization-building than on any specific project. The particular issue that affiliates work on depends largely on the concerns of local residents. Yet the sway of regional processes in shaping inequality and the value of regional power are evident in the efforts of local affiliates.

Perhaps the best example of this regional focus is in San Antonio, the home of Citizens Organized for Public Service (COPS). Founded in 1974, and the oldest of the existing IAF affiliates, COPS worked in the

1970s and '80s on a variety of issues of concern to residents in the area, including housing, education, and infrastructure. In 1990, when a local Levi Strauss plant that employed more than 1,000 people announced that it was closing, COPS was galvanized to address employment issues. Responding to both the immediate Levi's shutdown and a far-reaching trend of declines in manufacturing, transportation, and other industrial jobs, COPS worked with another IAF affiliate in the area to help create Project QUEST, a regional training and workforce development effort that is now one of the most celebrated regional workforce programs in the country. Its effectiveness has been characterized by three major factors: its strong community-based support for disadvantaged job-seekers; its strong ties with employers throughout the region; and its ability to induce systemic reforms in the region's community colleges to make them more responsive to the needs of Project QUEST's constituency.

Another IAF-affiliated regional organizing effort occurred in Baltimore, where Baltimoreans United in Leadership Development (BUILD) initiated the campaign in 1993 that resulted in passage of the first living-wage ordinance in the country. BUILD won by working in coalition with other organizations in the region, particularly the American Federation of State, County, and Municipal Employees (AFSCME). The stimulus for the campaign was the direct contrast between the downtown office and hotel developments, convention center, stadiums, and upscale commercial and residential developments that were part of efforts to revitalize Baltimore's Inner Harbor area, on the one hand, and on the other, the growing poverty and distress of predominantly African American residents in the neighborhoods immediately adjacent to these new developments (Fine 2000, 64). The living wage was an important step in holding the development of the Inner Harbor area accountable for its role as a major driver of the regional economy. BUILD highlighted the public subsidies that went into revitalizing the area and used them as a lever to demand that any government contracts also pay a living wage. The success of the Baltimore effort stimulated other IAF affiliates around the country likewise to become active in the living-wage movement.

As the examples illustrate, regional equity is not a key focus of the IAF federation, but local affiliates often play a critical role in regional equity efforts.[10] Both the resulting gaps and the interplay with more strategic

[10] The regional equity frame took a firmer hold in the IAF group in Santa Cruz and Monterey Counties, where two of us and a colleague who was a former research director

regional equity efforts can be seen in Los Angeles, where the IAF resurfaced in 1999. IAF actually had a long legacy in Los Angeles: affiliates such as United Neighborhoods Organizing (UNO), the South Central Organizing Committee (SCOC), East Valley Organization (EVO), and Valleys Organized in Community (VOICE) in the San Fernando Valley were established starting in the 1970s, and in 1986–87, they worked together to raise the state minimum wage. They then seemed to lose their path and their power even as SCOPE, LAANE, and more explicitly regional equity groups were on the rise in the early 1990s. Part of the problem, we would suggest, was that IAF was not a regional organization but rather a set of individual groups working independently throughout the region.

The clear opportunities in resurgent and insurgent Los Angeles induced IAF leader Ernesto Cortes to relocate from San Antonio to L.A. to facilitate the rebirth of the affiliates, this time under a single umbrella called One LA-IAF (formerly know as L.A. Metro). Previously, Cortes had been responsible for successfully growing COPS in San Antonio from a small neighborhood organizing effort into a regional-scale body called COPS/IAF Metro San Antonio. Unlike its sister organizing federation, Gamaliel, IAF is seeking to develop a regional voice without explicitly adopting the regional equity frame; it is instead prioritizing issues such as education reform, neighborhood safety, and community health—with the overall goal of rebuilding the social capital of communities and promoting racially inclusive, democratic participation.[11]

What helps One LA-IAF stand out is its geographic reach: it covers the city of Los Angeles, to be sure, but it also extends into the heavily Latino Southeast cities of Los Angeles County as well as out to the San Gabriel Valley and the Inland Empire. It does appear that One LA-IAF may be adopting a regional equity framework more openly in its efforts, at least as indicated by its organizational restructuring—and a 2008 foray into issues of workforce development. But it is too soon to tell whether the shift to a regional umbrella in L.A. can help the IAF achieve a presence

---

for the United Farm Workers combined forces to do a regional audit so that the emerging IAF organization could better understand the local political economy and identify salient organizing issues (see Pastor, Benner, and Rosner 2003).

[11] In 2008, One LA-IAF took up workforce development systems, more clearly a regional equity issue. More generally, Mark Warren (2001) has done extensive research and documentation of IAF and presents the argument connecting community organizing, social capital, and democracy.

parallel to that of other regional equity coalitions—or a success parallel to that in San Antonio.

Another prominent national network of groups using tactical regional equity organizing is ACORN, the Association of Community Organizations for Reform Now.[12] Since the mid-1990s, many local ACORN chapters have been valuable leaders in contributing to social movement, regional equity initiatives, primarily through their focus on living-wage campaigns. They are perhaps the strongest example of a national network that has contributed to building a national movement for regional equity without being strategically focused on it.

Founded in Arkansas in 1970, ACORN boasts over thirty years of experience in locally based, multiracial organizing, often linking low- and moderate-income people together in campaigns around a variety of social justice issues. Heavily influenced by Saul Alinsky, Fred Ross, and the organizing approach of founder Wade Rathke, ACORN is rooted in direct, individual memberships and focuses on bottom-up organizing and leadership development. It has grown into a network of around 850 neighborhood chapters with more than 175,000 members in over 100 cities across the United States, and it is the largest non-faith-based network of community organizing groups in the country (DeFilippis, Fisher, and Shragge 2007).[13]

Since Baltimore passed the first living-wage ordinance in 1994, more than 100 cities and counties across the country have passed municipal policies mandating that service contractors, economic development recipients, and other categories of employers pay wages and benefits to their employees well beyond those mandated by state or federal law. Among the many organizations involved in pushing for living-wage ordinances, ACORN is one of the most prominent: more than a dozen local chapters have led in local living-wage coalitions, including those in Chicago, Boston, New Orleans, Denver, Oakland, St. Louis, St. Paul, and Detroit. The national organization has created a Living Wage Resource Center and provided a national staff person almost exclusively devoted to supporting local groups in their living-wage organizing efforts with campaign materials, research, and training.

---

[12] Originally the Arkansas Community Organizations for Reform Now.

[13] A detailed history of ACORN (see http://www.acorn.org/index.php?id=2712) is attributed to Dan Russell, professor of political science, at Springfield College, Springfield, Mass. See also Delgado 1986.

ACORN has also achieved significant victories in other key policy initiatives that relate directly to a regional equity agenda. For example, ACORN chapters have secured municipal ordinances or agreements requiring developers to hire low-income and unemployed residents in projects in at least eight different cities. This is a strategy closely linked with the community benefits agreements that have been so important for regional equity organizing efforts in Los Angeles, San Jose, and elsewhere. Similarly, ACORN chapters have engaged in numerous campaigns aimed at bank lending in poor neighborhoods, helping to prevent the undermining of the Community Reinvestment Act and resulting in billions of dollars for loans in low-income neighborhoods (ACORN 2004; Fisher, Brooks, and Russell 2007). This is a clear example of targeting regional assets (in this case, banks) to promote opportunities for disadvantaged communities.

ACORN was an important leader in a regional (though failed) tax-sharing proposal in Sacramento, California, and its leaders have played important roles in pushing for affordable housing in Washington, D.C., and other areas around the country. For ACORN, these policies and organizing initiatives are not fundamentally rooted in an analysis of regional causes of inequality; or strategically focused on regional solutions to inequality; building regional alliances, however, has been a valuable tool for it in strengthening political power and pursuing social justice goals.

Among other, less developed networks of community groups that are also important is the Push Back Network. Formed in 2005, it is a multistate network anchored by SCOPE, whose own analysis is deeply rooted in a strategic view of regional equity. The network was primarily established to challenge traditional electoral approaches, which often focus on parachuting organizers into target regions and neighborhoods in order to mobilize voters tactically for a single event: voting day. Instead, it hopes to forge a new national network that uses this process more patiently to increase the general capacity of grassroots organizing institutions—and then leverages this community-based movement infrastructure into national-scale electoral outcomes and policy change. The Push Back Network, consisting of organizations in California, New Mexico, New York, Kentucky, Mississippi, and Alabama, is still in its nascent stages. Interestingly, though, its approach replicates exactly the strategy the right wing successfully utilized to dominate the national elections in 2004—that is, investing in local institutions to educate, invigorate, and mobilize national voters in an ongoing and sustained way.

Another network-based effort has come from environmental justice groups. It is telling that some of the regional equity efforts we have profiled were initially rooted in EJ issues: the Northwest Indiana Federation organized around environmental disparity; SCOPE had a long-running training program for environmental justice organizers; and Urban Habitat cut its teeth on environmental disparities before founding the Social Equity Caucus. Moreover, many of the most innovative efforts to gain transit fairness came from those associated with the EJ agenda (for example, the Bus Riders Union in Los Angeles).[14] Environmental justice and regional equity would seem to be a natural pairing—and understanding their network-building experience is instructive.

Following the movement's first 1991 People of Color Environmental Leadership Summit in Washington, EJ activists sought to establish a national presence by building from networks that are regional in scale—with region here denoting multistate areas—and that have as their sole purpose increasing the capacity and strength of grassroots organizing efforts.[15] Unfortunately, its attempts to secure a national voice—a Washington-based Office on Environmental Justice and an Environmental Justice Fund—both collapsed in the mid-1990s. And even though the EJ movement remains vibrant—and is actually experiencing substantial growth in such places as California—there seems to have been a relative deflation of the movement.

The reasons for this development are complex, including diminished resources from funders (Faber and McCarthy 2001). Still, the failure to launch—at least as much as early advocates had hoped—may be partly due to the fragmented nature of its national arm. Whereas its complicated network structure emerged from a healthy appreciation of local roots and local voice, and an accompanying distrust of rapid "scaling," we find it striking that most of the successful organizations of the regional

---

[14] For a particularly eloquent (and early) effort to build the connections between environment, transit, and regional development, see Bullard and Johnson 1997.

[15] This was a strategy decided at the First People of Color Environmental Leadership Summit in 1991; the networks are African American Environmental Justice Action Network (AAEJAN), Asian Pacific Environmental Network (APEN), Indigenous Environmental Network (IEN), Farm Workers Network for Economic and Environmental Justice (FWNEEJ), Northeast Environmental Justice Network (NEJN), Southern Organizing Committee for Economic and Social Justice (SOC), and Southwest Network for Environmental and Economic Justice (SNEEJ). Not all involve broad multistate regions; APEN is, for example, focused on building a regional network in the Bay Area rooted in the immigrant Asian Pacific Islander community.

equity movement were community-based but had few qualms about recognizing, engaging in, developing, and seizing the larger stage. There is something about confronting existing power that requires, well, power.

We do not mean to be too critical of the EJ experience. Two of us (Pastor and Matsuoka) came of age in this tradition, and its evolution has been inspiring: what began in many places as a single-issue, not-in-my-backyard style of organizing has evolved into a multiethnic, multiclass, multiissue movement that has mobilized people in local neighborhoods to function in regional contexts and carry their struggle across regional, state, and national borders. There is much to learn from this history, and there are current endeavors to recapture the national attention EJ once held in the 1990s. But to achieve a sustainable national scale, environmental justice proponents and others will need to be unafraid of creating and maintaining strong anchor organizations and nascent national groupings. And this means taking risks and engaging with other supporting institutions.[16]

Supporting the Work

Social movement organizations do not exist in a vacuum, and as social movement theory tells us, organizations often take action in relation to available resources (McCarthy and Zald 1977). Although we have made much of the distinction between social movement regionalists and others, this analytical slicing of the pie, however useful at a theoretical level, should not be misunderstood: we think that in the social ecology of change, one needs a healthy mix of various organizations.

Indeed, we have argued above that those pursuing regional equity as strategy and those pursuing regional equity as tactic are really part of the same family. We are further convinced that the three variants of regional equity groups we sketched in chapter 2—community developers, policy entrepreneurs, and social movement activists—can be stitched together. Community developers, after all, can demonstrate what is possible; policy entrepreneurs can show how the possible—through some tweaking of a regulation or a code—can be made standard operating practice; and social movement activists can use their combination of organizing and

---

[16] See Bullard (2007) for an analysis of how best to intersect EJ with Smart Growth and regional equity. For an earlier analysis of the social movement aspects of environmental justice, see Camacho 1998, and on network-building efforts, see Cordova et al. 2000.

framing to ensure that new policies and practices actually do become the lay of the land.

In assessing the potential for social movement regionalism to achieve a national level, it is important to understand the support available from other sources—in particular, policy intermediaries and funders—which can complement and complete movement-building. Probably the two strongest pieces of the policy infrastructure for social movement regionalism are the Brookings Institution and PolicyLink. The Metropolitan Policy Program at the Brookings Institution provides some of the best analysis in the country devoted to policy change on a metropolitan scale, frequently centered on promoting regional equity, although almost always under the unifying goal of "prosperity for all." Its focus is squarely on policymakers, not specifically on supporting social movement organizations, but many such organizations find the research extraordinarily useful.[17] PolicyLink has an explicit mission of supporting social movement organizations. The most visible aspect of this work has been its sponsoring of the two Regional Equity Summits in 2002 and 2005 (see chapter 2) and a third in the spring of 2008. PolicyLink has also designed an invaluable equitable development toolkit to help communities promote policy change.

Further, PolicyLink has worked with specific communities, helping to provide strategic support for social movement initiatives in locations across the country. Perhaps most prominent has been its engagement with the rebuilding process in Louisiana in the post-Katrina period. Some of this work is specifically policy oriented, working with state and local planners and policymakers to ensure that rebuilding decisions include promoting equity. Much of the work, however, supports local organizations and coalitions, including the local ACORN, IAF, and PICO affiliates, in their efforts to promote equitable rebuilding processes. PolicyLink has also been engaged in longer-term work in Atlanta, Boston, New York, Portland, and Washington, D.C. Leveraging their research, analysis, and technical support capabilities, PolicyLink staff have played important roles in supporting regional organizing efforts.[18]

[17] Although other important intermediaries working on either economic issues (such as the Economy Policy Institute) or urban problems (such as the Urban Institute) have some intersection with regional equity, their leaders do not generally see themselves squarely anchored in the midst of a metropolitan agenda whereas the Brookings effort does, and emphatically so.

[18] Useful university-based research centers that also play the intermediary role include the Kirwan Institute for the Study of Race and Ethnicity at Ohio State University, the

Though there are complexities involved in bringing together policy intermediaries and social movements, the most complex and problematic terrain for mixing and matching involves the relationship between funders and social movement regionalists. This relationship has an inherent dilemma: scholars who have examined social movement philanthropy frequently suggest that foundation funding for social movements is a conservative force, pushing social movement organizations in more moderate directions and thus diffusing social dissent—a moderating effect that may occur despite the stated intentions of foundations to support social movement work. One reason is simple: there are legal limitations on the amount of advocacy that nonprofit organizations can take on with philanthropic funding. Another is that foundation funding can induce nonprofit organizations to adopt conventional structures and practices in order to meet philanthropic expectations about ensuring organizational survival (Ostrander 1995; Chasin 2001; Jenkins and Eckert 1986; Magat 1999). But perhaps the most substantial factor is that it is frequently part and parcel of foundation culture to have a framework of "charity," which can work against social action to change the rules of the game.[19]

In some cases, we have seen funders pursue an explicit strategy to "seed" regional efforts, such as the example of the Irvine Foundation's effort to establish business-led civic regional collaborations.[20] An increasing number of funders seem to be engaged in regional equity policy debate and specific projects that attempt to achieve regional equity goals. Foundations that self-consciously promote social movement organizing and action, however, are few and typically small. Social justice–oriented

---

Institute on Race and Poverty at the University of Minnesota, and the Center for Justice, Tolerance and Community at the University of California–Santa Cruz. They have provided technical and research support to specific regions and, through convenings and networking, have brought together leading analysts and practitioners to learn from one another and to reflect on the evolution and future of the regional equity perspective. Given their university perches, however, they have had less latitude than Brookings or PolicyLink to be fully engaged in policy debates.

[19] There is also a tendency for foundations to sponsor demonstration projects without always thinking about the organizing that will be necessary to take the lessons learned into the highly political process of changing policy.

[20] Though these efforts have resulted in an expanded infrastructure of business regionalism in California, Jonas and Pincetl (2006) argue that they have functioned most often as regionalized chambers of commerce with limited inclusion of other community-based organizations.

foundations that have been prominent in early funding for social movement regionalism initiatives around the country include the New World
Foundation, the Liberty Hill Foundation (an affiliate of the national Funding Exchange and its network of sixteen activist-oriented, community-
based foundations around the country), and the McKay Foundation. For
many groups, even small grants can make a significant difference in early
organizing efforts, but building real capacity requires tapping into the
bigger grant pools distributed by the larger national foundations.

Many national foundations have stepped up to the plate, providing important financial support for the social movement organizations
and networks we've discussed, including, among others, the Ford, Rockefeller, and Annie E. Casey Foundations. Even when foundations are
generous, however, the resources available through philanthropy to address regional equity—or any issue, for that matter—are relatively minimal compared with resources available in the public and private sectors.
In David Rusk's words:

> According to the *Giving USA* annual report, private foundations granted
> over $25 billion in 2003...for all purposes. That amount is both impressive
> and pales in significance in the face of our society's unmet needs. For FY
> [fiscal year] 2004, for instance, the federal government's own budgetary
> outlays for "housing and community development" were $46 billion, but
> that was dwarfed by $476 billion in new residential construction by the
> private sector. (2005, 6)

Given limited resources and the sometimes moderating force of foundation funding, it is not surprising that the strongest national networks
of social movement–oriented regional equity organizations—namely,
the faith-based organizing networks and labor-linked efforts—all have
some base of financial support rooted in their own membership. This is
not to say that foundation funding is not important for them as well; they
have all relied on foundations to support their work in some capacity,
and foundations have been a valuable component of both their survival
and their growth. But with their own independent sources of funding,
they are more at liberty to stay on message than are groups completely
dependent on public or foundation funds.

Where funders have played one important role is in the education
of both their colleagues in the foundation world and practitioners in
the community. The Funders Network for Smart Growth has brought

together program officers to understand the regionalist frame and to promote better development decisions and growth policies, which frequently have the effect of supporting regional equity.[21] Other foundation projects have sought to bring regional efforts from across the country together so that each is not working in isolation. Philanthropic leadership can help craft a movement; however, there is a delicate balance between providing guidance through funding opportunities, and being considered heavy-handed in grant-making requirements. The funding of collaboratives, for example, has been central to many foundations' agendas—but although bringing allied groups together can create more powerful outcomes within regions, and potentially across regions, forced collaborations are exactly that—forced. Striking the right balance in the years to come will be a challenge.

Talking Up Regional Equity

Why should funders, intermediaries, and others interested in building social movements support the work of regional equity proponents? In some ways, the regional choice is an odd one: with the exception of a few metro areas such as Portland and Minneapolis–St. Paul, and a few issue areas such as transportation, formal regional authority ranges from limited to nonexistent. Yet part of the attraction of working at the regional level is precisely this relative lack of governmental structure—it means that the democratic practice of sustained conversation and consensus-building is the required route to crafting solutions.

Iris Young (2000) has made a compelling case along these lines in her book, *Inclusion and Democracy*. She distinguishes between aggregative democracy, in which actors with set preferences sort them out via the voting and lobbying processes (a formula that often leaves minority groups behind), and deliberate democracy, in which citizens enter into relationship with one another and talk through the possible positions and strategies till common ground is found. Young's vision is not that a sort of conflict-free "kumbaya" moment will then reign; she celebrates the rough-and-tumble struggle between differing positions and understands the role of power. Still, she argues that respectful deliberation will

---

[21] This is indirect support, since the Funders Network's focus is generally on Smart Growth in general, land-use decisions, transportation, and the like. Still, it is important that the network's first policy brief was on regional equity (Blackwell and McCullough 1999).

produce an understanding of "the other" and create a more solid basis for achieving economic and social justice.[22]

She also suggests that one of the most promising venues for deliberative democracy is precisely the level at which few venues exist—the region. Like us, she believes that many of the problems of social inequality take their lived form at the regional level—and so the "scope of politics should be regional. Regional governance is deeply democratic, however, only if combined with neighborhood and community-based participatory institutions" (Young 2000, 9). This is precisely the balance between community power and regional scale that has preoccupied many social movement regionalists. The "federated regionalism" of powell, combining local authority and control with cooperative planning, moves in this direction as well, addressing concerns of racial and economic equity and also more efficient regional functions (Institute on Race and Poverty 2002, 32).[23] That said, the most profound opportunity that regional equity may offer is a chance to truly reinvigorate democratic practice.

Of course, the existing gap in regional institutions has bedeviled rather than bedazzled regional equity proponents: because there is generally no "regional table" at which to sit, regional equity proponents must constantly assess the geography of change—that is, analyze the multiple levels (federal, state, and local) at which policy must be addressed and determine which level is both most important and most amenable to pressure in any given moment.

Federal policy, for example, is remarkably important, setting the ground rules for much of what happens, yet the opportunities for change may seem more limited here than at the state and local levels.

---

[22] This view of the region as the scale of democratic conversation is similar in some ways to the sort of "civic collaboratives" celebrated by Henton, Melville, and Walesh (1997, 2004) and by the business-oriented Alliance for Regional Stewardship (ARS). But that vision tends to highlight collaboration and "regional stewardship" as ways of protecting the commons and synthesizing the three Es of economy, environment, and equity, while the organizations we have profiled fall squarely in the equity camp and, like Young, see social tension and power-building as parts of the process of deliberative democracy. Indeed, they have sometimes been in direct conflict with "civic collaboratives"—as when WPUSA consciously positioned itself as a counterweight to JV:SVN—but they have also found ways to work with business, environmentalists, and others (as did Urban Habitat with the Bay Area Council, the Milwaukee job-training programs with metal-working firms, and the Atlanta Neighborhood Development Partnerships with major employers on affordable housing issues).

[23] The Institute on Race and Poverty (2002) points to Seattle as an example where development is coordinated regionally but decision-making powers are retained by local government, which is responsible for day-to-day development decisions.

Consequently, some organizers argue that we should either scale up from specific efforts—such as community benefits agreements that promote equitable development in key urban areas—or build from policy reform in bellwether states where conditions are ripe for change.

Whichever level is right, we need to do *something*. Americans are a pragmatic lot: they are willing to accept the uneven outcomes of a free market or the frightening consequences of an outsized prison system if they are convinced that nothing else will work to either boost growth or slow crime. But show them a Social Security system that delivers for the elderly or a Head Start program that actually gives poor kids a leg up in school, and they quickly make these programs into sacred cows. Progressives may bemoan the underlying attitudes (if only the public could see the unfairness of current arrangements!); however, the task is not to insist but to convince. To do this, we need to put the "progress" back in progressive—to show people a way out of current conditions which looks more like a route to success than a path to ideological complaint.

Part of the strength of the regional equity movement has been its focus on changing real policies and delivering real outcomes—there is nothing like a living wage or a community benefits agreement to spotlight the possible. We would argue, therefore, that the policy focus for national networks should be on housing, transportation, and workforce development.[24]

Why do we not emphasize the policy stalwarts of many regionalist thinkers: cross-jurisdiction tax-pooling and stronger metropolitan planning? We concur that both strategies make great policy sense: a shared tax base reduces the incentives for sprawl; shared planning enhances the power to spread housing fairly, connect residents with opportunity, and steer growth back to older cities. But although regional tax-sharing has proved effective in the few places in which it has been implemented, it has generally been a tough sell around the country. Regional growth management and planning, including the strategic use of urban growth boundaries, has been more popular, but its political traction too is still coming up short.

Prioritization of strategies will have to take into account these realities—and we would suggest that housing, transportation, and workforce development are agenda items that are important to relevant

[24] We thank Bruce Katz of the Brookings Institution for highlighting (in the Conversation on Regional Equity) these three policy areas as opportunities; see CORE 2006.

communities and to state officials and regional business leaders worried about competitiveness and fiscal health. Although it is always important to challenge the basic parameters of metropolitan development—and efforts to jump-start regional tax sharing and strict urban growth boundaries fit that bill—it is often easier to channel reform efforts that are already under way than to introduce new issues to the policy discussion.

Since the policy movement in these arenas is generally driven by business, it is critical to shift policy so that it favors disadvantaged communities. Housing policy could expand opportunities for low- and moderate-income families in both cities and suburbs by using the concept of "workforce housing." Federal and state tax incentives could increase access to home ownership for working families, providing the stepping-stone to wealth that so many households lack. Deconcentration of poverty could be encouraged by offering more vouchers to give low-income renters more choices, and shifting governance of both public housing and vouchers to the metropolitan level. The federal government could also facilitate the allocation of low-income-housing tax credits to areas of growing employment in the suburbs, not just to areas of current distress in the inner city. At the local level, "inclusionary zoning" efforts can be useful at creating mixed-income and high-opportunity neighborhoods.[25]

One area of vast potential for policy change is transportation. Transportation funding could be reformed to promote better integration of systems, stir development near rail and bus transfer stations, encourage participation in planning, and create jobs for local residents, especially those in distressed communities. At a state level, the allocation of infrastructure dollars creates the opportunity for improving transportation access for lower-income communities and individuals. At a local level, organizations like the Bus Riders Union in Los Angeles have helped to better connect residents to the region's opportunities through its efforts to shift resources to bus lines and its Countywide New Service campaign, which seeks to expand bus service to reach job centers, schools, and hospitals. Such comprehensive planning with an eye to the needs of the

[25] New Jersey helped paved the way with the Mt. Laurel decision that required wealthier municipalities to make room for affordable housing. But the state also worked against its aims with the creation of Regional Contribution Agreements, which allow one municipality to pay another to take its share of lower-priced housing. Eliminating such loopholes and prompting real integration by income is essential to open up opportunities and choice to inner-city residents, and doing so has been a central focus of the work of Gamaliel affiliates in New Jersey.

poor is essential—and yet, as in northwestern Indiana, part of the politics of success involves coordinating and improving services to inner-city residents and suburban commuters alike.

In workforce and economic development, another area ripe for intervention, there are clearly issues of spatial mismatch, particularly the way suburbanization of employment has proceeded over several decades. Globalization has created new insecurities for workers and firms in both cities and suburbs, and business is interested in new regional strategies to compete. Communities and labor unions are rightly worried that this is a cover for cutting wages and benefits yet an effective strategy for living wages will require more than rhetoric and legislation focused on fairness. It will also necessitate developing a new vision of the economy that combines (a) strategic growth to promote industries that provide family-sustaining wages; (b) the development of jobs that are accessible to large sectors of the population, not just the highly educated; (c) improving economic mobility and thereby creating cross-employer career ladders in regional labor markets; and (d) raising the base level of wages in low-wage jobs.

In all this policy work, the regional equity movement will have to define success more boldly. Among the toughest questions to answer is whether regional equity is about reducing disparities between people or between places. If it is primarily about people, then encouraging residents to move from distressed areas, perhaps by opening up affordable housing in the suburbs, is a great idea. But what if the community from which they depart becomes more distressed and the people who remain become even less connected and less well off? What if some areas are simply abandoned? Yet, if we instead adopt a place-based approach, what risks do we run of encouraging gentrification that results in displacement anyway?

This is more than an academic debate. In the aftermath of Hurricane Katrina, some New Orleans residents have insisted that fairness requires returning them to their neighborhoods of origin, whereas some analysts have suggested that mixed-income communities would be a superior, more sustainable outcome. Both strategies involve equity; both involve the region; and each seems in competition with the other for primacy in planning priorities. And it isn't just New Orleans. In Atlanta, regional equity proponents associated with the Atlanta Neighborhood Development Partnership have advocated for mixed-income housing, which others see as a recipe for simply forcing current residents out of their neighborhoods.

We do not pretend to have answers to these sets of questions. Our own formulation is that regional equity should create places of choice *and* places with choice. But we also recognize that this response is too facile. As the movement matures, the thorny issues of how much to stress mobility and how much to stress community development will continue to preoccupy analysts and activists who live in real cities with real trade-offs. Still, we would insist that this is a far more interesting set of questions than some that have preoccupied urban scholars in the past—and the promise of regional equity as a policy prescription is that it keeps issues of inclusion and issues of equality central to both regional and community approaches.

Picking Up the Pace

The overall picture we have painted is both encouraging and discouraging. Across the country, regional equity organizing is growing in both breadth and depth. In many places, groups are discovering that the regional scale is valuable for understanding the roots of social problems, for developing valuable solutions to social problems, and for building significant social power. Efforts to create national networks among those groups organizing around regional equity are ongoing, and there are natural synergies with other networks that have regional bases and related equity focuses. At the same time, those national organizations that focus on regional equity have predominantly organized within particular constituencies (labor, community, faith-based) rather than across constituencies. Although cross-constituency regional equity coalitions have formed in many regions around the country, there has yet to emerge, at a national level, a cohesive network of cross-constituency organizations focused on building regional equity.

Perhaps the current state of affairs simply reflects a natural process of social movement evolution. In the 2003 New World Foundation document *Funding Social Movements,* the authors outline four stages in the life span of a social movement:

- *Stage One: Building Movement Infrastructure:* A core group of activists, usually those with the most at stake in an issue, is motivated. New organizations and transformed organizations serve as anchors for the movement to grow. Internal networks materialize, then thicken, broaden, and

deepen. Eventually infrastructure is created that serves as the foundation of the movement.

- *Stage Two: Building Identity and Intention:* Activists in the movement begin
  to identify the vision, form an integrated agenda, and more explicitly state
  goals. Tensions begin to emerge—the movement goes through "growing
  pains" as questions regarding issues of expansion or contraction of the
  base and other problems become more pressing. The formation of movement leadership is critical at this stage.
- *Stage Three: Social Combustion—The Movement Moment:* This is the peak moment when the movement-building work pays off, and social, political,
  or policy goals are achieved. According to the New World Foundation:
  "Social movements change our concepts of possibility and nature—of
  what is possible in the human condition and what is natural to life on
  the planet" (2003, 9).
- *Stage Four: Consolidation or Dissipation:* Reform or repression or ebbing
  of civic energy causes the movement to dissipate (modest reform causes
  some satisfaction, leadership is co-opted, or the bottom is sold out) or to
  consolidate (structural change, new organizations, and new laws replace
  the need for active mobilization).[26]

Where is social movement regionalism located in this spectrum? We
see things fluctuating primarily between Stages One and Two, a sort of
uneven development not atypical of the metropolitan landscapes so
many regionalists seek to change. Activities within regions are heating
up, helping to build new identities and intentions, but the ability of the
different national networks to coordinate and work together has to date
been much more limited. PolicyLink's efforts to bring different constituencies together at a national level through its Regional Equity Summits
have created an important venue for connecting disparate parts of a
national movement. But otherwise, there seem to be few spaces where
different national networks come together to develop a common vision,
strategy, and supportive organizational structure; they tend to focus instead on building their own constituencies.

---

[26] The document draws on social movement theory, some of which we have mentioned
earlier. We use the NWF interpretation here as a "voice from the field" which has "seeded"
and supported several of the regional equity efforts we profile; New World Foundation
2003; and see: www.newwf.org/.

Ultimately, for a regional equity movement to capture the national imagination fully and contribute to a revitalization of progressive politics around the country, the varying constituencies need to develop a closer communication and coordinating structure throughout the country. They need to build on the telling moments of social combustion—starting at a local and regional scale with the modest epiphanies that come when city dwellers and suburbanites reach out to each other about more sustainable development, when the working poor and the middle class see a common fate resulting from economic insecurity, and when blacks, whites, Latinos, Asians, and others find identity not only in their ethnicity but also in their regional or community connections. And they need to tie such realizations to national events such as the Hurricane Katrina disaster—when for an all-too-short few weeks, attention by the media reminded us of the vulnerability created by a society when the geographic disparities in environmental protection, transit service, and household income are accepted as natural.

From the experience of living-wage campaigns, community benefit agreements, and inclusionary zoning ordinances as achieved by activists, can we build from the local level to create a new sense of national good? Can the lessons from faith-based, labor, and community organizations' efforts to fight together for more equitable urban development processes help to develop a vision that progress is possible? In a sense, the first four chapters of this book are about the Stage One profile of this movement—how it started, who's in the game, and what's exciting about it. Chapter 5 is primarily about the tensions that have begun to emerge: the differences in agendas, the role of race and regionalism, the challenges of making people's everyday experiences relevant to the movement—problems that are part of Stage Two. The final task, of course, is to more fully specify and achieve Stage Three, the "Movement Moment" in which the epiphanies and awakenings are not so modest but instead constitute the basis for a new understanding of America, social justice, and the need to come together.

Part of what often propels movements to Stage Three is leadership. For some, the regional equity bandwagon is not a natural fit. The frame it offers may be powerful, weaving together issues such as transportation, housing, environmental, and educational equity. However, any analysis of the whole package of causes and strategies, including tax-sharing, urban annexation, concentrated poverty, and cross-jurisdictional coalition building, can be overwhelming and lead to lack of interest for some.

Moreover, while a sense of urgency is felt when confronting local issues, a regional approach can sometimes feel less immediate and more academic.

This is where leadership comes in—actors who can truly attract people, speak to their life experiences, and connect with all sorts of constituencies. The continual debate, of course, is whether such leaders need to be singular—a Martin Luther King or a Cesar Chavez—or whether they can be collective and community-based leaders, the kind that have characterized, for example, the environmental justice movement. We are a bit agnostic on that issue, but we have a firmer position with regard to another leadership debate: are leaders just born, or can they be made?

In 2004, the nation was surprised by the rise of a new political star—Barack Obama. In a state where two-thirds of the residents—and an even larger share of the voters—are white, a black state senator from Chicago ran a startlingly successful campaign to become one of Illinois's two senators in Washington. His summer speech to the Democratic National Convention in Boston revealed part of his secret: arguing that "there is not a Black America and a White America and Latino America and Asian America—there's the United States of America." His soaring rhetoric and open manner showed why he had been able to connect to white suburbanites and rural voters. In January 2008, he stunned political pundits by winning the first contest of the presidential season: the Democratic caucuses in Iowa, a state that was 96 percent white (U.S. Census 2006). He went on to win the Democratic nomination and the Presidency, gaining votes in unexpected places and building a coalition that seemed to transcend traditional racial barriers.

In typical media fashion, Obama's ability to communicate across the lines of color and culture was ascribed to either his mixed racial heritage or some magical talent with which he alone was born. Who else, it seemed, could have figured out the memorable "We worship an 'awesome God' in the Blue States...and yes, we've got some gay friends in the Red States?"[27] Well, we also admire his talent and his way with words, but we think we know where he learned to talk like that: he was a community organizer in Chicago for the Gamaliel Foundation, exactly as

---

[27] These quotations are from Barack Obama's speech to the Democratic Convention at the Fleet Center in Boston on July 27, 2004. For the text, see http://www.americanrhetoric.com/speeches/convention2004/barackobama2004dnc.htm.

the network was trying to lift up regional equity as a new organizing framework, strategy, and language (Moberg 2007).

This, we think, is the hope of the new regional equity movement. Still forming, still evolving, it has begun to offer a way to create new language, bridge old divides, and fashion original policies and politics. It has taken off with particular strength in certain regions for reasons we have suggested: some places have more receptive structures, more similar city-suburb demographics, and more vibrant economies. Can the array of regional equity networks and efforts be fashioned into the fabric of a mass-scale social movement? Can this set of ideas and groups gain prominence in the national political consciousness in a way that significantly transforms American society? Could this be the start of something big?

Our answer is yes! We are aware of the problems with predictions—economists, it is said, have successfully predicted ten of the last two recessions. We plead guilty to having too much economic training spread among us, but we think that others might also be missing the signs that are sprouting, the hope that is stirring, the times that are a-changin'.

In the 1950s, after all, when the Montgomery bus boycott commenced, and the Southern Christian Leadership Conference was established, few observers would have predicted the evolution of a civil rights movement that entirely reshaped American politics and values. In the 1960s and 1970s, when offshore oil spills, worsening air pollution, and toxic contamination in such places as the Love Canal stirred the national consciousness, few could have known just how mainstream the principles and policies of environmental sustainability would become.

It is possible for regional equity proponents to follow in these footsteps of movement-building. But to do so means understanding that regional equity is not just about the technical details of transit-oriented development, cross-jurisdictional tax-sharing, or employer-oriented job training; it is about power-building, organizing, and social change. It is not just about demonstrating that the growth we prefer is "smarter" than that proposed by the other guys; it is about offering a vision of America in which cities are strong, racial conflict is superseded, and millions more join the middle class. And it is not just about devising new forms of metropolitan collaboration and public-private partnerships; it is about reflecting back to America a moral claim that we really are all in this together.

Can the regional equity movement become another transformative force for a better America? With vision and strategy born from honest conversation, we believe it can. With commitment and collaboration among unexpected partners, we believe it will. And with the challenges of racial and economic inequality still confronting us as we proceed into the twenty-first century, we believe it must.

References

Abbot, Carl. 1997. "The Portland Region: Where the City and Suburbs Talk to Each Other and Agree." *Housing Policy Debate* 8 (1): 11–51.

ACORN. 2004. *Separate and Unequal 2004: Predatory Lending in America*. Washington, D.C.: ACORN.

Agnew, John. 2000. "From the Political Economy of Regions to Regional Political Economy." *Progress in Human Geography* 24:101–10.

Altshuler, Alan, William Morrill, Harold Wolman, and Faith Mitchell. 1999. *Governance and Opportunity in Metropolitan America*. Washington, D.C.: National Academy Press.

Amin, Ash. 1999. "An Institutionalist Perspective on Regional Economic Development." *International Journal of Urban and Regional Research* 23 (2): 365–78.

——. 2004. "Regions Unbound: New Politics of Place." *Geografiska Annaler* 86B (1): 33–44.

Amin, Ash, and Nigel Thrift. 1995. "Globalization, 'Institutional Thickness,' and the Local Economy." In *Managing Cities: The New Urban Context*, ed. Patsy Healey, Stuart Cameron, Simin Davoudi, Stephen Graham, and Ali Madani-Pour, 91–108. Chichester, U.K.: Wiley.

Anglin, Roland V., and Susanna C. Montezemolo. 2004. *Supporting the Community Development Movement: The Achievements and Challenges of Intermediary Organizations*. Washington, D.C.: U.S. Department of Housing and Urban Development.

Atlantic Neighborhood Development Corporation. 2006. Interview. May 9.

Auerhahn, Louise, Bob Brownstein, Brian Darrow, and Phaedra Ellis-Lamkins. 2007. *Life in the Valley Economy: Silicon Valley Progress Report*. San Jose: Working Partnerships USA. http://www.wpusa.org/live/get/LIVE_2007.pdf.

Bacon, David. N.d. "Organizing Silicon Valley's High Tech Workers." http://dbacon.igc.org/Unions/04hitec0.htm.

Bailey, Robert. 1972. *Radicals in Urban Politics: The Alinsky Approach*. Chicago: University of Chicago Press.

Barnes, William, and Larry C. Ledebur. 1998. *The New Regional Economies: The U.S. Common Market and the Global Economy.* Thousand Oaks, Calif.: Sage.

Bay Area Economics. 1999. *The 7th Street/McClymonds Corridor Neighborhood Improvement Initiative: Community Plan.* Emeryville: Bay Area Economics.

Benhamou, Eric. 2000. "Valley Must Narrow the Wage Gap." *San Jose Mercury News,* May 31, 7B.

Benman, Keith. 2005. "RDA Money Could Land at Gary Airport." *Northwest Indiana and Illinois Times.* December 15.

——. 2006. Gary Airport Lands a Big One. *Northwest Indiana and Illinois Times.* January 17.

Benner, Chris. 1996. *Shock Absorbers in the Flexible Economy: The Rise of Contingent Employment in Silicon Valley.* San Jose: Working Partnerships.

——. 1998a. *Growing Together or Drifting Apart? Working Families and Business in the New Economy.* San Jose: Working Partnerships USA, with Economic Policy Institute.

——. 1998b. "Win the Lottery or Organize: Economic Restructuring and Union Organizing in Silicon Valley." *Berkeley Planning Journal* 12, 50–71.

——. 2002. *Work in the New Economy: Flexible Labor Markets in Silicon Valley.* Oxford: Blackwell.

Benner, Chris, Bob Brownstein, and Amy Dean. 1999. *Walking the Lifelong Tightrope: Negotiating Work in the New Economy.* San Jose: Working Partnerships USA, with Economic Policy Institute.

Benner, Chris, Laura Leete, and Manuel Pastor. 2007. *Staircases or Treadmills: Labor Market Intermediaries and Economic Opportunity in a Changing Economy.* New York: Russell Sage.

Berbeo, Dominic. 1999. "Council Panel Approves Tax Cut-for-Jobs Deal with DreamWorks." *City News Service, Inc.,* May 10.

Berger, Renee, Maggie Sale, and Liz Vasile Galin. 2006. *One East Palo Alto Neighborhood Improvement Initiative, Final Report: Year Five Implementation.* Report for the William and Flora Hewlett Foundation. San Francisco: Teamworks Consulting.

Berman, Lee Lucas. 1998. "Geographies of Organizing Justice for Janitors in Los Angeles." In *Organizing the Landscape: Geographical Perspectives on Labor Unionism,* ed. Andrew Herod. Minneapolis: University of Minnesota Press.

Bernhardt, Annette, Laura Dresser, and Joel Rogers. 2004. "Taking the High Road in Milwaukee: The Wisconsin Regional Training Partnership." In *Partnering for Change: Unions and Community Groups Build Coalitions for Economic Justice,* ed. David Reynolds. Armonk, N.Y.: M.E. Sharpe.

Bernstein, Scott. 1997. "Community-based Regionalism Key to Sustainable Future." *Neighborhood Works* 20:6.

Bhargava, Shalini, Bob Brownstein, Amy Dean, and Sarah Zimmerman. 2001. *Everyone's Valley: Inclusion and Affordable Housing in Silicon Valley.* San Jose: Working Partnerships USA.

Blackwell, Angela Glover, and Radhika Fox. 2004. *Regional Equity and Smart Growth: Opportunities for Advancing Social and Economic Justice in America.* Funders' Network for Smart Growth and Livable Communities. Translation Paper 1, ed. 2:

http://www.fundersnetwork.org/usr_doc/Regional_Equity_and_Smart_Growth_2nd_Ed.pdf.

Blackwell, Angela Glover, Stewart Kwoh, and Manuel Pastor. 2002. *Searching for the Uncommon Common Ground: New Dimensions on Race in America.* New York: Norton.

Blackwell, Angela Glover, and Heather McCullough. 1999. *Opportunities for Smarter Growth: Social Equity and the Smart Growth Movement.* Funders' Network on Smart Growth and Livable Communities. Translation Paper 1. Oakland, Calif.: PolicyLink.

Blume, Howard, and Duke Helfand. 2007. "Multiple Choice for Reform Path." *Los Angeles Times,* December 10.

Bollens, Scott. 2003. "In through the Back Door: Social Equity and Regional Governance." *Housing Policy Debate* 13 (4): 631–57.

Booza, Jason C., Jackie Cutsinger, and George Galster. 2006. *Where Did They Go? The Decline of Middle-Income Neighborhoods in Metropolitan America.* Washington, D.C.: Brookings Institution.

Boudreau, Julie-Anne. 2000. *The Megacity Saga: Democracy and Citizenship in This Global Age.* Montreal: Black Rose Books.

Bratt, Rachel G., and William M. Rohe. 2005. "Challenges and Dilemmas Facing Community Development Corporations in the United States." *Community Development Journal Advance Access* 42 (1): 63–78.

Braun, Henry, Frank Jenkins, and Wendy Grigg. 2006. *A Closer Look at Charter Schools using Hierarchical Linear Modeling (NCES 2006–460).* Washington, D.C.: U.S. Government Printing Office, U.S. Department of Education, National Center for Education Statistics, Institute of Education Sciences.

Brecher, Jeremy, and Tim Costello. 1990. *Building Bridges: The Emerging Coalition of Labor and Community.* New York: Monthly Review Press.

Brenner, Neil. 2002. "Decoding the Newest 'Metropolitan Regionalism' in the USA: A Critical Overview." *Cities* 19 (1): 3–21.

Broder, John. 2004. "Los Angeles Groups Agree to Airport Growth, for a Price." *New York Times,* December 17, A22.

Brookings Institution Center on Urban and Metropolitan Policy. 2003. *Back to Prosperity: A Competitive Agenda for Renewing Pennsylvania.* Washington, D.C.: Brookings Institution.

Brown, Jeffrey. 1998. "Race, Class, Gender, and Public Transportation." *Critical Planning* (UCLA), 5:3–20.

Brown, Prudence, and Leila Fiester. 2007. *Hard Lessons about Philanthropy and Community Change from the Neighborhood Improvement Initiative.* Prepared under contract to the William and Flora Hewlett Foundation. March.

Brownstein, Bob. 2000. "Working Partnerships: A New Political Strategy for Creating Living Wage Jobs." *Working USA* 4 (1): 35–48.

Bruegmann, Robert. 2005. *Sprawl: A Compact History.* Chicago: University of Chicago Press.

Buchsbaum, Peter. 1985. "No Wrong without Remedy: The New Jersey Supreme Court's Effort to Bar Exclusionary Zoning." *Urban Lawyer* 17 (1): 59–90.

Bullard, Robert D., ed. 2007. *Growing Smarter: Achieving Livable Communities, Environmental Justice, and Regional Equity.* Cambridge: MIT Press.

Bullard, Robert D., and Glenn S. Johnson. 1997. *Just Transportation: Dismantling Race and Class Barriers to Mobility.* Gabriola Island, B.C.: New Society.

Bullard, Robert D., Glenn S. Johnson, and Angel O. Torres, eds. 2004. *Highway Robbery: Transportation Racism and New Routes to Equity.* Cambridge: South End Press.

Burawoy, Michael. 2005. "2004 ASA Presidential Address: For Public Sociology." *American Sociological Review* 70 (1): 4–28.

Butler, Gregory. 2006. *Disunited Brotherhoods: Race, Racketeering, and the Fall of the New York Construction Unions.* Lincoln, Neb.: iUniverse.

CBP (California Budget Project). 2006. *Left Behind: Workers and Their Families in a Changing Los Angeles.* Sacramento: California Budget Project.

Calhoun, Craig. 2005. "The Promise of Public Sociology." *British Journal of Sociology,* 56(3).

Camacho, David E. ed., 1998. *Environmental Injustices, Political Struggles: Race, Class, and the Environment.* Durham, N.C.: Duke University Press.

Camden Reports. 2006. *Camden Demographics.* CAMConnect. http://www.cam connect.org/documents/camden_facts_2006.pdf.

Card, David, and Alan Kreuger. 1997. *Myth and Measurement: The New Economics of the Minimum Wage.* Princeton: Princeton University Press.

Carnoy, Martin, Manuel Castells and Chris Benner. 1997. "Labour Markets and Employment Practices in the Age of Flexibility: A Case Study of Silicon Valley." *International Labour Review* 136 (1): 27–48.

Castells, Manuel. 1983. *City and the Grassroots.* Berkeley: University of California Press.

——. 1997. *The Power of Identity: The Information Age,* vol. 2, *Economy, Society, and Culture.* Cambridge: Blackwell.

Center for Transit-Oriented Development. 2006. *Preserving and Promoting Diverse Transit-Oriented Neighborhoods.* Collaboration of the Center for Neighborhood Technology, Reconnecting America, and Strategic Economics. http://www. cnt.org/repository/diverseTOD_FullReport.pdf.

Chasin, Alexandra. 2001. *Selling Out: The Gay and Lesbian Movement Goes to Market.* New York: Palgrave Macmillan.

Chavez, Cesar. 1966. "The Organizer's Tale." *Ramparts,* July 1966.

Cieslewicz, David J. 2002. "The Environmental Impacts of Sprawl." In *Urban Sprawl: Causes, Consequences, and Policy Responses,* ed. Gregory Squires, 23–38. Washington, D.C.: Urban Institute Press.

Cleeland, Nancy. "L.A. Janitors OK Contract." *Los Angeles Times,* April 25, 2005.

Clifford, Frank. "AQMD Plan Will Target Pollution in Poor Areas." *Los Angeles Times,* October 11, 1997, A1.

Community Farm Alliance. 2003. *Bringing Kentucky's Food and Farm Economy Home.* Frankfort, Ky.: Community Farm Alliance. http://www.foodroutes.org/doclib/cfa_kentucky.pdf.

Community Scholars Program. 2005. *A "Just" Redevelopment: Lessons from the Figueroa Corridor Coalition for Economic Justice.* Los Angeles: UCLA Department of Urban Planning.

Conte, Christopher R. 2000. "The Boys of Sprawl: Free-market Think Tanks Are Working Hard to Convince Americans That Smart Growth Is a Stupid Idea." *Governing Magazine,* May. http://www.governing.com/archive/2000/may/sprawl.txt

Corcoran, Thomas, and Nathan Scovronick. 1998. "More than Equal: New Jersey's Quality Education Act." In *Strategies for School Equity: Creating Productive Schools in a Just Society,* ed. Marilyn J. Gittell. New Haven: Yale University Press.

Cordova, Teresa, Jose T. Bravo, Jeanne Gauna, Richard Moore, and Ruben Solis. 2000. "Building Networks to Tackle Global Restructuring: The Environmental and Economic Justice Movement." In *The Collaborative City: Opportunities and Struggles for Blacks and Latinos in U.S. Cities,* ed. John J. Betancur and Douglas C. Gills, 177–96. New York: Garland.

CORE (Conversation on Regional Equity). 2006. *Edging toward Equity: Creating Shared Opportunity in America's Regions.* Santa Cruz: University of California, Center for Justice, Tolerance and Community. http://cjtc.ustc.edu

Cox, Kevin. 1995. "Globalisation, Competition, and the Politics of Local Economic Development." *Urban Studies* 32 (2): 213–24.

Crowell, Charlene. 2005. *Living for the City: Developing Smart Growth Leadership in Detroit.* Detroit: National Association for the Advancement of Colored People (NAACP) and the Michigan Land Use Institute. http://www.mlui.org/downloads/naacp.pdf.

Darnovsky, Marcy, Barbara Epstein, and Richard Flacks. 1995. *Cultural Politics and Social Movements.* Philadelphia: Temple University Press.

Davies, James C. 1962. "Toward a Theory of Revolution." *American Sociological Review* 27 (1): 5–19.

Davis, Mike. 1990. *City of Quartz: Excavating the Future of Los Angeles.* London: Verso.

Dean, Amy B., and David B. Reynolds. 2008. "Labor's New Regional Strategy: The Rebirth of Central Labor Councils." *New Labor Forum* 17 (1): 46–55.

DeFilippis, James, Robert Fisher, and Eric Shragge. 2007. "What's Left in the Community? Oppositional Politics in Contemporary Practice." *Community Development Journal* 42 (2).

Delgado, Gary. 1986. *Organizing the Movement: The Roots and Growth of ACORN.* Philadelphia: Temple University Press.

——. 1994. *Beyond the Politics of Place: New Directions in Community Organizing in the 1990s.* Oakland, Calif.: Applied Research Center.

Delgado, Hector L. 1993. *New Immigrants, Old Unions: Organizing Undocumented Workers in Los Angeles.* Philadelphia: Temple University Press.

Dorsey, Hattie, and von Nkosi. 2006. Personal interview, Atlanta Neighborhood Development Corporation, Atlanta, Ga. May 9.

Downs, Anthony. 2005. "Smart Growth: Why We Discuss It More Than We Do It." *Journal of the American Planning Association* 71 (4): 367–78.

Dreier, Peter, John Mollenkopf, and Todd Swanstrom. 2001. *Place Matters: Metropolitics for the Twenty-First Century.* Lawrence: University Press of Kansas.

Dreier, Peter, and Beth Steckler. 2007. "Not Just for the Gentry." *The American Prospect* 18(1).

Drury, Richard Toshiyuki, Michael E. Belliveau, J. Scott Kuhn, and Shipra Bansal. 1999. "Pollution Trading and Environmental Injustice: Los Angeles' Failed Experiment in Air Quality Policy." *Duke Environmental Law and Policy Forum* 231.

Eaken, Elizabeth. 2002. "Hundreds Oppose Location of Facility." *The Lake County Times*, September 30, 2002, sec B.

Early, Steve, and Larry Cohen. 1994. "Jobs with Justice: Building a Broad-Based Movement for Workers' Rights." *Social Policy* 25:7–18.

———. 1997. "Jobs with Justice: Mobilizing Labor-Community Coalitions." *Working USA* 1:49–57.

Eberts, Randall, George Erickcek, and Jack Kleinhenz. 2006. *Dashboard Indicators for the Northeast Ohio Economy: Prepared for the Fund for Our Economic Future.* Cleveland, Ohio: Federal Reserve Bank of Cleveland.

Ellis-Lamkins, Phaedra. 2008. Personal communication, January 15.

Empowerment Research. 2004. *Mayfair Improvement Initiative Worker Survey.* East Palo Alto: Community Development Institute.

Environmental Defense. 2006. *L.A. Live: Community Benefits Program: Status Update.* http://www.environmentaldefense.org/documents/5196_LALive_CBA update.pdf.

Ethington, Philip, William H. Frey, and Dowell Myers. 2001. *The Racial Resegregation of Los Angeles County, 1940–2000.* Los Angeles and Ann Arbor: Race Contours 2000 Public Research Report 2001–5, University of Southern California and University of Michigan.

Faber, Daniel R., and Deborah McCarthy. 2001. *Green of Another Color: Building Effective Partnerships between Foundations and the Environmental Justice Movement.* Boston: Northeastern University, Philanthropy and Environmental Justice Research Project; accessible at www.precaution.org/lib/05/green of another color.pdf.

Fairris, David, David Runsten, Carolina Briones, and Jessica Goodheart. 2005. *Examining the Evidence: The Impact of the Los Angeles Living Wage Ordinance on Workers and Businesses.* Los Angeles: Los Angeles Alliance for a New Economy.

Ferman, Barbara. 1996. *Challenging the Growth Machine: Neighborhood Politics in Chicago and Pittsburgh.* Lawrence: University Press of Kansas.

Fine, Janice. 2000. "Community Unionism in Baltimore and Stamford." *Working USA* 4 (3): 59–85.

Fisher, Robert. 1994. *Let the People Decide.* Rev. ed. New York: Twayne.

Fisher, Robert, Fred Brooks, and Daniel Russell. 2007. "'Don't Be a Blockhead': ACORN, Protest Tactics, and Refund Anticipation Loans." *Urban Affairs Review* 42 (4): 553–82.

Flaming, Daniel, Patrick Burns, and Brent Haydamack. 2006. *From the Pockets of Strangers: Economic Impacts of Tourism in Los Angeles and Five Competing Metropolitan Destinations.* Los Angeles: Economic Roundtable.

Fogelson, Robert M. 1967. *The Fragmented Metropolis: Los Angeles, 1850–1930.* Cambridge: Harvard University Press.

Folmar, Kate. 2003. "Accord Expected on S.J. Project: Labor, Housing Changes Sought Downtown." *San Jose Mercury News*, March 27,1B.

Fox, Radhika, and Sarah Treuhaft. 2005. *Shared Prosperity, Stronger Regions: An Agenda for Rebuilding America's Older Core Cities*. Oakland, Calif.: PolicyLink.

Frank, Thomas. 2004. *What's the Matter with Kansas? How Conservatives Won the Heart of America*. New York: Henry Holt.

Frege, Carola, Edmund Heery, and Lowell Turner. 2003. Proceedings of the 55th annual meeting, in *Comparative Coalition Building and the Revitalization of the Labor Movement*, 122–30. Champaign, Ill.: Industrial Relations Research Association.

Frey, William. 2001. *Melting Pot Suburbs: A Census 2000 Study of Suburban Diversity*. Washington, D.C.: Brookings Institution Center on Urban and Metropolitan Policy.

Friedman, Thomas L. 2005. *The World Is Flat: A Brief History of the Twenty-first Century*. New York: Farrar, Straus & Giroux.

Friedmann, John, and Clyde Weaver. 1979. *Territory and Function: The Evolution of Regional Planning*. Berkeley: University of California Press.

Fulton, William, Jenifer Wolch, Antonio Villaraigosa, and Susan Weaver. 2003. *After Sprawl: Action Plans for Metropolitan Los Angeles*. Los Angeles: Southern California Studies Center, University of Southern California.

Funders' Network for Smart Growth and Livable Communities. 2005. *Signs of Promise: Stories of Philanthropic Leadership in Advancing Regional and Neighborhood Equity*. Coral Gables, Fla.: Funders' Network.

FutureWorks. 2004. *Minding Their Civic Business: A Look at the New Ways Regional Business-Civic Organizations Are Making a Difference in Metropolitan North America*. Arlington, Mass: FutureWorks.

Gahegan, Patrick. 2006. Interview by Chris Benner, February 2.

Gans, Herbert J. 1989. "Sociology in America: The Discipline and the Public American Sociological Association." 1988 Presidential Address. *American Sociological Review* 54 (1):1–16.

Geddes, Robert. 1997. "Metropolis Unbound: The Sprawling American City and the Search for Alternatives." *American Prospect* 35:40–46.

George, Alexander L., and Andrew Bennett. 2005. *Case Studies and Theory Development in the Social Sciences*. Cambridge: Belfer Center for Science and International Affairs, John F. Kennedy School of Government, Harvard University.

German, Jeff. 2006. "Labor Sees a New Day in Southern Nevada." *Las Vegas Sun*, December 10.

Glaser, Barney G., and Anselm L. Strauss. 1967. *The Discovery of Grounded Theory: Strategies for Qualitative Research*. Chicago: Aldine.

Goering, John. 2005. "Expanding Housing Choice and Integrating Neighborhoods: The MTO experiment." In *The Geography of Opportunity: Race and Housing Choice in Metropolitan America*, ed. Xavier de Sousa Briggs, 127–50. Washington, D.C.: Brookings Institution Press.

Goldsmith, William, and Edward J. Blakely. 1992. *Separate Societies: Poverty and Inequality in U.S. cities*. Philadelphia: Temple University Press.

Goldstein, John. 2006. Interview, March.

Gottlieb, Robert, Mark Vallianatos, Regina M. Freer, and Peter Dreier. 2005. *The Next Los Angeles: The Struggle for a Livable City*. Berkeley: University of California Press.

Grengs, Joe. 2002. "Community-Based Planning as a Source of Political Change: The Transit Equity Movement of Los Angeles' Bus Riders Union." *Journal of the American Planning Association* 68 (2).

———. 2005. "Fighting for Balanced Transportation in the Motor City." *Progressive Planning* 163 (Spring).

Grigsby, J. Eugene, and Goetz Wolff. 1995. *Economic Strategies for Multi-ethnic Communities in Los Angeles*. Los Angeles: Planning Group.

Groarke, Margaret. 2004. "Using Community Power against Targets beyond the Neighborhood." *New Political Science* 26 (2): 171–88.

Gurr, Ted. 1968. "A Causal Model of Civil Strife: A Comparative Analysis Using New Indices." *American Political Science Review* 62:1104–24.

Haas, Gilda. 1999. *Creating Creative Windows to the Banking Industry*. San Francisco: Federal Reserve Bank of San Francisco.

———. 2002. "Economic Justice in the Los Angeles Figueroa Corridor." In *Teaching for Change: Popular Education and the Labor Movement*. Los Angeles: UCLA Center for Labor Research and Education.

———. 2004. *We Shall Not Be Moved*. Los Angeles: Strategic Actions for a Just Economy.

———. 2005. "Visioning What Regional Efforts Look Like." Paper presented to Miami [Fla.] Community Benefits Initiative Workshop, April 17.

Halpern, Robert. 1995. *Rebuilding the Inner City*. New York: Columbia University Press.

Hamilton, David. 2004. "Developing Regional Regimes: A Comparison of Two Metropolitan Areas." *Journal of Urban Affairs* 26 (4): 455–77.

Harrison, Bennett. 2000. "It Takes a Region (or Does It?). In *Urban-Suburban Interdependencies*, ed. Rosalind Greenstein and Wim Wiewel, 141–60. Cambridge, Mass.: Lincoln Institute for Land Policy.

Heckscher, Charles, and David Palmer. 1993. "Associational Movements and Employment Rights: An Emerging Paradigm?" In *Research in the Sociology of Organizations: Special Issue on Labor Relations and Unions 12*, ed. Samuel B. Bacharach, Ronald Seeber, and David Walsh. Greenwich, Conn.: JAI Press.

Henton, Douglas, John Melville, and Kimberly Walesh. 1997. *Grassroots Leaders for a New Economy: How Civic Entrepreneurs Are Building Prosperous Communities*. San Francisco: Jossey-Bass.

———. 2004. *Civic Revolutionaries: Igniting the Passion for Change in America's Communities*. San Francisco: Jossey-Bass.

Herod, Andrew. 1991. "Local Political Practice in Response to a Manufacturing Plant Closure." *Antipode* 23 (4): 385–402.

Hertz, Judy. 2002. "Organizing for Change: Stories of Success; Saving the Heart of Hammond." Paper presented to the On-Line Conference on Community Organizing and Development. http://comm-org.wisc.edu/papers.htm.

Hirsch, Barry T., and David A. Macpherson. 1986. *Union Membership and Coverage Databases from the CPS*. http://www.unionstats.com.

——. 2003. "Union Membership and Coverage Database from the Current Population Survey: Note." *Industrial and Labor Relations Review* 56 (2): 349–54. http://www.unionstats.com/.

Holloway, Steven R., and James O. Wheeler. 1991. "Corporate Headquarters Relocation and Changes in Metropolitan Corporate Dominance, 1980–1987." *Economic Geography* 67 (1): 54–74.

Horwitt, Sanford D. 1989. *Let Them Call Me Rebel: Saul Alinsky, His Life and Legacy.* New York: Knopf.

Hughes, Elizabeth Blish. 2004. *In Transit.* New York: Ford Foundation.

Hyung, Je Jo. 2002. *Regional Restructuring and Urban Regimes: A Comparison of the Pittsburgh and Detroit Metropolitan Areas.* Working paper UMTRI 2002–20, Office for the Study of Automotive Transportation. Ann Arbor: University of Michigan, Transportation Research Institute.

Imbroscio, David L. 2006. "Shaming the Inside Game: A Critique of the Liberal Expansionist Approach to Addressing Urban Problems." *Urban Affairs Review* 42:224–48.

Institute on Race and Poverty. 2002. *Racism and Metropolitan Dynamics: The Civil Rights Challenge of the 21st Century.* Minneapolis: Institute on Race and Poverty.

Ito, Jennifer. 2007. Personal interview, January.

Jackson, Pat. 2006. Personal interview, February 22.

Janis, Madeline. 2005. Interview, June.

Jargowsky, Paul A. 1997. *Poverty and Place: Ghettos, Barrios, and the American City.* New York: Russell Sage Foundation.

Jenkins, J. Craig, and Craig M. Eckert. 1986. "Channeling Black Insurgency: Elite Patronage and Professional Social Movement Organizations in the Development of the Black Movement." *American Sociological Review* 51:812–29.

Joassart-Marcelli, Pascale, and Jennifer R. Wolch. 2003. "The Intrametropolitan Geography of Poverty and the Nonprofit Sector in Southern California." *Nonprofit and Voluntary Sector Quarterly* 32 (1): 70–96.

Johnston, Paul. 1994. *Success while Others Fail: Social Movement Unionism and the Public Workplace.* Ithaca: ILR Press.

Jonas, Andrew E. G., and Stephanie Pincetl. 2006. "Rescaling Regions in the State: The New Regionalism in California." *Political Geography* 25:482–505.

Jones, Martin, and Gordon MacLeod. 2004. "Regional Spaces, Spaces of Regionalism: Territory, Insurgent Politics, and the English Question." *Transactions of the Institute of British Geographers* 29 (4): 433–52.

Joseph, Peniel, ed. 2006. *The Black Power Movement: Rethinking the Black Power–Civil Rights Era.* London: Routledge.

——. 2007. *Waiting 'til the Midnight Hour: A Narrative History of Black Power in America.* New York: Holt.

JV:SVN (Joint Venture: Silicon Valley Network). 1995. *Integrating Silicon Valley's Defense and Commercial Economies: A Community-Based Action Plan.* Palo Alto: Joint Venture: Silicon Valley Network, and Center for Continuing Study of the California Economy.

——. 2003. *2003 Index of Silicon Valley.* San Jose: Joint Venture: Silicon Valley Network.

——. 2006. *2006 Index of Silicon Valley.* San Jose: Joint Venture: Silicon Valley Network.

Kain, John. 1968. "Housing Segregation, Negro Employment, and Metropolitan Decentralization." *Quarterly Journal of Economics* 25:110–30.

Katz, Bruce. 1998. "Reviving Cities: Think Metropolitan." Brookings Policy Brief, no. 33, Brookings Institution, June.

——, ed. 2000. *Reflections on Regionalism.* Washington, D.C.: Brookings Institution Press.

Katznelson, Ira. 1981. *City Trenches: Urban Politics and the Patterning of Class in the United States.* Chicago: University of Chicago Press.

Kazin, Michael. 1987. *Barons of Labor: The San Francisco Building Trades and Union Power in the Progressive Era.* Urbana: University of Illinois Press.

Keating, W. Dennis. 1986. "Linking Downtown Development to Broader Community Goals: An Analysis of Linkage Policy in Three Cities." *Journal of the American Planning Association* 52 (2): 133–141.

Kennedy, Randall. 1989. "Martin Luther King's Constitution: A Legal History of the Montgomery Bus Boycott." *Yale Law Journal* 98 (6): 999–1067.

Kenney, Martin, ed. 2000. *Understanding Silicon Valley: The Anatomy of an Entrepreneurial Region.* Palo Alto: Stanford University Press.

Klandermans, Bert. 1989. *Organizing for Change: Social Movement Organizations in Europe and the United States.* International Social Movement Research: A Research Annual. London: JAI Press.

Kleidman, Robert. 2004. "Community Organizing and Regionalism." *City and Community* 3 (4): 403–21.

Kornhauser, William. 1959. *The Politics of Mass Society.* Glencoe, Ill: Free Press.

Kreisi, Hanspeter. 1996. "The Organizational Structure of New Social Movements in Political Context." In *Comparative Perspectives on Social Movements,* ed. Doug McAdam, John D. McCarthy, and Mayer N. Zald, 152–85. Cambridge: Cambridge University Press.

Kretzmann, John P., and John L. McKnight. 1993. *Building Communities from the Inside Out: A Path toward Finding and Mobilizing a Community's Assets.* Evanston Ill.: Northwestern University Institute for Policy Research, ACTA Publications.

Kriesky, Jill. 2001. "Structural Change in the AFL-CIO: A Regional Study of Union Cities' Impact." In *Rekindling the Movement: Labor's Quest for Relevance in the 21st Century,* ed. Lowell Turner, Henry Katz, and Richard Hurd. Ithaca: ILR Press.

Kruglik, Mike, and Rich Stolz. 1999. "Organize! National Collaboration Drives Transportation Policy." *Shelterforce Online,* no. 103 (January/February).

Krugman, Paul R. 2003. *The Great Unraveling: Losing Our Way in the New Century.* New York: Norton.

LAEDC (Los Angeles Economic Development Corporation). 2002. *Los Angeles–Inland Empire Railroad Main Line Advanced Planning Study.* Los Angeles: Los Angeles Economic Development Corporation. Available at http://www.scag.ca.gov/goodsmove/pdf/LABasinMainLine2002.pdf.

——. 2005. "A Trade Congestion Reduction Program." Report prepared for the West Coast National Freight Gateway (WCNFG). Los Angeles: LAEDC. Available at http://www.laedc.org/consulting/projects/2005 WCNFGProgram-Full Report.pdf.

Lakoff, George. 2004. *Don't Think of an Elephant: Know Your Values and Frame the Debate.* White River Junction, Vt.: Chelsea Green.

Lang, Robert E., and Steven P. Hornburg. 1997. "Planning Portland Style: Pitfalls, and Possibilities." *Housing Policy Debate* 8 (1): 1–10.

Lawson, Steven. 2003. *Civil Rights Crossroads: Nation, Community, and the Black Freedom Struggle.* Lexington: University Press of Kentucky.

Leavitt, Jacqueline. 2005. *The Community Benefits Agreement and Figueroa Corridor Coalition for Economic Justice: A Tool for Linking Housing to Community Economic Development.* Los Angeles: Center for Labor Research and Education, Department of Urban Planning, UCLA.

Lee, Amy. 2006. "County Commission Approves Land Bank." *Detroit News,* June 16. http://www.detnews.com/apps/pbcs.dll/article?AID=200660616 0364.

Lee, Chong-Moon, William Miller, Marguerite Gong Hancock, and Henry Rowen, eds. 2000. *The Silicon Valley Edge: A Habitat for Innovation and Entrepreneurship.* Palo Alto, Calif.: Stanford University Press.

Lefebvre, Henri. 1996. *Writings on Cities.* Malden, Mass.: Blackwell.

Lerner, Michael. 2006. *The Left Hand of God: Taking Back Our Country from the Religious Right.* San Francisco: Harper.

Levine, Mark V., and Sandra J. Callaghan. 1998. *The Economic State of Milwaukee: The City and the Region.* Milwaukee: Center for Economic Development, University of Wisconsin–Milwaukee.

Lichtenstein, Nelson. 2003. *State of the Union: A Century of American Labor.* Princeton: Princeton University Press.

Long, Peter. 2001. *A First Glance at the Children's Health Initiative in Santa Clara Country, California.* Los Angeles: UCLA School of Public Health.

Lubove, Roy. 1996. *Twentieth Century Pittsburgh,* vol. 2, *The Post-Steel Era.* Pittsburgh: University of Pittsburgh Press.

Luce, Stephanie, and Mark Nelson. 2004. "Starting Down the Road to Power: The Denver Area Labor Federation." *Working USA* 8 (2). http://www.laborstud ies.wayne.edu/power.html.

Magat, Richard. 1999. *Unlikely Partners: Philanthropic Foundations and the Labor Movements.* Ithaca: ILR Press.

Mann, Eric. 1996. *A New Vision for Urban Transportation: The Bus Riders Union Makes History at the Intersection of Mass Transit, Civil Rights, and the Environment.* Los Angeles: Labor/Community Strategies Center.

——. 1999. Interview with Manuel Pastor, August 18.

Mann, Eric, Cynthia Hamilton, Anthony Thigpenn, Dean Toji, Laura Pulido, Geoff Ray, Robin Cannon, Lian Hurst Mann, and the Urban Strategies Group. 1993. *Reconstructing Los Angeles—and U.S. Cities—from the Bottom Up.* Los Angeles: Labor/Community Strategies Center.

Manning, Thomas. 1997. *Redevelopment and Race: Planning a Finer City in Postwar Detroit.* Baltimore: Johns Hopkins University Press.

Marcelli, Enrico A., Sundari Baru, and Donald Cohen. 2000. *Planning for Shared Prosperity or Growing Inequality?* San Diego: Center on Policy Initiatives. http://www.onlinecpi.org/downloads/planning.pdf.

Marcelli, Enrico A., and Pascale M. Joassart. 1998. *Prosperity and Poverty in the New Economy.* San Diego: Center on Policy Initiatives.

Martin, Deborah G. 2003. "'Place-framing' as Place-making: Constituting a Neighborhood for Organizing and Activism." *Annals of the Association of American Geographers* 93 (3): 730–50.

Martinez, Ramiro, Jr., and Abel Valenzuela Jr., eds. 2006. *Immigration and Crime: Ethnicity, Race and Violence.* New York: New York University Press.

Matsuoka, Martha. 2005. "From Neighborhood to Global: Community-based Regionalism and Shifting Concepts of Place in Community and Regional Development. Ph.D. diss. University of California–Los Angeles.

McAdam, Doug. 1982. *"The Political Process Model" in Political Process and the Development of Black Insurgency, 1930–1970.* Chicago: University of Chicago Press.

McCarthy, John, and Mayer Zald. 1977. "Resource Mobilization and Social Movements." *American Journal of Sociology* 82 (6): 1212–41.

McKnight, John L. 1987. "Regenerating Community." *Social Policy* 17 (3): 54–58.

Medoff, Peter, and Holly Sklar. 1994. *Streets of Hope: The Fall and Rise of an Urban Neighborhood.* Boston: South End Press.

Melucci, Alberto. 1996. *Challenging Codes: Collective Action in the Information Age.* Cambridge: Cambridge University Press.

Melucci, Alberto, Hanspeter Kriesi, Bert Klandermans, and Sydney Tarrow. 1988. *Getting Involved: Identity and Mobilization in Social Movements.* Greenwich Conn.: JAI Press.

Meyerson, Harold. 2004. "Las Vegas as a Workers' Paradise: The Hotel Workers Union Boosted Wages and Transformed Dead-end Jobs into Middle Class Careers in the Very Belly of the Casino Economy." *American Prospect* 15 (1): 38–42.

Milkman, Ruth. 2006. *L.A. Story: Immigrant Workers and the Future of the U.S. labor Movement.* New York: Russell Sage Foundation.

Milkman, Ruth, and Kent Wong. 2001. "Organizing Immigrant Workers: Case Studies from Southern California." In *Rekindling the Movement: Labor's Quest for 21st Century Relevance,* ed. Lowell Turner, Harry Katz, and Richard Hurd, 99–128. Ithaca: ILR Press.

Milwaukee Jobs Initiative. 2002. *Milwaukee Jobs Initiative: Five Years of Better Jobs.* Madison: Center on Wisconsin Strategy, University of Wisconsin.

Minkoff, Debra C. 1995. *Organizing for Equality: The Evolution of Women's and Racial-Ethnic Organizations in America, 1955–1985.* New Brunswick: Rutgers University Press.

Mintrom, Michael. 1997. "Policy Entrepreneurs and the Diffusion of Innovation." *American Journal of Political Science* 41 (3): 738–70.

Moberg, David. 2007. "Obama's Community Roots." *The Nation,* April 16.

Muller, Sarah, Sarah Zimmerman, Bob Brownstein, Amy B. Dean, and Phaedra Ellis-Lamkins. 2003. *Shared Prosperity and Inclusion: The Future of Economic Development Strategies in Silicon Valley.* San Jose: Working Partnerships USA.

Muro, Mark, and Robert Puentes. 2004. *Investing in a Better Future: A Review of the Fiscal and Competitive Advantages of Smarter Growth Development Patterns.* Discussion Paper. Washington, D.C.: Brookings Institution Center for Urban and Metropolitan Policy.

National Organizers Alliance. 2008. "US Social Forum Reflections." http://www.noacentral.org/page.php?id=170.

Neil, William J. V. 1991."Industrial Policy in Detroit: The Search for a New Regional Development Model in the Home of Fordism." *Local Economy* 6 (3): 250–70.

Nelson, Mary. 2006. Personal interview, February 22, 24.

Ness, Immanuel, and Stuart Eimer. 2001. *Central Labor Councils and the Revival of American Unionism: Organizing for Justice in Our Communities.* Armonk, N.Y.: M. E. Sharpe.

New World Foundation. 2000. *A New Look at Intermediaries* New York: New World Foundation.

——. 2003. *Funding Social Movements: The New World Foundation Perspective.* New York: New World Foundation.

——. 2005. *Building the New Majority: The New World Foundation Perspective.* New York: New World Foundation.

Nicholls, Walter Julio. 2003. "Forging 'New' Organizational Infrastructure for Los Angeles' Progressive Community." *International Journal of Urban and Regional Research* 27 (4): 881–96.

Nicholls, Walter Julio, and Justin Beaumont. 2003. "The Urbanisation of Justice Movements? Possibilities and Constraints for the City as a Space for Contentious Politics." Paper for the 99th Association of American Geographers Annual Meeting, New Orleans, March 4–8.

Nichols, John. 2005. "Progressive Cities in a Conservative Sea." *The Nation,* June 20.

Nissen, Bruce. 2004. "The Effectiveness and Limits of Labor-Community Coalitions: Evidence from South Florida." *Labor Studies Journal* 29 (1): 67–89.

Nowak, Jeremy. 1997. "Neighborhood Initiative and the Regional Economy." *Economic Development Quarterly* 11:1.

O'Connor, Alice. 1999. "Urban and Community Development." In *Swimming against the Tide: A Brief History of Federal Policy in Poor Communities,* ed. R. F. Ferguson and W. T. Dickens. Washington, D.C.: Brookings Institution Press.

Oliver, Melvin L., James H. Johnson Jr., Walter C. Farrell Jr., and Robert Gooding-Williams. 1993. *Anatomy of a Rebellion: A Political Economic Analysis.* New York: Routledge.

Ong, Paul, Eulalio Castellanos, Luz Echavarria, Ann Forsyth, Yvette Galindo, M. Richardson, Sarah Rigdon-Bensinger, Paul Schimek, and Holly Van Houten. 1989. *The Widening Divide: Income Inequality and Poverty in Los Angeles.* Los Angeles: Graduate School of Architecture and Urban Planning, University of California, Los Angeles.

Orfield, Myron. 1997. *Metropolitics: A Regional Agenda for Community and Stability.* Lincoln Institute of Land Policy. Washington, D.C.: Brookings Institution Press.

———. 2002. *American Metropolitics: The New Suburban Reality.* Washington, D.C.: Brookings Institution Press.

Orr, Marion, ed. 2007. *Transforming the City: Community Organizing and the Challenge of Political Change.* Lawrence: University Press of Kansas.

Orr, Marion, and Gerry Stoker. 1994. "Urban Regimes and Leadership in Detroit." *Urban Affairs Quarterly* 30 (1): 48–73.

Osterman, Paul. 2002. *Gathering Power: The Future of Progressive Politics in America.* Boston: Beacon Press.

Ostrander, Susan. 1995. *Money for Change: Social Movement Philanthropy at the Haymarket People's Fund.* Philadelphia: Temple University Press.

O'Toole, Randal. 2001. *The Folly of Smart Growth.* Bandon, Ore.: Thoreau Institute.

Pastor, Manuel. 1995. "Economic Inequality, Latino Poverty, and the Civil Unrest in Los Angeles." *Economic Development Quarterly* 9:3.

———. 2001. "Common Ground at Ground Zero? The New Economy and the New Organizing in Los Angeles." *Antipode* 33:2.

———. 2006. "Cohesion and Competitiveness: Business Leadership for Regional Growth and Social Equity." In *OECD Territorial Reviews: Competitive Cities in the Global Economy.* Paris: Organisation for Economic Co-Operation and Development.

———. 2007a. "Doing Good and Doing Well: Making the Business Case for Regional Equity and Racial Inclusion." Focus publication of the Joint Center for Political and Economic Studies, March–April, 12–13.

———. 2007b. "¿Quién es Más Urbanista? Latinos and 'Smart Growth.' " In *Growing Smarter: Achieving Livable Communities, Environmental Justice, and Regional Equity,* ed. Robert Bullard, 73–103. Cambridge, Mass.: MIT Press.

Pastor, Manuel, and Chris Benner. 2008. "Been Down So Long: Weak Market Cities and Regional Equity." *In Retooling for Growth: Building a 21st Century Economy in America's Older Industrial Areas,* ed. Richard M. McGahey and Jennifer S. Vey, 89–118. Washington, D.C.: Brookings Institution Press.

Pastor, Manuel, Chris Benner, and Martha Matsuoka. 2006. "The Regional Nexus: The Promise and Risk of Community-based Approaches to Metropolitan Equity." In *Jobs and Economic Development in Minority Communities,* ed. Paul Ong and Anastasia Loukaitou-Sideris. Philadelphia: Temple University Press.

Pastor, Manuel, Chris Benner, and Rachel Rosner. 2003. "'An Option for the Poor': A Research Audit for Community-Based Regionalism in California's Central Coast." *Economic Development Quarterly* 17 (May): 2.

———. 2006. *Edging toward Equity: Creating Shared Prosperity in America's Regions.* Santa Cruz: University of California Center for Justice, Tolerance, and Community.

Pastor, Manuel, Peter Dreier, Eugene Grigsby, and Marta López-Garza. 1997. *Growing Together: Linking Community and Regional Development.* Los Angeles: Occidental College.

———. 2000. *Regions That Work: How Cities and Suburbs Can Grow Together.* Minneapolis: University of Minnesota Press.

Pastor, Manuel, and Crystal Hayling. 1990. *Economic Development: The New Majority in Los Angeles.* Los Angeles: Occidental College International and Public Affairs Center.

Pastor, Manuel, T. William Lester, and Justin Scoggins. 2007. *Why Regions?* Berkeley: University of California Institute for Urban and Regional Development.

Pastor, Manuel, and Enrico Marcelli. 2004. "Somewhere over the Rainbow? African American, Immigration, and Coalition-Building." In *The Impact of Immigration on African Americans,* ed. Steven Schulman. New Brunswick, N.J.: Transactions.

Pastor, Manuel, and Justin Scoggins. 2007. *Working Poor in the Golden State: A Multi-measure Comparison Using the 2000 and 1990 Public Use Microdata Samples.* Santa Cruz: University of California Center for Justice, Tolerance, and Community.

Peirce, Neal R., Curtis W. Johnson, and John Stuart Hall. 1993. *Citistates: How Urban America Can Prosper in a Competitive World.* Washington, D.C.: Seven Locks Press.

Pincetl, Stephanie, Andrew E. G. Jonas, and David Wilson. 1999. *The Politics of Influence: Democracy and the Growth Machine in Orange County, U.S.* Albany: State University of New York Press.

Piore, Michael, and Charles Sabel. 1984. *The Second Industrial Divide: Possibilities for Prosperity.* New York: Basic Books.

Piven, Frances Fox, and Richard A. Cloward. 1967. "Black Control of Cities II: How Negroes Will Lose." *New Republic,* October 7, 15–19.

———. 1972. "The Case against Urban Desegregation." In *The Politics of Turmoil,* ed. Richard A. Cloward and Frances Fox Piven. New York: Pantheon.

———. 1979. *Poor People's Movements: Why They Succeed and How They Fail.* New York: Random House.

PolicyLink. 2002a. "Building a Healthier Sacramento Region: An Analysis of Assembly Bill 680." Oakland, Calif.: PolicyLink. http://www.policylink.org/pdfs/AB%20680.pdf.

———. 2002b. *Promoting Regional Equity: A Framing Paper.* Oakland, Calif.: PolicyLink.

Pollin, Robert, and Stephanie Luce. 1998. *The Living Wage: Building a Fair Economy.* New York: New Press.

Porter, Michael E. 1995. "The Competitive Advantage of the Inner City." *Harvard Business Review* 73:3.

powell, john. 2000. "Addressing Regional Dilemmas for Minority Communities." In *Reflections on Regionalism,* edited by Bruce Katz, 218–246. Washington, D.C.: Brookings Institution.

———. 2004. "Equity and Regionalism: The Impact of Government Restructuring on Communities of Color in Pittsburgh." Keynote Address for Sustainable Pittsburgh, November 19.

powell, john, Jason Reece, Christy Rogers, and Samir Gambhir. 2007. *Communities of Opportunity: A Framework for a More Equitable and Sustainable Future for All.* Columbus, Ohio: Kirwan Institute for the Study of Race and Ethnicity, Ohio

State University. Accessible at http://kirwan.gripserver3.com/publicationspresentations/publications/index.php.

Proscio, Tony. 2003. "Community Development and Smart Growth: Stopping Sprawl at Its Source." Translation Paper 13, Funders' Network for Smart Growth and Livable Communities. Available at http://www.fundersnetwork.org/usr_doc/TP_13_Community_Development_&_SG.pdf.

Puentes, Robert, and David Warren. 2006. *One-Fifth of the Nation: America's First Suburbs.* Washington, D.C.: Brookings Institution. http://www.brookings.edu/metro/pubs/20060215_FirstSuburbs.pdf.

Purcell, Mark. 2003. "Citizenship and the Right to the Global City." *International Journal of Urban and Regional Research* 27 (3): 564–90.

Putnam, Robert D. 2000. *Bowling Alone: The Collapse and Revival of American Community.* New York: Simon & Schuster.

Ranghelli, Lisa. 2002. *Replicating Success—The Alameda Corridor Job Training and Employment Program: A Replication Manual for Winning and Implementing Community-based Jobs Programs on Public Construction Projects.* Washington, D.C.: Center for Community Change.

Rast, Joel. 2006. "Environmental Justice and the New Regionalism." *Journal of Planning Education and Research* 25:249–63.

Rathke, Wade. 2004. "Majority Unionism: Strategies for Organizing the 21st Century Labor Movement." *Social Policy* 35 (1): 18–30.

Rhee, Nari, and Julie A. Sadler. 2007. "Labor Community Coalitions and Urban Power Building in San Jose." In *Labor in the New Urban Battlegrounds: Social Solidarity in a Global Economy,* ed. Lowell Turner and Daniel Cornfield, 178–92. Ithaca: ILR Press.

Richmond, Henry. 1997. "Comment on Carl Abbott's 'The Portland Region: Where City and Suburbs Talk to Each Other—and Often Agree.'" *Housing Policy Debate* 8(1).

Rivera, Cheryl. 2003. Keynote Speech at "Bridging the Bay," conference organized by Social Equity Caucus, Santa Cruz, Calif., April.

——. 2006. Personal interview, February 22.

Roberts, Nancy C., and Paula J. King. 1991. "Policy Entrepreneurs: Their Activity Structure and Function in the Policy Process." *Journal of Public Administration Research and Theory* 1 (2): 147–55.

Rogers, Reuel R. 2004. "Race-based Coalitions among Minority Groups: Afro-Caribbean Immigrants and African-Americans in New York City." *Urban Affairs Review* 39 (3): 283–317.

Rosenblum, Jonathan. 2001. "Building Organizing Capacity: The King County Labor Council." In *Central Labor Councils and the Revival of American Unionism,* ed. Immanuel Ness and Stuart Eimer. Armonk, N.Y.: M. E. Sharpe.

Rosenfeld, Stuart A. 2001. *Networks and Clusters: The Yin and Yang of Rural Development.* Kansas City: Federal Reserve Bank of Kansas City. http://www.rtsinc.org/publications/KCFed.pdf.

Rosner, Rachel, and Chris Benner. 1997. *Living Wage, an Opportunity for San Jose: A Report on the Benefits and Impact of a Living Wage Ordinance on the City of San Jose.* San Jose: Working Partnerships USA.

Rusk, David. 1993. *Cities without Suburbs.* Washington, D.C.: Woodrow Wilson Center Press.

——. 1999. *Inside Game, Outside Game: Winning Strategies for Saving Urban America.* Washington, D.C.: Brookings Institution Press.

——. 2005. "Measuring Regional Equity." Manuscript prepared for Conversations on Regional Equity.

——. 2006. *Annexation and the Fiscal Fate of Cities.* Washington, D.C.: Brookings Institution Survey Series. http://www.brook.edu/metro/pubs/20060810_fate ofcities.pdf.

Sabel, Charles F. 1988. "Flexible Specialization and the Reemergence of Regional Economies." In *Reversing Industrial Decline,* ed. Paul Hirst and Jonathan Zeitlin. Oxford: Berg.

Sanchez, Thomas. 2005. *Patterns of MPO Representation and Board Structure in Relation to Transportation Planning and Decision Making.* Washington, D.C.: Brookings Institution.

Sanyika, Mtangulizi K. 1986. "Balanced Development, Part Two: A Classification of Existing Linkages and Partnerships." *Economic Development and Law Center Report,* Fall, 19–22.

Sanyika, Mtangulizi K., and James W. Head. 1990. *Communities at Risk: Regional Transportation Issues in the Bay Area: The Concerns of Communities of Color and Low-Income Neighborhoods.* Issue Brief #6. San Francisco: San Francisco National Economic Development and Law Center, August. Discussion: http://www. transact.org/report.asp?id=32.

——. 1991. *Regionalism and Community Economic Development: The Nonprofit Sector Tackles Regional Issues in the San Francisco Bay Area.* Berkeley: National Economic Development and Law Center.

Santow, Mark. 2007. "Running in Place: Saul Alinsky, Race and Community Organizing." In *Transforming the City: Community Organizing and the Challenge of Political Change,* ed. Marian Orr. Lawrence: University Press of Kansas.

Savage, Linda A. 1998. "Geographies of Organizing: Justice for Janitors in Los Angeles." In *Organizing the Landscape: Geographical Perspectives on Labor Unionism,* ed. Andrew Herod. Minneapolis: University of Minnesota Press.

Savitch, H. V. and Ronald K. Vogel. 2004. "Suburbs without a City: Power and City-county Consolidation." *Urban Affairs Review* 396:758–90.

Saxenian, AnnaLee. 1994. *Regional Advantage: Culture and Competition in Silicon Valley and Route 128.* Cambridge: Harvard University Press.

SCOPE (Strategic Concepts in Organizing and Policy Education). 2003. *Power Tools: A Manual for Organizations Fighting for Justice.* Los Angeles: SCOPE.

——. 2006. *2006 Year in Review.* Los Angeles: SCOPE.

Scott, Allen J., and Edward W. Soja. 1996. *The City: Los Angeles and Urban Theory at the End of the Twentieth Century.* Berkeley: University of California Press.

Shields, Brian. 2003. "Lake County Council Supports RTA Tax Resolution." *Northwest Indiana and Illinois Times.* January 15.

Siegel, Lenny. 1994. "The Silicon Valley Experience: Why Labor Law Must Be Brought into the Twenty-First Century." Testimony before the U.S. Commission on the Future of Worker-Management Relations.

Sierra Club. 1998. *1998 Sierra Club Sprawl Report. 30 Most Sprawl-threatened Cities: Number Ten-Chicago.* http://www.sierraclub.org/sprawl/report98/chicago.asp.

Silver, Beverly. 2003. *Forces of Labor: Workers' Movements and Globalization since 1870.* Cambridge Studies in Comparative Politics. Cambridge: Cambridge University Press.

Simon, William H. 2001. *The Community Economic Development Movement: Law, Business, and the New Social Policy.* Durham, N.C.: Duke University Press.

Skocpol, Theda. 1997. "Building Community Top-Down or Bottom-Up? America's Voluntary Groups Thrive in a National Network." *Brookings Review* 15 (4): 16.

——. 2000. *The Missing Middle: Working Families and the Future of American Social Policy.* A Century Foundation Book. New York: Norton.

Skocpol, Theda, Marshall Ganz, and Ziad Munson. 2000. "A Nation of Organizers: The Institutional Origins of Civic Voluntarism in the University States." *American Political Science Review* 94 (3): 527–46.

Smith, Sabrina. 2006. Organizing director, SCOPE. Personal interview, Los Angeles, May.

Snow, David A., and Danny Trom. 2002. "The Case Study and the Study of Social Movements." In *Methods of Social Movement Research,* ed. Bert Klandermans and Suzanne Staggenborg. Minneapolis: University of Minnesota Press.

Soja, Edward W. 1989. *Postmodern Geographies: The Reassertion of Space in Critical Social Theory.* New York: Verso.

——. 2000. *Postmetropolis: Critical Studies of Cities and Regions.* Oxford: Blackwell.

Sotelo, Rhonnel. 2003. Telephone interview.

Stone, Deborah. 2000. "Why We Need a Care Movement." *The Nation,* March 13, 13–15.

Storper, Michael. 1997. *The Regional World: Territorial Development in a Global Economy.* New York: Guilford Press.

Suro, Robert, and Audrey Singer. 2002. *Latino Growth in Metropolitan America: Changing Patterns, New Locations.* Washington, D.C.: Brookings Institution.

Swanstrom, Todd. 1996. "Ideas Matter: Reflections on the New Regionalism." *Citiscape: A Journal of Policy Development and Research* 2 (2): 5–21.

Swanstrom, Todd, and Brian Banks. 2007. *Possibilities for Progressive Regionalism: Federal Transportation Policy and Local Hiring Agreements.* Berkeley: University of California Institute of Urban and Regional Development.

Swanstrom, Todd, and Laura Barrett. 2007. "The Road to Jobs: The Fight for Transportation Equity." *Social Policy,* Spring–Summer. http://www.socialpolicy.org/index.php?id=1833.

Swanstrom, Todd, with Laura Barrett, Shantha Ready, Michele Fontaine, Scott Krummenacher, and Ruth Sergenian. 2007. *The Road to Jobs: Patterns of Employment in the Construction Industry in Eighteen Metropolitan Areas.* Report for the Transportation Equity Network. St. Louis: RegionWise. http://sgusa.convio.net/site/DocServer/TEN_Road_to_ Jobs_study-complete.pdf?docID=3821.

Swanstrom, Todd, Colleen Casey, Robert Flack, and Peter Drier. 2004. *Pulling Apart: Economic Segregation among Suburbs and Central Cities in Major Metropolitan*

Areas. Living Cities Census Series. Washington, D.C.: Brookings Institution Metropolitan Policy Program.

Swyngedouw, Erik, and Kevin R. Cox. 1997. *In Neither Global nor Local: "Glocalization" and the Politics of Scale*. New York: Guilford Press.

Tarrow, Sydney. 1991. *Struggle, Politics, and Reform: Collective Action, Social Movements, and Cycles of Protest*. Western Societies Program occasional paper no. 21, 2nd ed. Ithaca, N.Y.: Center for International Studies, Cornell University.

Taylor, Dorceta E. 2000. "The Rise of the Environmental Justice Paradigm: Injustice Framing and the Social Construction of Environmental Discourses." *American Behavioral Scientist* 43 (4): 508–80.

Taylor, Julia. 2006. Interview. March 10.

Themba, Makani N. 1999. *Making Policy, Making Change: How Communities Are Taking Law into Their Own Hands*. Oakland, Calif.: Chardon Press.

Thigpenn, Anthony. 2004. Personal interview with Manuel Pastor July 9.

Thomas, June Manning. 1997. *Redevelopment and Race: Planning a Finer City in Postwar Detroit*. Baltimore: Johns Hopkins University Press.

Thompson, Edward P. 1978. "Eighteenth-century English Society: Class Struggle without Class?" *Social History* 3 (2): 133–65.

Thompson, J. Phillip. 2002. "Review of *Place Matters: Metropolitics for the Twenty-First Century* by Peter Dreier, John Mollenkopf, and Todd Swanstrom." *Urban Affairs Review* 37:442–51.

———. 2005. "Seeking Effective Power: Why Mayors Need Community Organizations." *Perspectives on Politics* 3 (2).

Tides Foundation. 2007. *The Right to the City: Reclaiming Our Urban Centers, Reframing Human Rights, and Redefining Citizenship*. San Francisco.

Tilly, Charles. 1979. "Repertoires of Contention in America and Britain, 1750–1830." In *The Dynamics of Social Movements: Resource Mobilization, Control, and Tactics*, ed. Mayer Zald and John McCarthy, 567–89. Cambridge: Winthrop.

Touraine, Alain. 1971. *The Post Industrial Society*. New York: Random House.

Turner, Lowell. 2005. "From Transformation to Revitalization: A New Research Agenda for a Contested Global Economy." *Work and Occupations* 32: 383–99.

UNCTAD (United Nations Conference on Trade and Development). 2007. *Review of Maritime Transport 2007*. Geneva: UNCTAD. Available at http://www.unctad.org/en/docs/rmt2007 en.pdf.

University of Wisconsin–Milwaukee, 2006. *The Economic State of Milwaukee's Inner City 2006*. Milwaukee: Center for Economic Development, University of Wisconsin–Milwaukee.

Urban Habitat Program. 1995. *Reintegrating the Flatlands: A Regional Framework for Military Base Conversion in the San Francisco Bay Area*. San Francisco: Urban Habitat Program.

———. 1998. *What If We Shared? Findings from Myron Orfield's San Francisco Bay Area Metropolitics: A Regional Agenda for Community and Stability*. San Francisco: Urban Habitat Program.

U.S. Census (United States Bureau of the Census). 1997. Exporter Location Series. Washington, D.C.: U.S. Department of Commerce.

——. 2000. *Census, Summary Files 1, 3, and 4.* Washington, D.C.: U.S. Department of Commerce.

——. 2004. *2004 American Community Survey.* Washington, D.C.: U.S. Department of Commerce.

——. 2005. *2005 American Community Survey.* Washington, D.C.: U.S. Department of Commerce.

——. 2006. *2006 American Community Survey.* Washington, D.C.: U.S. Department of Commerce.

V-8 Collaborative. 2006. Interview with leaders, February 3.

Voith, Richard. 1998. "Do Suburbs Need Cities?" *Journal of Regional Science* 38 (3): 445–65.

Waldinger, Roger, and Thomas Bailey. 1991. "The Continuing Significance of Race: Racial Conflict and Racial Discrimination in Construction." *Politics & Society* 19: 291–323.

Waldinger, Roger, and Mehdi Bozorgmehr. 1996. *The Making of a Multicultural Metropolis: Ethnic Los Angeles.* New York: Russell Sage Foundation.

Waldinger, Roger, Chris Erickson, Ruth Milkman, Daniel J. B. Mitchell, Abel Valenzuela, Kent Wong, and Maurice Zeitlin. 1996. *Helots No More: A Case Study of the Justice for Janitors Campaign in Los Angeles.* Los Angeles: Lewis Center for Regional Policy Studies, School of Public Policy and Social Research, UCLA.

——. 1997. "Justice for Janitors: Organizing in Difficult Times." *Dissent* 44 (1).

Wallis, Jim. 2005. *God's Politics: Why the Right Gets It Wrong and the Left Doesn't Get It.* New York: HarperCollins.

Walsh, Joan. 1997. *Stories of Renewal: Community Building and the Future of Urban America.* New York: Rockefeller Foundation.

Warren, Mark R. 2001. *Dry Bones Rattling: Community Building to Revitalize American Democracy.* Princeton: Princeton University Press.

Weaver, Clyde. 1984. *Regional Development and the Local Community: Planning, Politics and Social Context.* Chichester, U.K.: Wiley.

Weber, Rachel N., and Janet L. Smith. 2003. "Assets and Neighborhoods: The Role of Individual Assets in Neighborhood Revitalization." *Housing Policy Debate* 14 (1–2): 169–202.

Weir, Margaret. 2001. *Metropolitan Coalition-Building Strategies.* Prepared for the Urban Seminar Series on Children's Health and Safety, Cambridge, Mass. December 6–7.

Weir, Margaret, and Jane Rongerude. 2007. "Multi-level Power and Progressive Regionalism." In *Research Network on Building Resilient Regions.* Berkeley: University of California Institute of Urban and Regional Development.

Weir, Margaret, Jane Rongerude, and Christopher K. Ansell. 2007. "Collaboration Is Not Enough." In *MacArthur Foundation Research Network on Building Resilient Regions,* ed. Institute of Urban and Regional Development. Berkeley: University of California.

Weir, Margaret, Harold Wolman, and Todd Swanstrom. 2005. "The Calculus of Coalitions: Cities and States and the Metropolitan Agenda." *Urban Affairs Review* 40.

Wilson, William Julius. 1987. *The Truly Disadvantaged: The Inner City, the Underclass, and Public Policy.* Chicago: University of Chicago Press.

Wilton, Robert D., and Cynthia Cranford. 2002. "Toward an Understanding of the Spatiality of Social Movements: Labor Organizing at a Private University in Los Angeles." *Social Problems* 49 (3): 374–94.

Winslow, Ward, Ed. 1995. *The Making of Silicon Valley: A One Hundred Year Renaissance.* Palo Alto, Calif.: Santa Clara Valley Historical Association.

Wolch, Jennifer, Manuel Pastor, and Peter Dreier. 2004. *Up Against the Sprawl: Public Policy and the Making of Southern California.* Minneapolis: University of Minnesota Press.

Wolf, James, and Mary Beth Farquar. 2005. "Assessing Progress: The State of Metropolitan Planning Organizations under ISTEA and TEA-21." *International Journal of Public Administration* 28 (13–14): 1057–79.

Wood, David E., Myron Orfield, and Joel Rogers. 2000. *Milwaukee Metropatterns: Sprawl and Social Patterns in Metro Milwaukee.* Madison: Center on Wisconsin Strategy and Metropolitan Area Research Corporation.

Wood, Richard. 2007. "Higher Power: Strategic Capacity for State and National Organizing." In *Transforming the City: Community Organizing and the Challenge of Political Change,* ed. Marion Orr. Lawrence: University Press of Kansas, 162–92.

WPUSA (Working Partnerships USA). 2006. *An Historical Analysis of Tax and Fiscal Propositions in California, 1978–2004.* San Jose: Working Partnerships USA.

Young, Iris Marion. 2000. *Inclusion and Democracy.* New York: Oxford University Press.

Younis, Mona. 1998. "San Antonio and Fruitvale." *Citiscape: A Journal of Policy Development and Research* 4 (2): 221–44.

Zeidenberg, Matthew. 2004. *Moving Outward: The Shifting Landscape of Poverty in Milwaukee.* Madison: Center on Wisconsin Strategy (COWS).

Zlolniski, Christian. 2006. *Janitors, Street Vendors, and Activists: The Lives of Mexican Immigrants in Silicon Valley.* Berkeley: University of California Press.

Index